THE DYNAMIC DECADE

Promoting Science Complex Connections: Bridges Between New Venable and Murray. Source: Wilson Architects, Photographer Anton Grassl

THE DYNAMIC DECADE

CREATING THE SUSTAINABLE CAMPUS FOR THE UNIVERSITY
OF NORTH CAROLINA AT CHAPEL HILL, 2001–2011

DAVID R. GODSCHALK AND JONATHAN B. HOWES

THE UNIVERSITY OF NORTH CAROLINA AT CHAPEL HILL

Copyright © 2012 University of North Carolina, Chapel Hill

Distributed by
The University of North Carolina Press
116 South Boundary St.
Chapel Hill, North Carolina 27514
1-800-848-6224
www.uncpress.unc.edu

Paper ISBN 978-1-4696-0725-2
E-book ISBN 978-1-4696-0726-9

Contents

	List of Illustrations, Tables, Sidebars	vi
	Foreword. The Chancellor's View *James Moeser, Chancellor Emeritus*	1
1.	Sustaining the Campus: UNC's Dynamic Decade of Campus Development	7
2.	Creating the Framework: The Campus Master Plan	17
3.	Setting Priorities: The Development Plan	30
4.	Designing Projects: Siting and Architectural Issues	49
5.	Preserving the Historic Campus: Buildings and Landscapes	62
6.	Enhancing the Historic North Campus	85
7.	Recasting the Twentieth Century Southeast Campus	103
8.	Growing the Health Services Southwest Campus	119
9.	Visualizing a New Research Campus at Carolina North	129
10.	Lessons for Creating a Sustainable Campus	144
	Afterword *Holden Thorp, Chancellor*	153
	Appendix A. Development Project Chronology	155
	Appendix B. Carolina North	159
	References	162
	Acknowledgments	163
	Authors' Biographies	164

Illustrations, Tables, Sidebars

Frontispiece. Promoting Science Complex Connections: Bridge Between New Venable and Murray.

Students on Polk Place   6

1. Sustaining the Campus: UNC's Dynamic Decade of Campus Development

    Fig. 1-1. Construction Underway for the Sciences Complex   11
    Fig. 1-2. The Sustainable Campus   12
    Fig. 1-3. Book Outline   14

2. Creating the Framework: The Campus Master Plan

    Fig. 2-1. Proposed Open Space Plan   18
    Sidebar. Adam Gross, Master Planner   19
    Fig. 2-2. Master Plan Phases   20
    Table 2-1. Campus Building Floor Area Growth   21
    Fig. 2-3. Campus Topography   22
    Fig. 2-4. Conceptual Design   25
    Fig. 2-5. Final Proposed Campus Master Plan   27

3. Setting Priorities: The Development Plan

    Fig. 3-1. Construction Underway Inside Memorial Hall   31
    Fig. 3-2. Development Plan Components   32
    Sidebar. Rosemary Waldorf, Mayor   34
    Sidebar. Bruce Runberg, Associate Vice Chancellor for Facilities Planning and Construction   36
    Table 3-1. Proposed Development Summary   37
    Fig. 3-3. Environmental Plan Map   39
    Fig. 3-4. Students Walking in McCorkle Place   40
    Table 3-2. Anticipated Employee and Student Growth 2000–2010   41
    Fig. 3-5. Existing Main Campus Parking Facilities   42
    Fig. 3-6. Pedestrian Corridors   44
    Fig. 3-7. Proposed Utilities   45
    Fig. 3-8. Perimeter Transition Areas   47

4. Designing Projects: Siting and Architectural Issues
    Fig. 4-1. Project Design Process   50
    Fig. 4-2. Project Review and Approval Process   53
    Sidebar. Pete Anderson, Design Reviewer   54
    Sidebar. Bill Wilson, Architect   56
    Fig. 4-3. Plan of Science Complex, Phase II   57
    Fig. 4-4. Plan of Cobb Parking Deck and Adjacent Area   59
    Fig. 4-5. Cobb Tennis Courts and Parking Deck   60

5. Preserving the Historic Campus: Buildings and Landscapes
    Fig. 5-1. Students Enjoying McCorkle Place   63
    Sidebar. Paul Kapp, Historic Preservation Architect   64
    Fig. 5-2. UNC'S Historic Buildings Map   65
    Fig. 5-3. Old Well and Old East   66
    Fig. 5-4. Playmakers Theatre   67
    Fig. 5-5. Hill Hall, Originally the Carnegie Library   68
    Fig. 5-6. Wilson Library   68
    Fig. 5-7. South Building   69
    Fig. 5-8. National Register Historic Districts Surrounding
        the UNC Campus   70
    Fig. 5-9. Rendering of Campus YMCA   71
    Fig. 5-10. West House   72
    Fig. 5-11. Murphey Hall   72
    Fig. 5-12. Spencer Love House   73
    Fig. 5-13. Coker Arboretum   75
    Fig. 5-14. Map of UNC's Landmark Spaces   77
    Sidebar. Peter Schaudt, Landscape Architect   79
    Fig. 5-15. Potential McCorkle Place Extension   80
    Fig. 5-16. Restored Manning Hall Side Quad   81
    Fig. 5-17. Possible Bell Tower Integration   81
    Fig. 5-18. Kenan Woods Opportunities   82
    Fig. 5-19. Forest Theatre Potential   83

6. Enhancing the Historic North Campus
    Fig. 6-1. Old Venable   86
    Fig. 6-2. The Three Major North Campus Communities   87
    Fig. 6-3. Science Community Map   88
    Fig. 6-4. Caudill Laboratories   90
    Sidebar. Tom Clegg, Science Planning Team Leader   91
    Fig. 6-5. Rendering of Genomic Sciences Building   93
    Fig. 6-6. Arts Community Map   94
    Fig. 6-7. Kenan Music Building   95
    Sidebar. Tom Kenan, Private Donor   96
    Fig. 6-8. Renovated Memorial Hall on Opening Night   97
    Fig. 6-9. North Student Residence Life and Services Community   98
    Fig. 6-10. Renovated Cobb Residence Hall   99
    Sidebar. Anna Wu, Campus Architect   100

7. Recasting the Twentieth Century Southeast Campus
   - Fig. 7-1. The Twentieth Century Southeast Campus with New Projects — 104
   - Fig. 7-2. Southeast Campus Communities — 105
   - Fig. 7-3. Student Family Housing and Residence Halls on Southeast Campus — 106
   - Fig. 7-4. South Student Residence Life and Services Community — 107
   - Fig. 7-5. Koury Residence Hall — 108
   - Fig. 7-6. Rams Head Center — 109
   - Fig. 7-7. Student Academic Services Building — 110
   - Fig. 7-8. Student Family Housing Community — 111
   - Fig. 7-9. Baity Hill Student Family Housing Complex — 112
   - Sidebar. Ken Broun, Neighborhood Advocate — 113
   - Fig. 7-10. Athletics and Visitors' Complex Map — 115
   - Fig. 7-11. Boshamer Baseball Stadium, Rams Head Center, and Kenan Football Stadium — 116

8. Growing the Health Services Southwest Campus
   - Fig. 8-1. Southwest Campus Communities — 120
   - Fig. 8-2. North Carolina Cancer Hospital and Health Affairs and Health Research Communities — 121
   - Sidebar. Mary Beck, Senior Vice President, Planning and Program Development, UNC Hospitals — 122
   - Fig. 8-3. Health Affairs Community — 123
   - Fig. 8-4. North Carolina Cancer Hospital — 124
   - Fig. 8-5. Health Research Community — 126
   - Fig. 8-6. Dental Sciences Building and Bridge over Manning Drive — 127
   - Fig. 8-7. South Columbia Streetscape Improvements — 128

9. Visualizing a New Research Campus at Carolina North
   - Fig. 9-1. 1998 Horace Williams Land Use Plan — 133
   - Sidebar. Jack Evans, Executive Director — 135
   - Fig. 9-2. Carolina North Plan, 2007 — 136
   - Sidebar. David Owens, Honest Broker — 139
   - Fig. 9-3. Land Use Arrangement in the Development Agreement Plan of Carolina North — 142
   - Fig. 9-4. Future Carolina North Greenway — 143

10. Lessons for Creating a Sustainable Campus
    - Fig. 10-1. Sustainable Campus Development — 145
    - Sidebar. Luanne Greene, Implementation Planner — 149

THE DYNAMIC DECADE

Foreword

THE CHANCELLOR'S VIEW

James Moeser, Chancellor Emeritus

"We shape our buildings, and afterwards, our buildings shape us."
Winston Churchill to the House of Commons, October 28, 1943

I arrived in Chapel Hill in August, 2000, at the beginning of "the Dynamic Decade" that David Godschalk and Jonathan Howes describe in this book. In many ways, the appointment to the chancellorship of the University of North Carolina at Chapel Hill was the pinnacle of my career. I had long admired UNC, first as a faculty member and Dean at the University of Kansas, where UNC was designated as one of KU's aspirant peer institutions. Later, as Provost of the University of South Carolina, I had an opportunity to view UNC from the perspective of a neighbor state that had never supported its universities as well as North Carolina. I knew that Carolina was one of America's great universities. The first time that my wife, Susan, and I walked on the historic brick paths in April, 2000, just after my election as Chancellor by the Board of Governors, I got goose bumps.

August, 2000, was a propitious moment to begin. While Carolina had a great reputation nationally, it was a university with a decaying infrastructure. Little construction had taken place in the previous thirty years. The deferred maintenance backlog was staggering. Two years prior to my arrival, a construction bond issue had been defeated. However, in 2000, an enormous $3.1 billion Higher Education Bond Issue for the UNC system and the North Carolina Community College system was set to go before the voters in the November election. It would not be an overstatement to say that the future of the University hung in the balance of the November election.

I started my first day on the job accompanied by a group of reporters and photographers on a tour of what the local newspaper described as

"Chapel Hill's Chamber of Horrors" to see for myself some of the worst physical facilities on campus. I saw labs in the School of Medicine where researchers were conducting experiments using sophisticated equipment, where the only means of adjusting the ambient temperature in the room was by opening a window and where buckets were placed on the floor because of leaky roofs. I toured Venable Hall, the cavernous 1929 home of our world-class chemistry department. Ed Samulski, the chemistry department chair, invited me to imagine that I was the CEO of a major company considering funding to support research in this aging facility. The *Chapel Hill News* article quoted Holden Thorp, then a young professor of chemistry, "We're at the point where we are able to compete [for graduate students] with the top names like MIT and Stanford," he said. "But when they come to the interview, the condition of the labs can be a big part of the decision. They take one look at this place and say, 'What the heck is going on?'"

In my installation address on University Day, October 12, 2000, I pledged to the voters that, if they approved the bond issue, we would triple their investment through private fundraising. (I made this rather audacious pledge, I must confess, wondering if it would come back to haunt me. Ultimately, we raised $2.4 billion through the Carolina First Campaign, and our faculty received many millions in grant funding, both of which we used to leverage the $515 million from the bond funds toward a total construction budget of $2.3 billion.)

In November, 2000, the voters of North Carolina overwhelmingly approved the largest higher education construction bond issue ever passed by any state, passing in all 100 counties with a seventy-five percent plurality. This was an incredible statement of support for the University. It also carried with it a mandate for responsible implementation. I felt this responsibility very keenly.

Fortunately, before my arrival, work had begun on a comprehensive Master Plan for the campus. Indeed, I was able to give that plan a final review and approval before it was sent on to the Board of Trustees for adoption. The Ayers Saint Gross campus Master Plan was an absolutely essential prerequisite to building the equivalent of the entire Wake Forest University campus in the midst of Carolina's campus. It also gave us the framework for our next major hurdle: negotiating a development agreement with the Town of Chapel Hill.

As Godschalk and Howes point out, UNC is almost unique in the degree to which its host community controls its physical development. The Town of Chapel Hill not only controls the zoning for the campus, in 2000 it also had in place a maximum square footage cap which the University could not exceed. Indeed, it would have been impossible to build out the envisioned first phase of the Master Plan without exceeding the Town's cap. Absent a new agreement with the town, every single construction project would have to have been taken to the Town government for approval, a process that would have caused major delays and substantially increased cost.

If the sales pitch to the State of North Carolina for the passage of the bond had been relatively easy, the political situation in Chapel Hill was just the opposite. Shortly after I arrived, someone repeated to me a saying that I would hear over and over, namely, that "people remember Chapel Hill the way it never was, and they want it to stay that way."

Chapel Hill is a lovely college town. The University is surrounded by beautiful neighborhoods, most of which were originally faculty neighborhoods, but which with the passage of time, have become so upscale that few faculty now can afford to live in them. These neighbors were intensely suspicious of the University's plans to expand and grow. Moreover, the recent history of town/gown relationships was marked by poor communication, distrust, and cynicism.

Godschalk and Howes correctly report the difficult and tedious negotiations that ultimately led to the ten-year development plan, a manageable portion of the Board of Trustees-approved campus master plan, which allowed us to move through the projects without having to take each one separately to the Town government for approval. Former Mayor Waldorf, in her sidebar, reports the phone call I made to her to inform her that a rider had been attached to the budget in the N.C. Senate that would have stripped the town of its zoning authority. While that rider was later removed, the Town knew that the threat was real. The State of North Carolina was not going to allow a town to stand in the way of its flagship university's need to expand and grow.

Ten years later, the town/gown relationship matured from those early days of confrontation and threat to a new environment of trust and collaboration. I think this is, at least in part, due to the fact that the University really did commit itself to responsible implementation of everything it agreed to do in the development agreement with the Town. In some cases we made concessions that I still think were unwise, most notably, the decision not to seek the widening of the South Columbia Street bottleneck from the 15-501 Bypass to South Campus. We made this concession in order to win town approval for the completion of the Cobb Chiller and Parking Deck, which was strongly opposed by the Gimghoul neighborhood, even though this project resulted in cleaning up a blighted area of campus near that neighborhood and improving the intersection with Country Club Drive.

For me, the design guidelines were the most important element of the Ayers Saint Gross Master Plan. They strengthened my hand in demanding quality work from first-rate architects. Early on the process, I saw the first list of proposed architects for the multi-phased physical science project, the largest project in the plan. It was not, in my opinion, a distinguished list. I sent it back and asked the planners to do two things. First, I said, let's establish a Design Review Board, which can help us choose great architects and help them create good projects. And second, let's cast our net nationally. We are building for the next century. We need to build well. I think the results speak for themselves. For the science complex, we got Bill Wilson and a group of buildings that are world-class in terms of their aesthetic beauty, their respect for historical context, and their capacity to support great science.

The Design Review Board has played a critical role in every one of these projects. Made up of architects and designers, this group has worked with project architects and with our own staff and faculty to make sure that these buildings are not only well designed, but appropriate for their setting, and really functional. As a result of this additional step in the internal design and review process, the Board of Trustees has a much higher degree of confidence in the integrity and quality of the projects that it has the ultimate responsibility to approve.

The faculty led the programming process. (One of the lessons learned here is that letting faculty plan the facilities that they will use is one of the strongest retention tools in the box.) This was particularly true in the physical science complex. These buildings were literally shaped by our academic visions. In this enormous complex, we wanted to facilitate interdisciplinary collaboration, so we built buildings that literally connect with each other. Ultimately, when this project is completed, we will have built physical connections to and among all of the physical sciences in the College of Arts and Sciences and to the health sciences further south.

Public higher education began in Chapel Hill. This is a very old campus, and therefore, much of the work during the Dynamic Decade had to do with restoring and repurposing old buildings. I was determined that we were going to do this well. Unfortunately, our track record was not the best in this area. As I took the oath of office on October 12, 2000, I had only to look a few feet to my right to catch a glimpse of the Campus Y, a derelict, partially condemned building designed by Frank Milburn in 1909. It had barely escaped demolition a few years earlier, and some Trustees still wanted it removed.

Polk and McCorkle Place were filled with buildings that cried out for help. Therefore, we created the position of Campus Historic Preservation Manager and appointed Paul Hardin Kapp to provide leadership in this area. I am proud of the painstaking work that has restored buildings to their original color and preserved their integrity, while modernizing them and making them useful for a twenty-first century university. Murphey Hall, with its restored hardwood floors and state-of-the-art classrooms is a good example. So is Memorial Hall, which has become the home of a truly world class performing arts program. Unfortunately, the work is not finished. Roughly half of the McKim and Mead buildings on Polk Place have been touched, the remainder waiting for the next round of funding. My favorite old building on campus, the A. J. Davis-designed Old Playmakers Theatre, has seen only an exterior renovation. Its interior, cleaned up though barely usable without air conditioning, quietly waits.

Perhaps the genius of the Master Plan is its recognition that the essence of the Carolina campus lies not in grand, heroic architecture, but in its landscape – in the connective tissue between buildings. I think back to Chancellor Robert House, who famously said, "My first impression of Chapel Hill was trees. My last impression was trees." My favorite summary of all that we accomplished in this dynamic decade is that while we added 6 million square feet of building space, we took twenty acres of asphalt and turned ten of those acres into green spaces. There was really no magic here. It just involved a major investment in parking structures to eliminate many acres of surface parking lots. Here again, I felt it was essential that we have the leadership on staff to advocate for the landscape —that landscape architecture was the functional equal to architecture.

While we wanted to preserve the beauty that existed in North Campus between Franklin Street and South Road, we wanted to create a similar area of beauty and reflection in the urbanized South Campus. The Rams Head deck and plaza was the cornerstone of this achievement. We have accomplished much of our goal with South Campus, but this, too, is incomplete. It is critical that we stay with the plan in the decades to follow.

Unseen in all of this development, but equally important, is UNC's incredible investment in infrastructure and its commitment to sustainability as evidenced in mammoth underground steam tunnels, cisterns for captured water runoff, and pipelines for treated water reuse. The appointment of a full-time Sustainability Coordinator was a key signal that we were making a serious and lasting commitment to sustainability. I am proud of the "green" buildings we built: Carrington, the FedEx Global Education Building, and the N.C. Botanical Garden. But the real demonstration of UNC's commitment to sustainability will be demonstrated in the build out of Carolina North, our campus of the future.

We express our values in what we build. We express our values in how we build. I like to think that the build out of the UNC campus during this dynamic decade truly expresses the values of this great University, that in these buildings and in the spaces that hold them, we find truth and integrity. *Lux. Libertas.*

Students on Polk Place. Source: Dan Sears, UNC Master Plan

CHAPTER 1

Sustaining the Campus

UNC'S DYNAMIC DECADE OF CAMPUS DEVELOPMENT

The university campus is a central feature in urban development. While driven by its educational mission, campus growth reflects many of the precepts of private real estate development in its quest for additional space. At the same time, the economic importance of the university casts it into a quasi-public role as community developer. The tensions between these internal and external roles can create substantial town/gown friction as the university seeks to expand and the community requires it to recognize and mitigate the impacts of its growth.

The *internal* logic of campus development stems from the university's core mission of teaching, research, and service; this requires attention to knowledge development, disciplinary excellence, and technological advance, as well as to the demands of faculty, student, and alumni constituencies. Arrayed against this is the *external* logic of the host community, which views the university campus as a very large activity center with associated neighborhood impacts, service demands, and land use implications. Because universities are among the community's largest landowners and employers, as well as major consumers of public services, they have an array of external constituents that assert claims related to physical location, economic impact, and political decisions (Perry and Wiewel 2005).

University growth, like that of private real estate development, is influenced by national and regional economic conditions. Universities must secure financing and therefore face the challenges posed by economic downturns. University developers are influenced by the same boom and

> ...the "dynamic decade of campus growth at the University of North Carolina at Chapel Hill is an intriguing mix of planning, politics, and designs

bust cycles that drive the private real estate development market. When economic conditions are favorable, as in the U.S. during the period up to the year 2008, campus growth takes off and local tensions escalate; when conditions are unfavorable, campus growth slows, along with local tensions. As Brutus remarked in Shakespeare's Julius Caesar, "There is a tide in the affairs of men, which taken at the flood, leads on to fortune."

University planners must be sensitive to the contending forces of market conditions, growth impacts, and local politics. At the same time, they must respond to the need to keep their campus facilities competitive with those of other universities seeking to outperform them in the arenas of research and teaching, faculty recruitment and retention, student quality and quantity, grant support and fund raising. In short, they must find ways to *sustainably develop* their campus environments with their blends of historic buildings, new projects, cherished landscapes, and typically inadequate infrastructure.

The purpose of this book is to tell the story of how one university met this complex sustainability challenge while catching the wave of the favorable economic boom during the late 1990's and early 2000's to renew itself and leap ahead. It recounts the ins and outs of creating and implementing the Master Plan at the University of North Carolina at Chapel Hill, and draws on this experience to lay out lessons for other universities concerned with planning for long-term sustainability.

UNC'S DYNAMIC DECADE OF DEVELOPMENT: 2001–2011

The story of the "dynamic decade" of campus growth at the University of North Carolina at Chapel Hill is an intriguing mix of planning, politics, and design. Thanks to a state bond issue that provided major capital funding passing at the same time as an innovative master plan was completed, and spurred by inspired political leadership and design guidance, this beautiful old campus was transformed into a sustainable new environment for 21st century teaching, learning, and research during ten fast-moving years of growth.

During that decade from 2001 to 2011, over six million square feet of new buildings were constructed, over a million square feet of existing buildings were renovated, over five million square feet of pedestrian paths and open space were created, a free bus system was initiated, and a new sustainability ethic was adopted. The UNC building boom was echoed across the nation. Nationally, college construction began to shift into high gear in 2000 and peaked in 2006, going from $7.3 billion to $15 billion per year (Abramson 2010).

This growth was catalyzed by $515 million in funding from a statewide Higher Education Bond Referendum in 2000, along with major private contributions. Then Chancellor James Moeser pledged to take that investment and triple it through private support to the University, generating in total some $1.5 billion in capital funding. With this funding boost, implementation of the Master Plan took off at a furious pace. By the end of the decade, between the bond funds, private donations, University investments, and ongoing State appropriations, UNC had invested $2.3 billion on a total of 165 projects.

Meanwhile, enrollment increased by 3,400 students, and 300 new faculty were recruited. Had this growth not been firmly guided and sensitively designed, the resulting impacts on the beautiful forested 18th century campus, chartered in 1789, could have been catastrophic. Fortunately, the University's newly prepared 2001 Master Plan set forth a powerful vision, generated through wide-ranging public participation, along with careful design guidelines to ensure that new projects would respect the beloved campus character. Realizing in 1998 that its old plan was no longer adequate to meet projected increases in student enrollment and building space, the University selected Ayers Saint Gross of Baltimore to undertake a new plan.

The resulting 2001 Master Plan was unanimously adopted by the UNC Board of Trustees and became the guiding beacon for the development made possible by the bond issue. However, because growth on the campus is subject to concurrent jurisdiction by the University and the Town of Chapel Hill, the story has an important second chapter.

The scale of the massive proposed campus growth ratcheted up political concern and conflict within the community of Chapel Hill. Neighbors of the campus, fearful of the impacts of growth on their neighborhoods, organized the Neighborhood Alliance, which lobbied the Chapel Hill Town Council to intervene on their behalf. Candidates for the Town Council actively sought the endorsement of the Neighborhood Alliance, crafting their platforms on a basis of controlling campus growth.

With a pro-neighborhood majority, the Council took a more active interest in campus development, broadening the scope of their zoning regulations and approval procedures to consider the impacts of campus development from the perspective of community costs and benefits. The Council also pressured the University to provide more on-campus housing to reduce conflicts between student and town residents in existing neighborhoods. Fear of political intervention by Chapel Hill prompted a state legislator to introduce a bill removing the Town's zoning control over campus development.

Town/gown politics could have short-circuited the planned campus growth. Chapel Hill elected officials like to oversee the details of all development in the Town, subjecting the University to a lengthy and rigorous Special Use Permit process with multiple committee reviews and public hearings. Had this process been applied to each proposed campus building, new development would have proceeded at a snail's pace. To avoid this gridlock, a new zoning category, Office/Institutional – 4 (OI-4), was negotiated in 2001. That zoning category required Town review and approval of a Development Plan that laid out a ten-year schedule of campus construction.

This new tool, the Development Plan, had to include extensive analyses of the impacts of the proposed ten-year projects in order to assure the community and the Town Council that development impacts were understood and would be mitigated. Once the Development Plan was approved by both the University and the Town, then the Town Manager could approve applications for individual Site Development Permits as an administrative action.

To manage the internal growth issues, the University relied on a multicentered institutional structure. The Board of Trustees used its Buildings and Grounds Committee to assess new projects prior to formal decision-making by the full Board membership. The existing Chancellor's Buildings and Grounds group, made up of faculty, staff, and students, provided advice to the Chancellor on plans and projects. At the direction of the Chancellor, the University Architect also formed an outside Design Review Board to work with architects from the early stages of new project designs. Finally, the University hired a new sustainability officer to advocate the inclusion of green development in all new plans and a historic preservation manager to oversee the renewal of the historic buildings, as well as a landscape architect, a stormwater manager, an environmental manager, a forest manager, and an accessibility manager.

Implementation succeeded so well that almost half of the plan's proposals moved forward in the first five years after completion of the 2001 Master Plan. Most of these were complete or under construction by 2009, as bulldozers and construction crews renewed and expanded the campus landscape.

Meanwhile, as development began to approach the responsible capacity of the existing campus, the University saw the need for a new research and teaching campus to ease space constraints and support new research and business relationships. Bringing the decade to a close, a second Master Plan and a Development Agreement with the Town of Chapel Hill for a new campus—Carolina North—were approved in 2009 after intense town/gown negotiations. At the same time, the national economy slowed, ending the development boom.

Campus growth followed the precepts of the Master Plan and Development Plan, but was continually adjusted in response to community concerns, design elaboration, and learning at each stage of implementation. During that planning and adjustment, important lessons were learned about sustainable campus development. While every campus has certain unique features, the basic sustainability principles are universal.

As we narrate the details of the UNC experience, we continually dig beneath that experience to bring out the more general lessons. These lessons should be relevant to all universities with historic campuses who are concerned with the planning, political, and design actions necessary to

1-1. Construction Underway for the Sciences Complex, 2004. Source: Dan Sears, UNC

update and refurbish existing buildings and common spaces with new buildings and green design standards from today.

LESSONS OF SUSTAINABLE CAMPUS DEVELOPMENT

Campus planners striving to retool the physical plants of older universities into sustainable environments for contemporary higher education face both challenges and opportunities. Master plan preparations demand widespread faculty, staff, and student participation to build consensus for innovative concepts. Town/gown politics demands patient and collaborative interaction with the community leaders who hold plan approval power. Furthermore, maintaining the consistent aesthetic appeal of a beautiful traditional campus requires clear and carefully considered design guidelines. However, the payoff for these efforts is a campus that combines the best of both the old and the new.

In this book, we view UNC's dynamic decade through the lens of *sustainable campus development*. Although the visionary 2001 Master Plan did not specifically discuss the concept of sustainability, it embodied basic sustainability principles. By viewing sustainability as broader than simply energy conservation and pollution reduction, UNC's resolution of the deeper issues of campus planning, politics, and design generated a

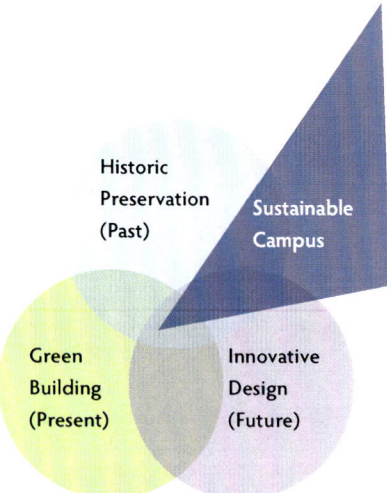

1-2. The Sustainable Campus

…the triple bottom line for a campus plan is sustaining the past, present, and future.

uniquely sustainable solution. Meanwhile, a parallel sustainability effort was growing through administrative channels.

Organized efforts to institutionalize sustainability at UNC began in 1999, leading to the formation of the UNC Sustainability Coalition. Executive Order 156 from the NC Governor called on state agencies to adopt sustainable practices. Simultaneously, students requested that the University community become more proactive on environmental issues. After two years of volunteer efforts, the University became the first in the state to employ a full-time Sustainability Coordinator. Cynthia Pollock Shea, LEED AP, was hired in 2001 and in 2003 the department grew to include an Energy Conservation Manager and an administrative assistant.

The sustainable development concept was set forth in 1987 by the Brundtland Commission of the United Nations: sustainable development is development that meets the needs of the present without compromising the ability of future generations to meet their own needs. That concept emphasizes the balance among environment, economy, and equity, sometimes called the "three Es" or the "triple bottom line."

The concept of campus sustainability requires a somewhat different perspective. Because the historic campus remains in place for generations, its maintenance must be a central focus of sustainable planning. Therefore, the triple bottom line for a campus plan is *sustaining the past, present, and future*. It is the *intersection* of these concerns that determines the beauty and functionality of a contemporary university campus.

Our findings can be summarized in terms of five general lessons. These are discussed in more detail in the following chapters and illustrated by experience in the design and implementation of different types of projects. However, we state them here to orient and prepare the reader for what is to come.

Lesson One. Define Sustainability as a Balance of Past, Present, and Future Needs

The master planning process started with recognition of the immense value of the traditional campus. In looking back at what was learned during the planning process, we find that sustainability was a major goal. Thus, our working definition of a sustainable campus is one that meets the needs of today's learning experience while balancing the need to preserve its historic resources, the need to be a contemporary model of green design and construction, and the need to innovate in order to meet future education capabilities. Its role is to lead in the generation and application of socially useful knowledge. Its plans are sensitive to the needs of both current and future stakeholders, on and off the campus. In short, the sustainable campus is an exemplar of forward-looking planning that does not lose sight of the past.

Lesson Two. Relate Development Proposals to the University's Mission

One of the foremost goals of the Master Plan was to assist in carrying out the University's mission, and that became a touchstone for assessing new development proposals. When funding becomes available for a major new construction program, there is a temptation to include many projects that are only marginally related to the mission of the University. Proponents of affordable housing, for example, argue that public funds and land should be devoted to solving the wider community's affordable housing problem. Environmentalists argue that it is the University's duty to set aside large tracts of open space. Campus decision-makers must evaluate such worthy proposals against their overall responsibility toward higher education goals.

Lesson Three. Build Consensus with All Stakeholders from the Start

A major effort from the start of the Master Plan process was to understand and work with all affected parties in order to generate a plan that met everyone's needs. University expansion necessarily generates impacts on both the external community and the internal schools and departments. Calculating the costs and benefits of growth is complex and contentious. If serious efforts are not made at the onset to understand and work with the many stakeholders, then plans will be derailed at the end of the process or watered down by unwise compromises. Money and time spent on building consensus through enlightened tradeoffs is well spent.

Lesson Four. Limit Growth to Responsible Campus Capacity

Most university campuses face space limitations and older campuses often approach build out on their sites. This underscores the value of a development strategy based on limiting growth to the *responsible capacity* of the campus. This is determined not simply by the number of square feet of land available for new building, but also by the availability of associated infrastructure and support institutions, in addition to the need to maintain the functions of natural systems. For example, at UNC the responsible capacity was expanded by an extensive stormwater management program, a free University/Town public bus system, thermal storage for chilled water, water reuse, recycling, tree replacement, and creation of a Sustainability Office.

Lesson Five. Review Projects for Consistency with Master Plan Principles Throughout Design

Investing in up-front and continuing design review maximizes stakeholder participation and understanding and improves final project designs. At UNC, all plans and building project designs were reviewed by three groups. The Board of Trustees' Buildings and Grounds Committee involved the University's top level decision-making body in design oversight. The Chancellor's Buildings and Grounds Committee involved faculty and staff in making formal recommendations to the Chancellor. A newly created Design Review Board of experienced architects and planners gave periodic critiques to project architects. Thus, all plans were thoroughly vetted internally to make sure that they followed the principles set forth in the Master Plan before going public for review by town-elected officials and community residents.

PLANNING, POLITICS, AND DESIGN AS INPUTS TO A SUSTAINABLE CAMPUS

Many books on campus planning or architecture focus on pictures of the attractive new buildings, along with colored plans of the projected growth. We include such images and plans, but we also look at what went on behind the scenes and during the linked sequences of planning, political negotiations, and architectural design. We interview some of the key players to capture their perspectives on important decisions and actions. In our view, it is not enough to simply tout the products of campus development without explaining their history. In some cases, the underlying history may be more important and enlightening than the as-built structures.

In looking back over the development decade at UNC, we discuss the process as well as the products of campus growth. We look at the full slate of issues, including development of planning strategies, negotiating the town/gown approval processes, and guiding the architectural, engineering, and landscape design activities. We describe the physical and institutional outcomes and derive the principles underlying the successful outcomes. We focus on the underlying theme of achieving sustainability in the face of sometimes daunting challenges.

The structure of the book follows the chronology of the dynamic decade. Chapters 2–5 deal with the planning, priority-setting, design, and preservation processes. Chapters 6–8 deal with the construction of new projects across the campus. Chapters 9–10 discuss future projects and conclusions about lessons for creating a sustainable campus.

The story starts in Chapter 2 with the preparation of the 2001 Master Plan, including the generation of proposals, the stakeholder participation process, and the governmental reviews. Master planning faced the challenge of creating a new vision of sustainability while rethinking the responsible capacity of the campus, building consensus on a strategy to meet projected growth demands, and respecting the existing constraints of the 200-year-old campus setting. In short, the big issue was figuring out how to create a framework that would allow the campus to grow substantially without doing serious harm to the beautiful old campus that alumni remember.

Chapter 3 describes the content of the Development Plan, including its guiding principles and its strategies for adding new construction as

---

Developing the Plan

CHAPTER 2
Creating the Framework

CHAPTER 3
Setting Priorities

CHAPTER 4
Designing Projects

CHAPTER 5
Preserving the Historic Campus

Building New Projects

CHAPTER 6
Enhancing the Historic North Campus

CHAPTER 7
Recasting the Twentieth Century Southeast Campus

CHAPTER 8
Growing the Health Services Southwest Campus

Future Projects and Conclusions

CHAPTER 9
Visualizing a New Research Campus at Carolina North

CHAPTER 10
Lessons for Creating a Sustainable Campus

1-3. Book Outline

well as renewing existing buildings. Development planning faced the challenge of escaping the Chapel Hill zoning straitjacket that had been accustomed to doing extensive and time-consuming public reviews of each individual building. It had to create a new zoning approach based on a single comprehensive review of a ten-year growth program. It also faced the challenge of reorienting the University's own decision-making process to analyze the threats and opportunities involved in setting priorities for a specific ten-year development plan.

Chapter 4 reviews the procedures and guidelines for the Project Design Process. Project design faced the challenge of reorienting the University's existing design review system to handle a flood of new projects while firmly guiding the individual project architects toward designs that were compatible with the historic Carolina aesthetic. Many nationally-known architectural firms were employed to design new buildings. The project design review process had to encourage design creativity without opening the door to an undisciplined array of flamboyant "starchitect" assemblages.

Chapter 5 looks at the campus renovation program that analyzed and preserved UNC's historic buildings and landscapes. To create a truly sustainable campus, new buildings and facilities must be planned to be compatible with, and contribute to, the important historic heritage of the older campus. The challenge of preservation was twofold: to modernize the older campus buildings without losing their historic character and charm, and to ensure the continuing ecological health and natural processes of the historic landscape.

The remainder of the book describes the ensuing plans and projects carried out during the dynamic decade. The description of these plans and projects is organized around the "communities" built up by locating and connecting related clusters of activities—a major tenet of sustainable design that encourages mixed uses within comfortable walking distance to reduce automobile traffic. For example, the Master Plan creates a new Southeast Campus community by linking new and existing student dormitories with student recreational and dining facilities by means of a new pedestrian walkway that bridges the North and South Campuses.

Chapter 6 discusses the North Campus projects for the sciences, arts, and student housing communities. All of the restoration projects and a limited number of new projects were fitted into the largely built-up North Campus. The North Campus challenge was to shoehorn major expansions of its arts and sciences facilities into the traditional central campus. It had to build walkable, mixed-use communities that connected old and new buildings and activity patterns, without disrupting the historic landscape and building patterns.

Chapter 7 discusses the Southeast Campus projects for student and student family housing and athletic facilities. More space for development allowed the construction of many more student residential projects on the Southeast Campus, where the challenge was to find ways to create attractive and convenient on-campus living facilities. Planners had to figure out how to blend the old and new dormitories and to provide accessible dining, recreation, and student services to the larger student population there.

Chapter 8 covers the planning for the Southwest Campus, home to the extensive health affairs and health research communities. Here the challenge was to humanize the existing sprawling agglomeration by giving more priority to pedestrian movements and outdoor commons areas and less priority to arterial roads and parking facilities. Planners had to ensure access for large numbers of patients and health affairs staff, while providing space for continuing expansion of health affairs and health research structures and activities.

Chapter 9 describes the planning for a future research and academic campus to be located on the University's Horace Williams Airport site. As it became clear that the existing campus would not be able to accommodate much growth beyond the needs identified in the Master Plan, the potential to develop the large University property adjacent to the airport was explored. The challenge for the planners of this new Carolina North campus was to work out an agreement with the Town of Chapel Hill on a development strategy that would satisfy the needs of both parties while preserving the valuable environmental resources on the land.

Chapter 10 returns to the book's original theme: planning the sustainable campus. It summarizes and reiterates the lessons learned from the experience of the dynamic decade. It points the way toward the campus of the future, where sustainability will be the touchstone for development decisions, town/gown relationships, and design concepts.

CHAPTER 2

Creating the Framework

THE CAMPUS MASTER PLAN

> *This is an elegant reinforcement of the original McKim, Mead & White plan. By maintaining its historic precepts, it gives new clarity while restoring the ground plan of the campus for the students and faculty. The open diagram respects the original grid system, reintroduces courtyard planning and the green flow so it again dominates the campus plan. This is an antidote to Joni Mitchell's lament on paving paradise to put up a parking lot.*
>
> 2002 Excellence in Design Award-AIA Baltimore

Creation of the award-winning 2001 Campus Master Plan was spurred by the need to update the 1988 Campus Framework Plan prepared by Johnson, Johnson, and Roy (1991) and by announcement of significant enrollment increases for the 16-campus University of North Carolina system. The three-year planning process began in 1998 with the hiring of the Baltimore-based architectural firm of Ayers Saint Gross. Charged with creating a plan for the physical development of the campus into the 21st century, the architectural consultants launched an intensive process during which hundreds of faculty, staff, students, administration, and campus neighbors engaged in over 500 planning meetings. A key concern of the participants was planning for preservation and extension of the existing open space. This chapter describes the information gathered and the actions taken during the planning process for the 2001 Campus Master Plan.

Campuses have been described as "ideal, independent villages that provide the setting for socially and culturally coherent communities …

2-1. Proposed Open Space Plan. Source: 2001 UNC Campus Master Plan

a distinctly American invention at once representing a search for a viable past and an embrace of the future." (Stern 2010, 11) The story of the UNC Master Plan preparation follows that process of searching for key elements of the viable past around which the University was built and then looking for the needs and aspirations of a forward-looking vision that would successfully embrace the future.

The sustainability challenge for master planners Adam Gross and his colleagues at Ayers Saint Gross was to build consensus on a future development vision that would meet the University's projected growth demands while respecting the responsible capacity of the campus, including its important environmental, physical, and social constraints. In the process, they would be developing settings for the overlapping social and cultural communities that support the many activities of campus life. Their task was to bring a diverse group of student, faculty, staff, and town stakeholders to agreement on a plan to grow the campus while doing no harm to its inherent values—a daunting assignment!

ADAM GROSS, MASTER PLANNER

A native of the Northeast, Adam Gross had no preconceived notions about UNC's campus before he started work on the Master Plan in 1998, but it didn't take long for Gross, a principal at the Baltimore design firm Ayers Saint Gross (ASG), to figure out that UNC was a special place.

"It was like a New England town in the South," he says, recalling first impressions of intellectual rigor, liveliness, and sports tradition, plus the "softness of the landscape" created by brick paths, wide quadrangles and giant trees.

It was also quickly apparent that the campus's winning qualities came to a more or less hard stop at South Road. "Everything north of South Road was very beloved, and everything south of it was the opposite, sprawl and concrete," Gross says.

His design team's challenge became how to export the best qualities of the North Campus to the South Campus, a task that some thought would be impossible given the utilitarian design of many of the existing buildings on the South Campus.

Nor did the doubts stop there. David Pardue, a UNC Trustee from 1995 to 2003 who was on the committee that selected Ayers Saint Gross, recalls hearing plenty of pessimism about whether any plan could accommodate the sheer scale of growth—the study plan called for UNC to add 6,000 students by 2010, going from 24,000 to 30,000—without damaging the beauty and feel of the campus.

"Many people in town and some on campus were against the effort, arguing that we shouldn't grow and therefore we didn't need a new plan," Pardue says. "From my perspective, the plan was absolutely essential. The growth was coming, like it or not, and the only issue was whether we properly planned or whether we let it happen haphazardly, as we had sometimes done in the past."

Ayers Saint Gross sought to allay these concerns one by one. On one front, they sought to improve the quality of the grounds on South Campus by "creating density in the best sense of the word," Gross says—a goal that was achieved in part through the construction of four new student residential halls that had the added benefit of blocking 1960s-era architecture from the views of passersby.

At the same time, they sketched out vital new pedestrian corridors to link the two campuses. One flowed through the new science campus—the collection of laboratory and classroom buildings (Murray, Venable, Caudill) that took the place of the old Venable Hall—and opened up a new route between north and south. A second was created by the new Rams Head Parking Deck, which gave students a more pleasant walking route to the one that formerly took them down one hill, across a parking lot, and up another hill.

In the course of the three-year process, Gross and his team faced their fair share of concerns about traffic, overcrowding, noise, and other common side effects of growth—"a lot of contentious neighborhood and town council meetings." And one element of the plan, UNC's proposed expansion south along Mason Farm Road, drew perhaps more opposition from residents than any other. But Gross and ASG were able to work through these objections step by step.

"We tried to see the campus from (the residents') point of view," Gross says. "We would meet in their neighborhoods, stand in their backyards and try to understand their concerns on the ground so that we could hopefully be sensitive and responsive to their issues. Patience is also necessary in these situations, as is a willingness to pull back and rethink solutions in a way that engages the neighbors and encourages them to be part of the solution."

Former Trustee David Pardue, for one, thinks that ASG's solutions were spot on. "Most important is the fact that eventually we were able to develop a workable, affordable plan that achieved great results," Pardue says. "I shudder to think what would have happened had we not had Adam's help."

> **Master Plan**
>
> **OBSERVATION**
> analyses of place, precedents, and programs
>
> **CONCEPTUAL DEVELOPMENT**
> principles, sketches, open space, conceptual plan
>
> **PRECINCT STUDIES**
> stakeholder tours/ workshops, option testing, preferred options
>
> **FINAL PLAN AND DESIGN GUIDELINES**
> campus-wide and district buildings and open space

2-2. Master Plan Phases

The UNC master planning process proceeded through four phases. During the *Observation phase*, existing data, studies, interviews, history, and programs were analyzed in order to understand what factors had shaped the campus over the past two centuries. During the *Conceptual Development phase*, guiding principles were generated, a conceptual plan was sketched out, and consensus was built about campus development directions. During the *Precinct Studies phase*, discrete areas of the campus were studied in workshops and stakeholder tours in order to test options and decide on preferred projects at a neighborhood scale. During the *Final Master Plan and Design Guidelines phase*, the preceding work was integrated into an overall plan and a set of development guidelines to guide growth. The four phases were carried out in sequence, although there was much looping back and forth during succeeding phases.

OBSERVATION PHASE—WHAT SHAPES THIS CAMPUS?

The Observation phase analyzed the place—its physical and activity systems, its precedents—comparison with peer institutions, and its programs—space use and needs. The goal was to understand the underlying factors that shape the existing campus before planning new buildings and facilities.

PLACE—the physical campus and its activity patterns represent the personality and soul of the University in the hearts and minds of its users. The beauty of sunlight pouring through the trees in McCorkle and Polk Places, the friendly conversations while sitting on a stone wall after class, the dignity of academic buildings clad in mellow red brick and white trim constitute unforgettable memories of one's time on the UNC campus. To capture this essence in drawings and numbers, the planners analyzed the historic buildings and their arrangement on the campus, the older neighborhoods adjacent to the campus, the natural systems underlying the campus, and the built systems and infrastructure serving the campus.

Historic Campus. Central to the forward thinking necessary for the plan was an in-depth understanding of the existing campus and its historic precedents during the past 200 years (Powell 1992; Allcott 1986). During this reconnaissance, four broad development epochs were identified, illustrating the sequence of development from the origin of the University in 1793 to the start of the 1990's planning process.

Epoch I: 1793–1914. The original concept of a people's university was realized through a small residential undergraduate college. Focused on the park-like quadrangle of McCorkle Place, the first buildings were arranged in formal axes parallel and perpendicular to Franklin Street, the main street of Chapel Hill. The hub of the layout was South Building, the location of the Chancellor's office.

Epoch II: 1915–1945. The University's first comprehensive plan, prepared by John Nolen in 1917–1919 and added to by McKim, Mead, and White in 1920, expanded the campus to the south and east. Polk Place, a formally laid out academic quadrangle, extended the main axial green space from South Building to Wilson Library.

Epoch III: 1946–1962. Following World War II, campus growth continued on Polk Place. In addition, major hospital and public health buildings were built in the south, along with a cluster of married student housing for the returning veterans.

Epoch IV: 1963–1997. Increased funding for medical research spurred Health Affairs growth on the south campus, including major hospital and research buildings and parking decks. New dormitories and athletic buildings also grew on the south campus, while some academic, housing, and student support facilities were added to the north. A Campus Framework Plan prepared by consultants Johnson, Johnson, and Roy (JJR) was approved.

During the four epochs, the floor area of the campus expanded from less than 800,000 square feet to 11.9 million square feet (Table 2-1). The 2001 Master Plan identified a modest increase of 767,000 square feet from 1998 to 2001, but this continued to grow as funding became available under the year 2000 statewide bond issue for higher education, bringing the total close to 13 million square feet.

Historic Neighborhoods. In addition to the historic buildings on the campus, the historic neighborhoods adjacent to the campus affect future campus growth. The UNC campus is ringed on three sides by Chapel Hill neighborhoods listed on the National Register. New construction in these neighborhoods is tightly regulated under the Town of Chapel Hill Historic District guidelines. Over time their composition has changed from including some student-friendly housing to more expensive upper income houses no longer affordable to students. While enjoying excellent proximity to university facilities and events, the residents of historic neighborhoods fiercely resist outward expansion of the campus, as well as new buildings on the outer edges of the existing campus. In effect, the campus is ringed with a historic neighborhoods collar.

Natural Systems. Topography, vegetation, and wa-

TABLE 2-1. Campus building floor area growth.
Source: Campus Master Plan 2001, pg. 6.

Epoch	Floor Area (square feet)	Added Cumulative Floor Area (square feet)
1793–1914	778,937	778,937
1915–1945	1,214,665	1,993,602
1946–1962	1,981,275	3,974,877
1963–1997	7,902,472	11,877,340
1998–2001	767,000	12,644,940
In design, Fall 2001	288,000	12,932,949

> In effect, the campus is ringed with a historic neighborhoods collar.

2-3. Campus Topography.
Source: Ayers Saint Gross

ter have affected past planning and are important determinants of future development. As part of the Triassic Basin, the existing landform was created some 200 million years ago. The original organization of the campus followed two ridge lines. The North Campus grid, centered on Polk and McCorkle places, runs at a right angle to Franklin Street, Chapel Hill's main east-west road, which follows the major ridge line. The Health Affairs campus to the south is located along a secondary ridge. Its layout is oriented at an angle to the North Campus grid.

The UNC campus sits in a green and wooded landscape. On the North Campus, buildings are integrated into this landscape and open spaces are defined by edges and ceilings of trees. Vegetation reinforces the relaxed, informal spatial character of the campus. The grove of trees around Kenan Stadium is a defining characteristic of Carolina. On the

South Campus, the larger buildings become objects placed in carved-out portions of the landscape. New development must respect the existing mature landscape and attempt to heal areas where the landscape has been damaged. The tree canopy must be continued from north to south.

Water flows along the natural contours of the land. As it leaves the campus, this water enters streams at the core of two major watersheds. Most of the campus drains into the Morgan Creek basin to the south. A portion of the North Campus drains into the Little Creek basin to the north. Water flows are important because the campus drainage must be contained and managed so as to avoid degrading water quality in the surrounding lakes and water supply reservoirs. Most of the original open creeks and streams had been placed in underground pipes to accommodate previous campus growth. Where possible, these were proposed to be returned to their open state, a process called "daylighting."

Built Systems. Making the campus work requires an array of built facilities and services, including roads, pedestrian paths, transit, parking, and utilities. Each one has a capacity, an influence on the others, and a relationship with systems outside the campus. The Observation phase of the planning process analyzed existing built systems patterns and characteristics as inputs to designing the future campus.

Planners concluded that there were in effect two campuses at the University of North Carolina at Chapel Hill. The historic North Campus was defined by buildings edging a strong central axis of green open space following Polk and McCorkle Places, resulting in an attractive, human-scale built environment based on pedestrian circulation. The newer South Campus, containing Health Affairs, athletic facilities, and high-rise student residential facilities, was defined by its streets and parking lots based on automobile circulation, as well as by some remnant forests. To create continuity between the two, the patterns of open space, paths, and streets of North Campus needed to be extended to South Campus.

North Campus streets were laid out in a coherent grid that was friendly to pedestrians, while South Campus streets did not follow a network, and were too wide and far apart. Pedestrian paths on North Campus focused on Polk and McCorkle Places. South Campus paths were scattered and less well connected, making it difficult to walk between the two areas as well as to various Health Affairs buildings.

Parking and traffic were seen by many as the biggest problems on campus. While remote park-and-ride lots served much of the demand, more than 20 acres were devoted to existing surface parking lots. Planners believed that future plans should minimize automobile traffic on the main campus, instead relying more on the joint University-Town bus system, the regional bus system, and the potential future fixed guide-way transit system connecting the campus to Durham and the Research Triangle Park.

In addition to the surface streets, paths, and parking areas, planners

> Parking and traffic were seen by many as the biggest problems on campus.

CREATING THE FRAMEWORK   23

mapped an underground system of major utility lines running through the campus. This underground network constitutes a hidden infrastructure framework that influences where new buildings can be placed. These water lines, steam lines, and electric lines are expensive to move and limit flexibility in siting new buildings.

PRECEDENT aspects compared the 1998 built campuses of UNC with those of peer institutions at the University of Georgia and the University of Virginia. Diagrams of the building footprint patterns of each university were drawn and compared in terms of scale and density, circulation and parking, open space, walkability, and relationship to neighboring communities.

These diagrams revealed that the UNC campus ground plan was denser and more clearly organized than its sister institutions. However, the diagrams also highlighted the disconnection between the built areas and streets of the North Campus and those of the South Campus.

PROGRAM aspects looked at campus space needs, including current shortfalls and demand for accommodating future enrollment increases. Two scenarios were estimated: a *moderate growth* increase from the total enrollment baseline of 24,189 to a new total of 27,500, and an *aggressive growth* increase to a new total of 30,175.

To support the moderate growth estimate, about 1.5 million gross square feet (GSF) of academic and support space would be needed to match average levels at six peer public universities (University of California at Berkeley, University of Georgia, University of Michigan-Ann Arbor, University of Virginia, University of Washington-Seattle, and University of Wisconsin-Madison). This increased to 1.8 million GSF when the effect of planned demolition was considered.

To support the aggressive growth estimate, about 2.34 million GSF would be needed to match average peer levels. This increased to 2.7 million with planned demolition included.

In response to Town concerns that the University was not providing enough student housing, former Chancellor Michael Hooker promised in 1998 that future plans would include "a bed for every undergraduate head." To fulfill this promise, about 1.3 GSF of residential space would be required under the moderate growth estimate. This would support some 2,900 students, the number of undergraduates added in that scenario and 90 percent of the total additional students, in suite-style housing. To accommodate 90 percent of the additional students under the aggressive growth estimate would require 5,400 beds or about 2.4 million GSF of residential space.

In addition to planning for the new space requirement, the space needs analysis recommended that the University move ahead with its plan to upgrade and renovate its existing instructional space, along with some research and library space.

CONCEPTUAL DEVELOPMENT PHASE

During the Conceptual Development phase, planning participants generated a set of guiding principles to guide preparation of the Conceptual Plan. Based on these principles, a number of conceptual sketches were prepared, along with an open space diagram. These were integrated into the Final Conceptual Plan, a broad brush approach described as a "sketch before painting."

GUIDING PRINCIPLES. The four guiding principles were:

- Support Carolina's mission of teaching research and public service.
- Export the qualities of McCorkle and Polk places by using their integration of built and natural systems as a model for future growth and renovation.
- Enhance the University's intellectual climate by removing barriers and creating new venues for intellectual life.
- Support local and regional planning strategies through University plans for housing, parking, transit, utilities, and growth.

CONCEPTUAL SKETCHES. A series of ideas was explored, based on findings from the Observation phase. The main ideas stemmed from visualizing the campus as a cluster of three academic villages: the historic North Campus core, a new Health Affairs village to the southwest, and a new housing and student life village to the southeast. In the Conceptual Design, the grid street system, pattern of buildings, paths, and connected open spaces of the North Campus would be extended to the new villages.

The new framework of streets and open space was to bring the human scale and orderly layout of the historic campus core to the new Health Affairs and student housing and life villages, while accommodating the requirements of a contemporary research university. These were powerful early ideas. While many refinements were made to this concept sketch as planning proceeded, the basic structure remained remarkably similar in the final Master Plan.

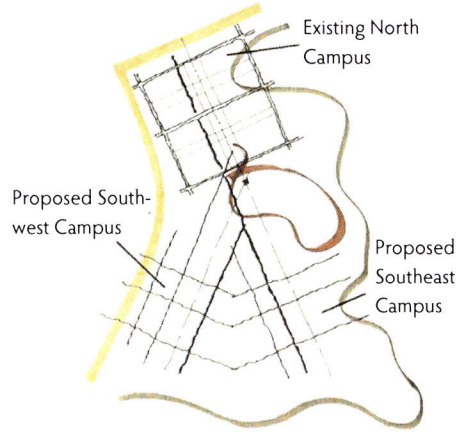

2-4. Conceptual Design. Source: 2001 UNC Campus Master Plan

CREATING THE FRAMEWORK   25

PRECINCT STUDIES PHASE

The Precinct Studies phase was crucial to the planning process because it built consensus for the major elements and details to be included in the Master Plan. During this phase, the planning process expanded to involve a comprehensive group of stakeholders: faculty, staff, students, neighbors, and local officials. Four precincts were defined for more detailed planning:

1. Sciences precinct
2. North Campus precinct
3. Health Affairs precinct
4. Academics/Housing/Athletics precinct

Stepping down from the overall campus concept plan, the Precinct Studies phase tested hundreds of planning proposals for discrete areas through intensive stakeholder discussions and critiques. Individuals who work and live in each precinct walked the campus and took part in two-day workshops led by the planning team. Participants met in an on-campus design studio which contained sketch plans and models. A unique visualization approach used alternative design ideas drawn on cut-outs of various campus areas, which could be pasted onto the overall campus plan for study. These so-called "paper dolls" could be quickly revised, providing a simple and flexible means for stakeholders to see and assess their ideas against the larger context. The planners used this technique to help participants visualize alternative layouts of new buildings.

This approach allowed the planners and the stakeholders to review building setbacks and scale, engineering systems, pedestrian and vehicular circulation, service points, open space and entrances, code compliance, and landscape composition. The resulting precinct plans hammered out the big ideas, as well as the details, for siting major new buildings and parking which were then carried forward into the work on the Final Master Plan.

FINAL PLAN AND DESIGN GUIDELINES

FINAL PLAN. The Final Plan section of the Master Plan laid out the proposed development on an overall plan drawing, as well as on side-by-side existing and proposed breakouts of key elements: open space, pedestrian circulation, vehicular circulation, parking, buildings, and building use. The Final Proposed Campus Master Plan highlighted the way that proposed buildings (shown in red) would fit into the existing campus fabric.

The Master Plan is a long-range vision for the ultimate development of the campus. It does not contain a specific date for completion. Rather, it is to be carried out over time through a ten-year Development Plan and through subsequent stages in later years.

The final plan relies on careful infill in the north and wholesale trans-

2-5. Final Proposed Campus Master Plan (new buildings in brown). Source: 2001 UNC Campus Master Plan

formation of parking lots in the south to accommodate growth while improving the physical character of the campus. Several existing surface parking lots will become building sites and lost parking will be made up in new decks. Buildings will be sited to create new quadrangles and improve walkability. New pedestrian bridges and ground-level walkways will connect north and south campus.

DESIGN GUIDELINES. Design Guidelines are included in the Plan to ensure that the future buildings and grounds are as well conceived and executed as those of the past. The goal is to set a framework for future designs so that the civic nature of the historic core is extended campus-wide. The guidelines recognize that the campus is unified by consistent elements such as low stone walls, brick walks, and landscape treatments. Architecture is more diverse, especially between north and south areas of the campus, but it tends to be consistent within precincts.

The guidelines send a strong, clear message about the importance of respecting the things that make the Carolina campus a beautiful and inspiring place. To maintain a unified and consistent built environment, future designers must fit their buildings into the existing context, rather than seeking to create radically diverging new architectural compositions. The guidelines are the tools to implement the recommendations of the Master Plan.

The organization of the Design Guidelines reflects the overall framework. Part I addresses campus-wide documentation of existing Carolina building styles, open space, and street types. Part II recommends specific guidelines for three districts—north, southeast, and southwest. Part III lays out a process for implementing the guidelines, including a schedule of review and approval meetings.

Campus-wide guidelines distinguish between "background" buildings that form the edges of quadrangles and "heroic" buildings that stand in places of honor or special focus. Preferred models of compatible buildings, based on existing examples, are identified. Building siting should use simple plans that create common outdoor spaces. Massing and scale should complement the rhythms and scale of surroundings. Fenestration and materials should reflect revered precedents from the UNC campus as well as successful buildings from other university campuses.

Open space is central to campus design, constituting places of interaction, study, and recreation. The UNC campus contains a full range of open space types, including paved courtyards, lawns, wooded open places, a managed arboretum, and an old growth forest. Future open space should reflect the geometry and organization of the campus. Natural woodlands, steep slopes, and streambeds should be preserved and highlighted. The primary palette of grass with hardwood shade trees, brick walks and stone walls should be extended throughout the campus.

District guidelines identify the distinctive nature generated by topography, history, and use. The north district goal is to reinforce the existing fabric of buildings and grounds that make this the most memorable area of campus. The southeast district goal is to establish a new fabric of buildings and grounds that support a mixed-use village of living and learning. The southwest district goal is to establish scale, create open spaces, and form edges that complement the needs of Health Affairs and its users.

ADDITIONAL PLANS. The Master Plan includes additional plans for specific functions. A Transportation and Parking section describes the conclusions of a supporting study prepared by Parsons Brinkerhoff Quade & Douglass and Martin/Alexiou/Bryson. An Environmental Master Plan section, prepared by landscape architects Andropogen Associates, and environmental consultants Cahill and Associates, describes the conclusions of a supporting study aimed at evaluating the impacts of increased development and impervious surface on land and water resources, protecting environmentally sensitive areas, and addressing water quality regulations. The Utilities Master Plan, prepared by Affiliated Engineers, analyzes the impact of build out of the Master Plan on the four major utility systems: steam, chilled water, electrical power, and data/telecommunications. The Stormwater Management Plan provides the basis for installing best management practices for controlling runoff.

The Environmental Master Plan tests the premise that the UNC campus could accommodate significant additional square footage while preserving and even enhancing critical natural resources of land and water. These resources include the campus setting, the Mason Farm Biological Reserve, and the regional water resources affected by the University's building program and stormwater management. The charge was to evaluate the campus land and water resources, guide their protection and restoration, and develop growth strategies that mitigate the impacts of development on the main campus and downstream. The Master Plan was revised to reflect recommendations from the Environmental Plan to protect significant natural landscapes from development, to daylight some existing buried streams, and to site new buildings in South Campus away from steep, forested slopes. According to Jill Coleman, the facilities planning landscape architect, the impact of the Environmental Master Plan was significant because "it clearly placed recognition and protection of the campus natural assets front and center of the campus planning effort."

How are the broad ideas and planning proposals of the Master Plan translated into feasible development projects? The next chapter on the Development Plan discusses how the Master Plan vision for the overall campus was broken out into separate projects for implementation over a ten-year period.

CHAPTER 3

Setting Priorities
THE DEVELOPMENT PLAN

The July 3, 2001, Development Plan took the first step in *implementing* the Master Plan. The Master Plan served as the big picture of University development extending over the long-range future, while the Development Plan was the medium view, extending through the coming decade. Development would be ubiquitous, with both old and new buildings facing construction crews. Not even venerable Memorial Hall would be exempt.

The Development Plan was an institutional innovation generated during the master planning process to replace the existing building-by-building review under Town zoning. Basically, the University's Development Plan said to the Town, "This is our ten-year list of expected projects that we would like you to review and approve as a comprehensive development program, rather than subjecting each new building to individual special use permit reviews." Its benefit to the Town was that decision-makers could address all of the impacts of anticipated development in one comprehensive review process. Its benefit to the University was that building could proceed more expeditiously once the Development Plan had received Town approval.

The sustainability challenge for the Development Plan was twofold. The first challenge was to convince Town elected officials that they should change their existing process of conducting Special Use zoning reviews for each separate University building proposal, with the months of advisory board discussions, public hearings, and Council debates that each review entailed. Not only did such reviews take as much as a year or more, but also they occupied large portions of the Council's agendas. However, given the hallowed role of public participation in Chapel Hill

3-1. Construction Underway Inside Memorial Hall, 2003. Source: UNC Facilities Planning & Construction

zoning decisions, the new ordinance needed to promise more than simply increased efficiency: it also needed to show the public benefit of a comprehensive review of a ten-year plan as a means of holding the University accountable for the impacts of its new growth.

The second sustainability challenge was to prepare the Development Plan itself, not a typical broad-brush general plan, but a detailed implementation program based on exacting impact analyses, building priorities, and cost estimates. The University was accustomed to planning projects based on annual budget cycles and State appropriations, rather than committing itself to a precise ten-year development program. Not only did this administrative shift take countless internal discussions, trade-offs, and financial juggling acts, but it also required engaging a raft of specialized consultants to project the feasibility, sustainability, and impacts of various development scenarios. The resulting plan had to be able to stand up under intensive public scrutiny and to respond to the approval conditions imposed by the Town. If the Development Plan could weather such an intensive, accelerated process, then it would open the door to an unprecedented campus building renaissance.

The Development Plan added the dimension of time to the Master Plan proposals, setting a ten-year schedule and sequence for construction. It described buildings and infrastructure that would begin construction during the next eight years and be completed within the next ten years. It included all types of projects: academic, research, student life, administration, utilities, parking, health care, and undergraduate and student family housing. It provided space to meet increased enrollment needs and

> The Development Plan was an institutional innovation…to replace existing building-by-building review under Town zoning.

> **Development Plan**
>
> **BUILDINGS**
> Construction date
> Function
> Size
>
> **INFRASTRUCTURE**
> Transportation
> Storm water
> Utilities
> Parking
>
> **IMPACTS**
> Streets
> Walkways
> Air quality
> Noise
> Lighting
>
> **MITIGATION**
> Storm water
>   management
> Parking replacement

3-2. Development Plan Components

addresses space deficiencies for existing programs. It sequenced development so as to support renovation projects with new construction.

The content of the Development Plan included a map and summary table listing all proposed buildings with the dates of construction, type of use, and size. It discussed the major types of infrastructure and their impacts. Finally, it outlined the mitigation proposed to deal with the anticipated impacts.

THE DEVELOPMENT PLAN PROCESS

When it became clear that the North Carolina statewide bond issue for higher education capital projects would be passed at nearly the same time as the completion of the 2001 Master Plan, it signaled an upcoming surge of new campus construction. To better accommodate reviews of the expected growth, the Town of Chapel Hill revised its development ordinance. The new Office/Institutional–4 (OI-4) Zoning District, approved in 2001, superseded the previous campus zoning district based on an overall campus-wide floor area ratio (FAR) limit.

A key feature of the OI-4 District was the preparation of a Development Plan that provided the community with an understanding of proposed development levels and their impacts so that mitigation measures could be designed and implemented. If the Development Plan was approved, then the Town Manager could approve applications for individual Site Development Permits as an administrative action, without the requirement of a Special Use Permit and its accompanying public hearing, saving months or even years of time dedicated to project reviews. Thus, the University submitted the 2001 Development Plan to the Town with extensive analyses of the anticipated impacts of its proposed projects.

A critical purpose of the Development Plan was to allow the University and the Town of Chapel Hill to look together at the University's comprehensive plan for controlled, responsible, and clearly defined growth. Under state zoning law, the University and Town hold concurrent jurisdiction over campus development. Because the University's development is subject to Town zoning, it was important to provide Town officials with ample time to understand, review, and approve in advance the proposed location, size, and uses of campus construction projects. The Development Plan was not only an internal planning document; it was also a critical tool for external communication, negotiation, and regulation.

The final Development Plan resulted from intense discussions and critiques of preliminary drafts by the Town and the public. Town staff reviewed proposals, submitted comments, and asked for additional information. Mayor Rosemary Waldorf and Chancellor James Moeser carried on extensive negotiations of fiscal equity, aimed at ensuring that the costs of mitigating the impacts of the proposed campus development would not be passed along to the Chapel Hill taxpayers and working out specific plans for mitigation of adverse impacts. Their joint memorandum on Town Gown Fiscal Discussions set forth a number of University commitments to compensate the Town for future municipal service loads, such as "providing a bed for every undergraduate head," cleaning up a former landfill on its Horace Williams tract, considering sites for new schools, and mitigating stormwater impacts.

The Development Plan was a new approach for the University and the Town, representing a very different way of dealing with planning and approval of campus development. It recognized that the myriad details involved in implementing a huge amount of new construction in the space of a single decade could not all be anticipated in advance. Hence, provision was made for addenda and modifications to the Development Plan as new data and information became available. In fact, two addenda and a modification were issued within two years of the completion of the 2001 Development Plan.

PREPARING THE DEVELOPMENT PLAN: INSTITUTIONAL CHALLENGES

Preparing the Development plan was a monumental task. At first, no one grasped the magnitude of the challenge. It gradually became clear that this would be an unprecedented institutional undertaking. Nancy Suttenfield, then UNC Vice Chancellor for Finance and Administration, remarked at the time that carrying out a 6 million square foot expansion was akin to building a Wake Forest University in the middle of the active UNC campus (Suttenfield 2005).

The task was complicated by the fact that the expansion would take place on top of the ongoing "normal" UNC building program. Not only did the Development Plan propose to use the Higher Education Bond funding to build fifty-one new projects during the dynamic decade, but also this new construction would be overlaid on about a hundred ongoing development projects. At the end of the dynamic decade in 2011, these ongoing projects (not in the Development Plan) included 14 new buildings and many renovated buildings, as well as a number of infrastructure projects.

This high growth period repeatedly challenged campus planners and architects to redefine how the campus would develop. The 1988 UNC plan, A Guide to Physical Development, prepared by Johnson, Johnson, and Roy, Inc. projected a campus building capacity of 14 million square feet; the 2001 Master Plan projected a capacity of 22–23 million square feet. In the first six years of the Development Plan, UNC added an additional 6 million square feet of new construction. As of 2011, approximately 20 million square feet have been developed, as the campus approaches its responsible capacity.

Preparation of the capital program for the Development Plan was

…carrying out a 6 million square foot expansion was akin to building a Wake Forest University in the middle of the active UNC campus.

ROSEMARY WALDORF, MAYOR

More than a decade after the fact, former Chapel Hill Mayor Rosemary Waldorf still remembers the low point in town/gown relations over the University's proposed development plan. On Memorial Day 2001, she was at home cooking supper when Chancellor James Moeser called to tell her that he had allowed a bill to be introduced in the state legislature that would strip the Town of its zoning authority over campus.

"There were people in the General Assembly who couldn't really see that Chapel Hill had a point of view in this plan," she recalls. "From the Town's perspective, that was highly unwelcome."

Fortunately for all parties, the bill would eventually be withdrawn. "It blew over, and we got back to the table," she says. "My mindset as mayor was always that it was necessary for the Town and the University to get along. I didn't see any other option for behavior."

Waldorf recalls a handful of issues that were critical to the town when weighing the University's plans. First, she says, was transportation. In the face of all this growth, the Town and the University could not function without an improved bus system and the University would have to cover the costs. Waldorf says that the decision to make the buses fare-free, which was only possible with the support of funds from the University and its students, was vital.

The Town also stipulated that stormwater runoff, and, in fact, any other infrastructure costs stemming from the proposed growth, would be managed and paid for by the University, not by the Town. Noting that UNC properties are exempt from local property taxes, Waldorf says, "The Town of Chapel Hill didn't need to pay for any of the infrastructure, and indeed we did not."

The part of the plan that involved, in the long term, taking over some residential properties in the Mason Farm area was equally important to the Town. "The plan's perimeter included some properties owned by people who had been in that neighborhood for decades," she says. "The whole neighborhood was pretty engaged in this process. My memory is that a boundary was established that included just a few properties."

Perhaps the trickiest issue, and the one that led to Moeser's Memorial Day phone call, was that the University did not want to be subjected to the Town's review and approval process for every building project. As it happened, Waldorf agreed with the University's position in principle. "If (the Town) got the parameters right on the big picture, why do we need to look at what they do to the interior of campus?" she says.

To navigate this concern, Waldorf was strategic when pulling together the Town Council committee that would work with the University on the development plan. To ensure that the committee's conclusions would stand up to scrutiny, she asked that it be composed of council members who had no connection to the University and were, in fact, most likely to be toughest on it. She recalls telling the group, over and over again, that "it was important for us to seem reasonable, and it was important for us to *be* reasonable."

"We weren't there to be just 'yes' people," she says. "But I think as a group we were always fair."

assigned to Bruce Runberg, Associate Vice Chancellor for Facilities Planning and Construction. He was charged with consolidating the plans for the ongoing projects with the new projects into a single working program and with building up the planning staff to deal with this additional surge of activity.

Together with Anna Wu, the Campus Architect, Runberg doubled the Facilities Planning staff, taking it from 30 up to 62, and hired a Historic Preservation Manager and a Landscape Architect. To honor the campus' commitment towards comprehensive sustainability, all staff designers were trained to become LEED accredited. To ensure that all new projects retained the Carolina character, a new Design Review Group was established to assist staff in reviewing projects and working with outside architects. To conduct the necessary supporting studies, outside consultants were engaged for specialized tasks, including stormwater master planning by Andropogen Associates and transportation management analyses by Martin Alexiou Bryson.

Not only was it necessary to set the development priorities, calculate the program needs, hire and supervise the architects and consultants, but also the Facilities Planning staff had to work out logistics for housing those ongoing educational programs whose buildings were being renovated or newly built. That logistics process was like a set of "daisy chains," since each renovation or demolition of an existing building required finding "swing space" to accommodate displaced faculty offices and teaching classrooms during construction. Swing space was created both in older buildings on campus and in rental quarters off campus, so that disruptions were held to a minimum.

Development Plan implementation was viewed as an opportunity to instill Carolina values, including emphasizing sustainability, preserving environmental resources, maintaining architectural consistency, and honoring historical integrity. Values were clearly stated in the Development Plan, through its parking policy, tree replacement policy, environmental policy, and open space corridors. To further the values during design, projects were explored to see how they provided chances to knit together "communities" of related projects or functions. Architects were encouraged to extend their designs to include sustainability and context: the connections and spaces between buildings, rather than simply limiting their scope to individual structures.

To obtain funds for this wider scope, a fee structure was set up for each project to pay for infrastructure, open space, and energy out of the building budget. Advisory committees, such as Buildings and Grounds, Pedestrian Safety, and the Design Review Board, reviewed project plans to ensure that they met Carolina standards. As projects proceeded, their review compliance was tracked with a computer program known as "Dr-Checks" (Design Review Checking System), which allows project reviewers to enter their comments so that the design team may respond through a web browser into a database.

BRUCE RUNBERG, ASSOCIATE VICE CHANCELLOR FOR FACILITIES PLANNING AND CONSTRUCTION

"It's like building a Wake Forest University in the middle of a very active campus."

That's how one of Bruce Runberg's colleagues described the scale of UNC's build out during the dynamic decade, and the phrase comes quickly to Runberg's mind when he is asked to recall that time.

"On the one hand we were overwhelmed, and on the other we were very glad," says Runberg, UNC's Associate Vice Chancellor for Facilities Planning and Construction. "We knew the University had a huge backlog of needs."

Before 2000, he says, the University was fortunate if it secured funds for two capital projects a year through the regular State appropriations process. The passage of the bond program, however, quite suddenly put 150 on his docket—some $1.5 billion worth of projects that had to get done. "It was very challenging and very surprising," he says.

With all that construction on the horizon, one of Runberg's first moves was to work with the Town to develop a new methodology for project review and approval. The old project-by-project system was simply too cumbersome and time-consuming given the numbers now involved. The University also needed to renegotiate a 14.5 million-square-foot cap on campus buildings, imposed by the Town and the Orange Water and Sewer Authority.

The negotiations were "very tough," Runberg recalls, with the Town pushing for a number of concessions from the university on transportation and water, among other issues. "At the time, it seemed like we were being called upon to do more than what was fair, but ultimately we were satisfied," he says. "Both parties felt like they gave up a lot, which usually means (the agreement) was reasonable."

All the upfront work—a frenetic four months of back-and-forth with the Town—paid lasting dividends. "You put a lot of energy into the front end to get the development plan approved, but there were savings on each individual plan later," he says.

With the methodology in place, Runberg found himself in need of a bigger team. In 2000, Runberg had some 30 people on his staff. By the time the University broke ground on projects two years later, he had twice that number. "We were able to beef up quickly," he says, noting that they used a management consultant to identify staffing gaps. "Fortunately, it was a time when we were able to hire excellent people."

Runberg's new team then confronted the logistics of the massive building campaign, starting with prioritizing and scheduling all the projects. "It was a big jigsaw puzzle at first. We had to do sequencing and develop several sets of daisy chains," he says. "You couldn't get at every single building at one time."

It would have been impossible, for example, to close all 120 classrooms scheduled for renovation at one time. Runberg's team had to stage them, 15 or so a year, turning what sounded like a relatively simple task into an eight-year process.

Tactics changed as lessons were learned. The planners initially tried to keep some buildings open during renovation, for example, but they saw how difficult that could be when working on Peabody Hall, the home of the School of Education.

That department "went through a lot of aggravation to stay in that building during the renovation," Runberg says. "It was a lesson learned. It is several times more difficult to do a renovation of a building while people are still in it."

On later projects, Runberg and his colleagues turned to what they called "swing spaces"—existing or leased buildings that served as temporary homes for a number of departments as their buildings were renovated or replaced. "We used Howell Hall for four different groups that we moved in and out," Runberg says. "That helped immeasurably."

Looking back, Runberg rates the exporting of North Campus qualities to the South Campus as the dynamic decade's biggest success. That process involved building the Rams Head complex that links the two campuses, hiding the less appealing architecture of older residence halls, and planting trees along Manning Drive, among other endeavors.

Runberg also cites the establishment of the Design Review Board as one of the enduring successes—and, in fact, reasons for success—of the dynamic decade. "We used them throughout the course of the decade to strengthen all of the designs," he says. "We get dozens of compliments on the buildings that were added and very few complaints. Each of them is a winner."

Table 3-1. Proposed Development Summary. Source: UNC Development Plan—05/19/10

Classification	Square Footage	Parking Spaces
Academic	1,383,090	—
Cultural	102,725	—
Housing	635,612	—
Infrastructure	135,600	—
Office	163,200	—
Parking	1,885,000	5,330
Research	457,400	—
Student Life	307,300	—
NC-Health Care	831,350	—
Total	5,901,277	5,330

Remarkably, this mammoth development agenda succeeded in bringing the huge slate of new projects in on-budget and on-time. Thanks to an efficient management process and an energetic effort by staff, committee members, designers, and consultants, the product of Development Plan implementation met the expectations of the town and gown for sustainable campus growth. As implementation proceeded, the UNC Board of Trustees regularly recognized the staff accomplishments in managing this demanding task.

DESCRIPTION OF PROPOSED DEVELOPMENT IN SPACE AND TIME

The 2001 Development Plan proposed to build almost six million square feet of new construction and 5,330 parking spaces during the decade ahead. This new space was spread among many types of uses. A spreadsheet listed each project with its use classification, area per floor, number of floors, parking spaces, and anticipated start and completion dates.

The remainder of the Development Plan accounted for the adopted standards governing campus development projects, the methodology for assessing their impacts, their calculated impacts, and the mitigation to be applied. These impacts were discussed in terms of noise and light, environmental, transportation, stormwater management, public utilities, historic districts, and perimeter transition areas. Among the most important influences on the Development Plan were the environmental resources and transportation standards.

DEVELOPMENT PROJECT STANDARDS

ENVIRONMENTAL RESOURCES STANDARDS. Development was required to minimize impacts on natural and man-made environmental resources, according to principles to address land and water resource management identified in the 2001 Environmental Master Plan:

- Balance growth with preservation of the natural drainage system.
    - Maximize water conservation. Enhance the natural beauty of the campus.
- Manage stormwater as an opportunity, rather than a problem.
    - Manage total stormwater volume on site. Maximize infiltration of stormwater.
    - Protect water quality, minimize erosion and sedimentation, and provide for rainwater reuse.
- Recognize that the University of North Carolina at Chapel Hill is part of the Cape Fear Watershed.
    - Enhance and protect water quality of streams to meet water quality standards.
    - Protect Jordan Lake, a major downstream drinking water supply and recreation area.
- Reinforce the University's role as a role model.
    - Optimize open space/habitat protection and management to restore ecological functions of natural areas along streams and on steep slopes adjacent to streams.
    - Implement Best Management Practices.

In addition to historic land and buildings, other unique and irreplaceable areas to be protected from development included Coker Arboretum, Coker Pinetum, Polk Place, McCorkle Place, Bell Tower Plaza, Kenan Stadium surrounding area, and the top of Baity Hill. These unique areas are shown on the Environmental Plan.

Site development plans were to be prepared in accordance with the Town's Resource Conservation District (stream protection area) and with UNC's Construction Guidelines, which incorporated the principles of the 2001 Environmental Master Plan, including the following guidelines:

- Design to reduce negative environmental impacts and restore natural systems.
- Use natural topography to minimize grading, preserve trees, reduce water runoff and soil erosion, increase water infiltration, and protect watershed.
- Use natural site features to reduce building energy requirements (passive heating, cooling, natural ventilation, daylight).
- Landscape should be self-sustaining and support conservation and restoration of biological and water resources, including species diversity and habitat protection, soil stability, fertility, and aeration.
- Site should support facilities for pedestrians, bicycling, carpooling, mass transit, and other less polluting forms of transportation.

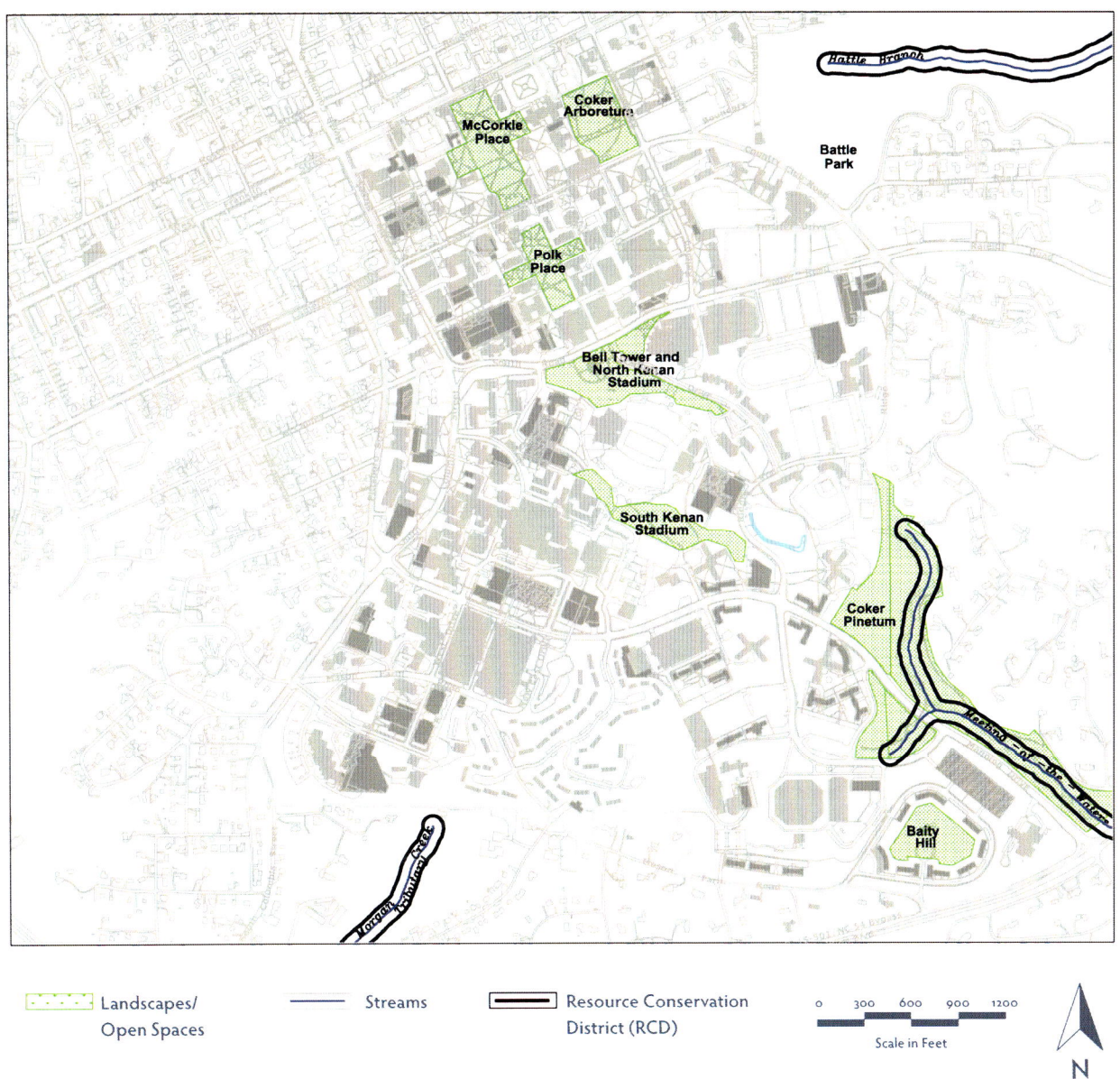

3-3. Environmental Plan Map. Source: 2001 UNC Development Plan

Tree protection during construction was of paramount importance. The campus was honored with an American Society of Landscape Architects' Centennial Medallion in 1999 and also received a national Green Star award for campus beauty from the Professional Grounds Management Society in 2005. The park-like setting of the historical quadrangles with their large trees contributes to the beauty of the campus.

Tree protection plans included:

- Size, species, and location of all affected trees, and those to be removed.
- Routes of trenches for underground utility liners.
- Areas for construction staging, outside of drip lines of trees.

TRANSPORTATION AND PARKING. Transportation and parking constituted the largest and most visible impacts attributable to the large-scale development proposed in the 2001 Development Plan. Thus the parking and trip generation analyses, trip reduction strategies, and plans for key intersections made up the largest section of the Development Plan. The initial transportation impact analysis relied on existing data, with new data to be collected for the first update in the fall of 2001.

In order to compute demand based on building square footage, the analysis subtracted buildings to be demolished (235,000 sq. ft.), parking decks (1,885,000 sq. ft.), and infrastructure projects (135,000 sq. ft.) from the overall total of 5,901,277 sq. ft. proposed. The net increase in new floor area was assumed to be approximately 3.6 million square feet,

3-4. Students Walking in McCorkle Place. Source: Dan Sears, UNC

TABLE 3-2. Anticipated Employee and Student Growth 2000–2010

	2000	2010	2000–2010	Growth Rate
Total Employees	14,303	19,337	+5,034	35%
On main campus	13,016	17,597	+4,581	35%
Off main campus	1,287	1,740	+453	35%
Total Students	25,872	29,249	+3,377	13%
Resident students	7,244	10,136	+2,892	40%
Commuting students	18,369	18,821	+452	2.5%

or an estimated 35 percent increase over existing occupied floor area. Employees were estimated to increase by 35 percent from 14,303 in 2000 to 19,337 in 2010, and students were estimated to increase by 13 percent from 25,872 in 2000 to 29,249 in 2010, with resident students increasing by 40 percent due to the policy of adding housing for each new undergraduate.

Existing main campus parking in the year 2000 was accommodated largely in surface lots, with the exception of four parking decks. The Development plan called for the elimination of many surface lots, with future parking located in structured spaces. Some 3,811 existing surface spaces would be permanently displaced, and 5,366 new structured spaces (in decks or lower levels of buildings) would be added under the Development Plan. The net parking impact would be an increase of 1,550 spaces, most of them designated for patients or visitors. Applying the existing ratio of main campus spaces to population resulted in a total shortage of 3,214 spaces in 2010.

Parking analyses showed an existing shortage of on-campus parking in the year 2000, with approximately 8,000 spaces for about 13,000 main campus employees, or 0.61 spaces per employee. With the oversell ratio, 0.77 employee parking permits were issued. On a typical day there was an employee parking "shortfall" of about 2,675 spaces. Freshman students were not eligible for a main campus parking permit, nor were students residing off-campus within a two-mile radius of the Bell Tower. The parking permit rate for students was less than 0.10 per student.

The total number of commuters to be diverted to alternative modes was 2,715. Estimated diversions were: Chapel Hill transit, 1,500; Regional transit, 250; Ridesharing, 150; and Park-and-Ride, 815. Trip reduction strategies included:

- Making Chapel Hill Transit buses fare-free, extending on-campus routes and headways, and increasing service to Park-and-Ride lots.
- Adding additional Park-and-Ride lots.
- Enhancing regional transit, ridesharing, teleworking, cycling, and pedestrian access.

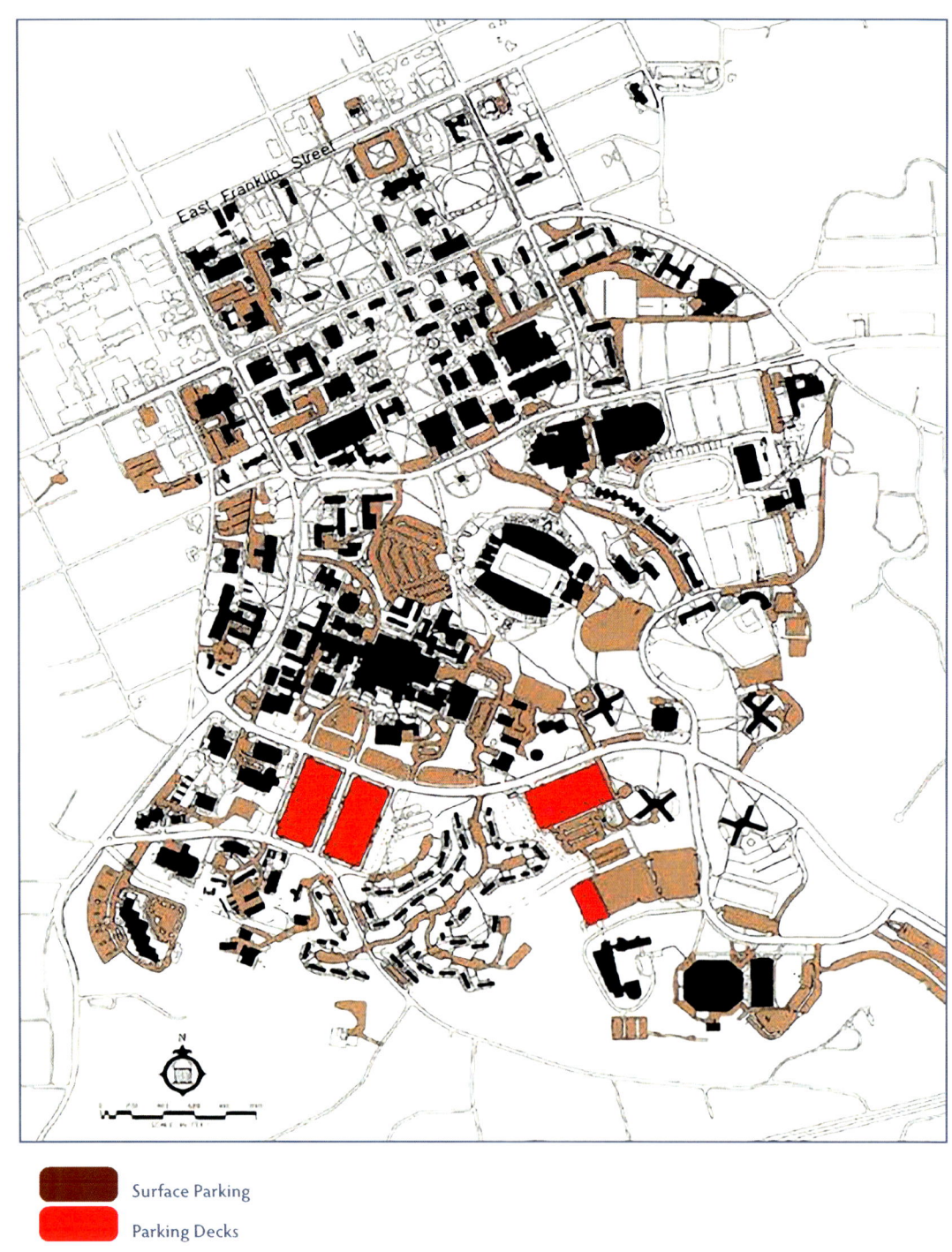

3-5. Existing Main Campus Parking Facilities. Source: 2001 UNC Development Plan

Pedestrian circulation improvements were aimed at increasing the network of paths on South Campus to emulate those on North Campus. Improvements proposed included new north-south linking paths, new parking decks with grassed roofs to reduce stormwater runoff, and pedestrian bridges over heavily-traveled roads. The Pedestrian Corridors map shows the proposed network.

STORMWATER MANAGEMENT. The University committed to a Development Plan that prevents any increase in the amount or rate of stormwater runoff leaving the campus, or the pollutant load conveyed in that runoff. The first step was to analyze current drainage conditions and then to compare them with future conditions under the Development Plan.

The campus is located in the upper reaches of five stream drainage sub-basins: Bolin Creek (20.2 acres), Battle Creek (133.6 acres), Chapel Creek (76.9 acres), Meeting of the Waters (550.1 acres), and Morgan Creek (57.6 acres). A Geographic Information Systems analysis was conducted to measure the amount of impervious surface in each basin. This measure provided an estimate of the amount of runoff generated during a storm event, when not only does the rate of stormwater runoff increase, but the volume also increases as the rainfall is no longer able to soak into the soil.

In order to implement the stormwater management goals of retaining and infiltrating stormwater, as well as reducing runoff and pollutants, a number of best practices were proposed. These included stormwater storage and infiltration methods, such as porous paving for parking areas, storage/infiltration beds beneath parking, playfield, and lawn areas, restoration of stream corridors, changes in landscape practices, protection and restoration of environmentally sensitive areas, vegetated (green) roofs, and other methods.

The impervious surface information was mapped and then overlaid with proposed projects in order to show the locations of existing and proposed buildings and existing and proposed pervious surfaces. A considerable amount of impervious surface was removed during the ten-year development period, thanks to implementation of the proactive stormwater management strategy.

PUBLIC UTILITIES. Campus utilities were provided both by the University and outside providers: The University operated a co-generation facility for combined heat and power, while Orange Water and Sewer Authority (OWASA) provided water and sewer service. PSNC supplied natural gas, Duke Power supplied electricity and BellSouth provided telephone service. As a consequence, planning for changes to the current systems required coordination with yet another host of important players. The resulting Utility Master Plan component of the Development Plan described new utility infrastructure required to support the physical growth of the campus. In particular, it identified new plant locations and utility corridors, which were later expanded to add a new corridor from the UNC cogeneration facility on the west.

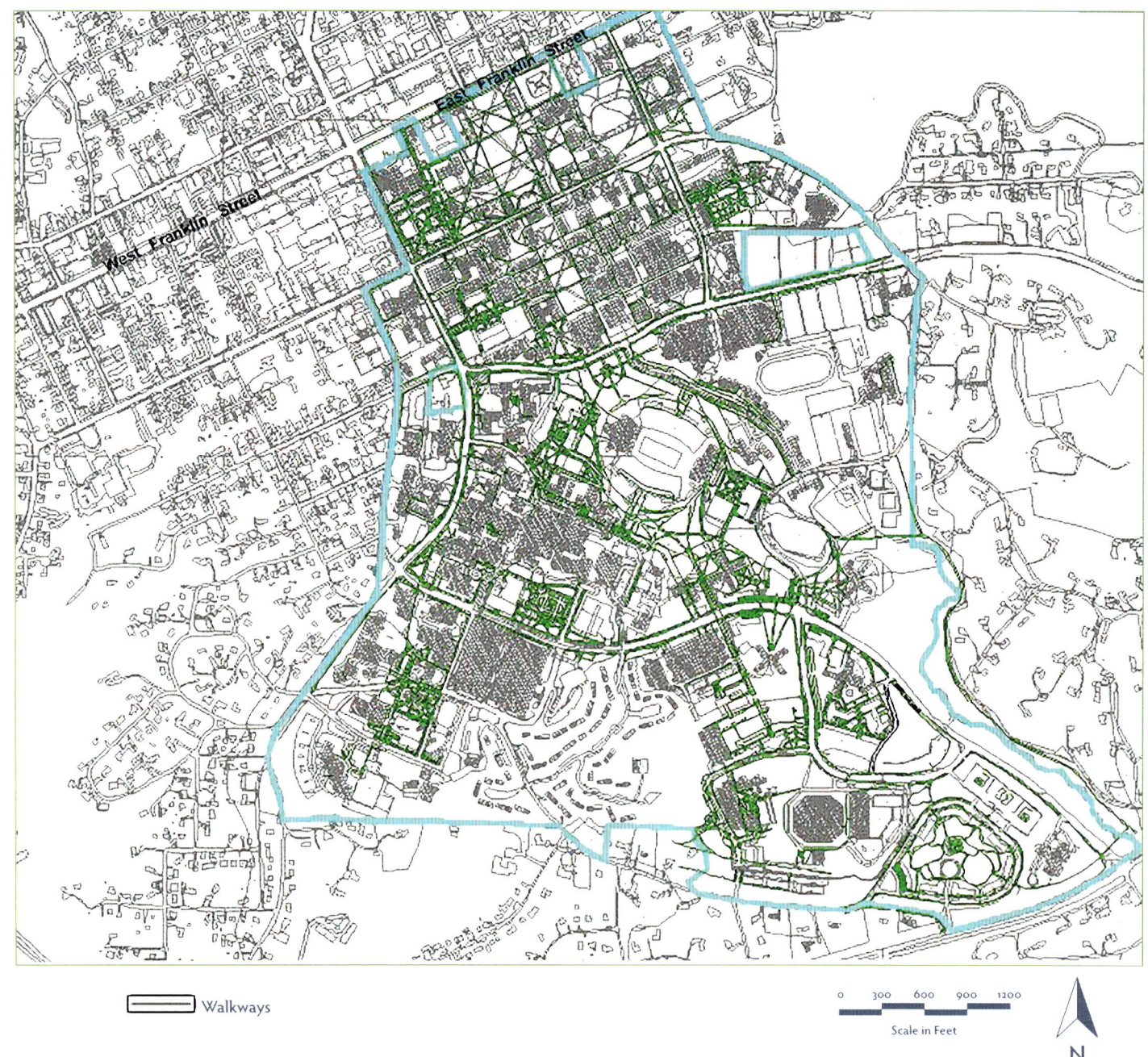

3-6. Pedestrian Corridors. Source: 2001 UNC Development Plan

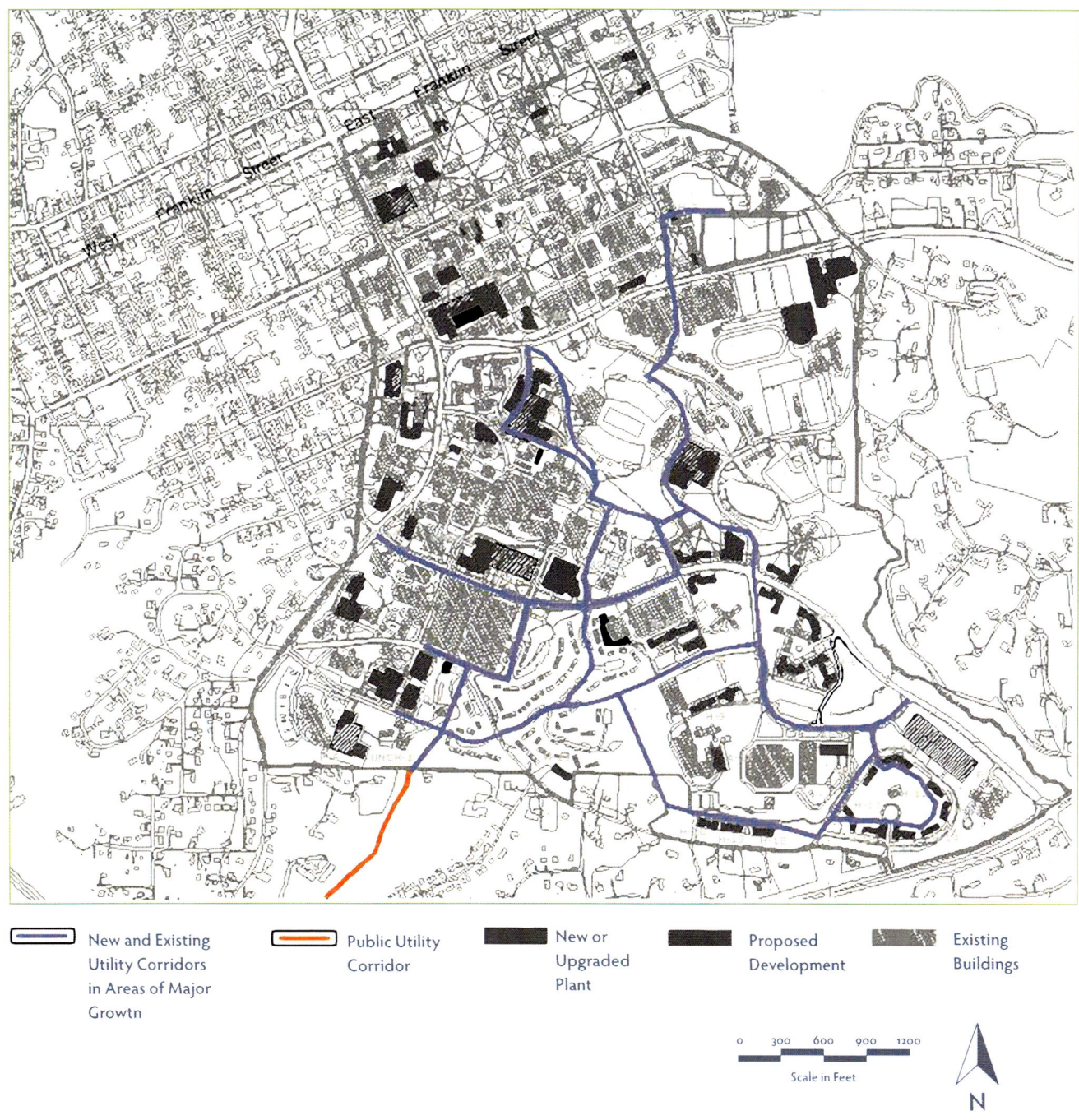

3-7. Proposed Utilities. Source: 2001 UNC Development Plan

HISTORIC DISTRICTS. Buildings in the Development Plan located within a local Historic District had to comply with the North Carolina General Statutes. The Chapel Hill Historic District was listed in the National Register of Historic Places in 1971. One of its three areas was the University Campus Area, described as the northern quadrangle centering on a tree-lined open space named McCorkle Place that includes the oldest campus buildings as well as some later ones. These structures provide an overview of the development of collegiate architecture from the late eighteenth to the early twentieth century. All campus development in the Historic District was subject to review by the NC Department of Cultural Resources. In addition, two buildings, Playmakers Theater and Old East, had been designated as National Historic Landmarks and the Carolina Inn individually listed on the National Register of Historic Places.

PERIMETER TRANSITION AREAS. To protect campus neighbors concerned about new buildings on the edge of the OI-4 Zoning District, seven perimeter transition areas were identified with special development standards. The designated Perimeter Transition Areas are Battle Lane, East Franklin Street, South Columbia Street, McCauley/Pittsboro Street, ACC Site, Student Family Housing West, and Student Family Housing East. The standards include screening of mechanical equipment, exterior lighting, building height limits, and landscaping. Standards were set for each situation depending on the proposed building, site conditions, and adjacent zoning.

DEVELOPMENT PLAN LESSONS

One of the most important institutional innovations to emerge from the master planning process was the creation of a "University" zoning district that enabled the University to submit, and the Town to review and approve, one unified ten-year development plan, rather than getting bogged down in endless Town public hearings and political fights over each new building project. It is difficult to overstate the importance of the town/gown agreement on this new procedure. Without it, it is doubtful that the full extent of development could have gone forward during the dynamic decade. And it is likely that the synergy of designing and building the projects as coordinated communities within the campus would not have been possible.

A major benefit of adopting the new zoning district was that it demonstrated the ability of the Town and the University to agree on a process for deciding about major development issues. Prior to adoption of the OI-4 district, there had been much pressure on Town officials to rein in University growth. Several efforts to create coordinating town/gown committees had failed to result in an acceptable approach. In the past, elected officials and town advisory committee members had attempted to micromanage each proposed University project. As a result, the new zon-

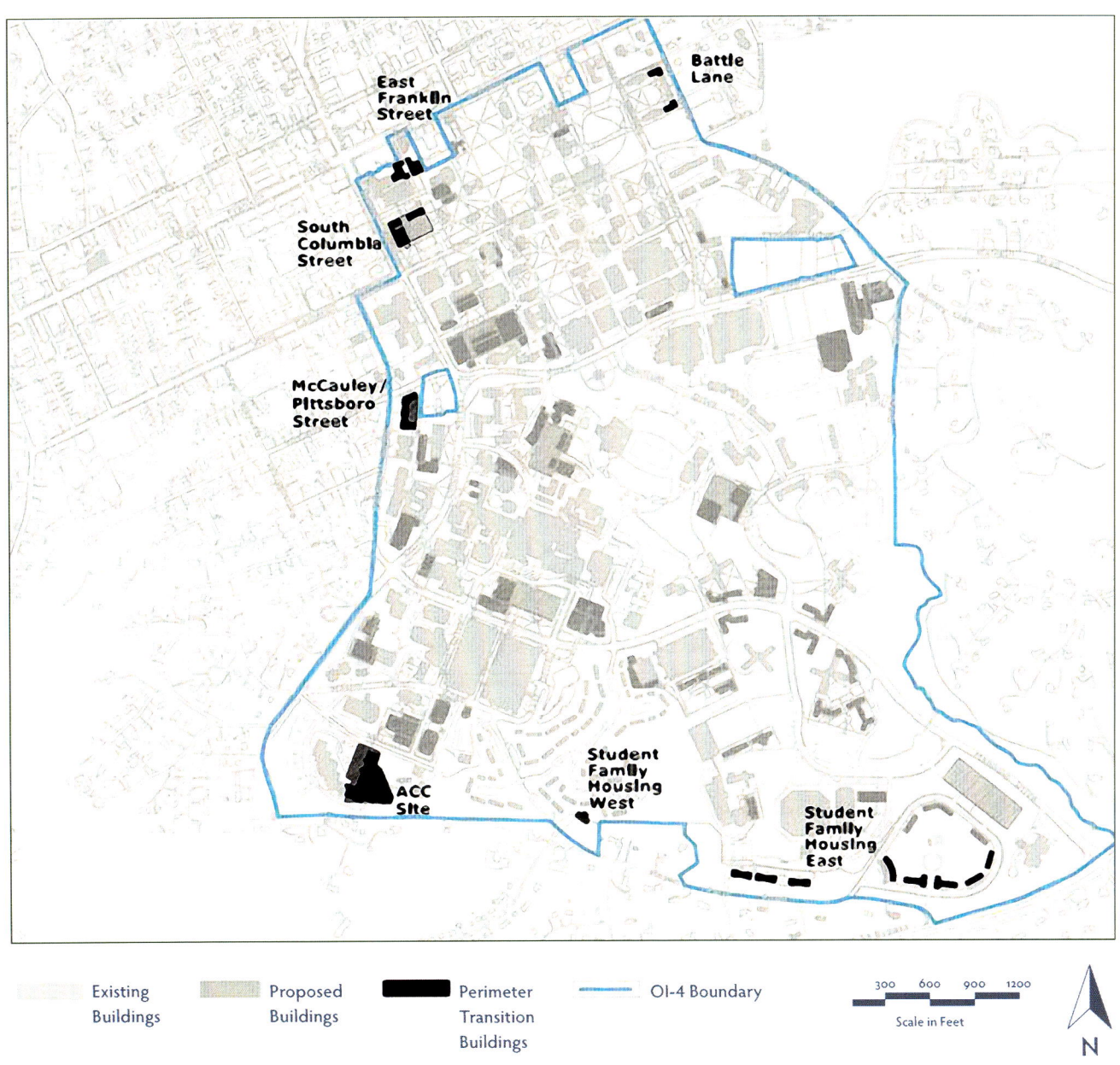

3-8. Perimeter Transition Areas. Source: 2001 UNC Development Plan

ing district represented a welcome break in the impasse and a clear example of the possibility of consensus that would have further long-term benefits when the time came time to approve the plan for Carolina North.

Another major benefit of the Development Plan was that it forced University planners to analyze and plan for large-scale development impacts during the master planning process, rather than tackling them as they occurred. The University invested in top-notch professional consultants to help solve the problems of traffic and environmental impacts, utility systems, historic preservation, architecture and landscape architecture. In the process, much valuable information was obtained and many useful concepts were tested. Without the required comprehensiveness of the Development Plan, the pressures of meeting project deadlines and the scrutiny of the Town made it unlikely that the full creativity that poured forth would have materialized.

Important lessons from the Development Plan were:

- In the face of major campus development growth, town/gown cooperation was essential in creating new types of plans and regulations aimed at collaborative management of growth that meets both university and community needs.
- Taking a comprehensive planning view, rather than a building-by-building or project-by-project view, enabled the University and the community to be more efficient and more effective in managing the large-scale development effort.
- Carrying out a very large campus development initiative required a corresponding investment in professional assistance to deal with the scale and complexity of the associated impacts.

As will be seen in the next chapter, the development planning process did not alleviate all conflicts over campus development, but it made the issues of siting and approval manageable. This new cooperative climate, in turn, encouraged the flowering of some outstanding design projects.

CHAPTER 4

Designing Projects

SITING AND ARCHITECTURAL ISSUES

Architecture and landscape shape the campus experience. Together, the buildings and open space determine the way that the campus is seen and used: its look and feel. While structures and common outdoor areas may appear to be a seamless fabric, in actuality that fabric is shaped by a myriad of decisions by planners, designers, and others with power over the project design process and its outcome.

This chapter describes the way that decisions were made about the sites where campus buildings and facilities were to be located and about how the design elements of the buildings and landscapes themselves were determined. It unpacks the project design process and its contribution to the goal of a sustainable campus.

Project design took the stage after the large-scale campus planning framework was set by the Master Plan and Development Plan. As noted previously, the Master Plan set the general location and type of future projects and the Development Plan set their timing and sequence within overall campus development priorities. When the time came to design an individual building or facility and the necessary funds were allocated, then the project design process began.

The sustainability challenge for project design was deciding how to enlist the nation's leading architectural firms in implementing the Master Plan while ensuring that their design projects would add up to a desirable overall campus aesthetic rather than a potpourri of individual buildings, each clamoring for attention. The existing internal design review system, staffed by individual University architects, had to be reconfigured to handle issues both of quantity, as the flood of new projects mounted, and of

Project Design

SITE SELECTION

DESIGNER SELECTION

PLAN PREPARATION AND REVIEW

FINAL APPROVAL

4-1. Project Design Process

quality, as the increased prestige of the outside design firms demanded firm but diplomatic review and guidance by a panel of their peers.

No matter how good the Master Plan and Development Plan were, without wise project design decisions the final campus environment ran the risk of leaving a heritage of missed opportunities and unappealing architecture. To succeed, project design had to integrate historic preservation, green building, and innovative design into a sustainable stream of new projects and restoration plans.

Project design followed a series of stages. To summarize, the first stage consisted of reviewing location options and selecting the site for the project. Next, a designer was chosen through interviews with firms successful in designing similar projects around the country. Once selected, the designer then prepared preliminary plans which were discussed and refined through a systematic review process, both on-campus and in the community. In the final stage, the plans were submitted to the University Board of Trustees, who held final intra-campus approval powers, and to the Chapel Hill town government, who held ultimate extra-campus approval power under the Town's zoning regulations, as described in the discussion of the Development Plan in Chapter 3.

Site selection entailed decisions about how to proceed with the general new building locations specified in the Master Plan and Development Plan. Even though these plans had been approved, actually proposing a project on a specific site could rouse new opposition, as adjacent stakehoders were mobilized. Arguments against buildings on particular sites could range from their impacts on existing neighborhoods to the style of their architecture.

Designer selection encompassed decisions about choosing from amongst available and qualified architectural teams. Given the unprecedented number and scope of new projects to be designed during implementation of the Master Plan, then-Chancellor Moeser decided to form a Design Review Board and to widen the list of potential design firms to include not just North Carolina firms, but also prominent firms from around the United States. Selection committees who interviewed prospective firms were made up of representatives from the Board of Trustees, Chancellor's Building and Grounds Committee, departments or programs who would inhabit the new buildings, and Facilities Planning and Construction staff.

Plan preparation and review involved decisions about the architecture of new projects—both their creative aspects and their analytical aspects. Design firms took up the challenge of solving the creative problems and integrating the building program, the site, and the guidelines of good design into alternative project plans. The review process worked in concert with designers to ensure that implications of feasibility and compatibility were accounted for. The result was typically a back-and-forth, trial-and-error design and review process that generated final plans, as exemplified in the design of the new Science Complex discussed below.

Final approval comprised decision-making under the concurrent jurisdiction system of UNC and the Town of Chapel Hill, in which both the Trustees and the Town Council ultimately ratified new campus plans and project designs. Prior to adopting the 2001 Office-Institutional-4 District, external reviews focused on individual buildings. Under the new OI-4 zoning district, the Town focused on the overall Development Plan. As with all such decisions, the composition of the approval group played a large role in the outcome. University Trustees with a preference for traditional architecture may be reluctant to approve a building with a more contemporary design. Town Council members with a strong neighborhood constituency may be reluctant to approve projects that have neighborhood impacts. Project designs must run a sometimes unpredictable gauntlet of stakeholders and institutional rules in order to be approved for construction, as will be seen in the example of the Cobb Parking Deck and Chiller Plant described later in this chapter.

At any stage of project design, complications or new considerations may change, delay, or cancel the project. As Bruce Runberg, Associate Vice Chancellor for Facilities Planning and Construction, is fond of saying, "The road to success is always under construction." We take up UNC's creative approach to steering project design through this dynamic whirlpool after a discussion of the way that the philosophy of community building permeated the design process.

> …UNC's campus planners used the opportunity of development to create campus communities.

PLACE-MAKING AS COMMUNITY BUILDING

Instead of viewing new buildings as stand-alone projects, UNC's campus planners used the opportunity of development to create campus communities. They linked new buildings and facilities into mini-neighborhood clusters of related structures, open spaces, and circulation routes. New student housing areas were placed near student recreation, dining, and administrative services, and were connected to the broader campus through accessible pedestrian walkways. This place-making approach went beyond the architecture of individual buildings to focus on tying together related activity patterns, such as enjoyment of the arts, conducting science research and teaching, attending athletic events and venues, providing medical research and patient care, and taking part in student life and housing. A university campus is an ideal microcosm to demonstrate the value of mixed-use neighborhoods to enhance accessibility.

Community building began during preparation of the Master Plan. Planning workshops were held in campus "precincts"—Science, North Campus, Health Affairs, and Academics/Housing/Athletics. Rather than focusing on individual new buildings, alternative layouts of groups of new buildings were created to help stakeholders understand the urban design possibilities. Planners sketched out potential designs showing different arrangements of buildings and open space to visualize the possibil-

DESIGNING PROJECTS 51

ities. For example, the old Bell Tower parking lot was envisioned as a site for new science buildings, linked to redevelopment of the area around the old Venable Hall.

While not formally designated in the plan, the community groupings were articulated and developed as new projects were designed. Smaller in scale than the precincts used in the planning process, these communities were distinguished by their major uses and activity patterns. The resulting groupings of structures, open space, and walkways were defined by function, proximity, and geographic location. Because they sometimes included proximate buildings planned before the Master Plan was prepared, not all the buildings in each community were related to the major use, and some communities overlapped. But the majority of new construction in each community was tied to its primary function, such as student life, classroom and research, athletics, and health affairs.

New project design processes were seized as opportunities to create walkable, mixed-use places where, for example, it would be possible for students to move easily between their dorms, classrooms, gyms, and dining halls, or for visitors to move easily between parking areas and arts or sports facilities. The result was eight user-based communities or complexes:

- An Arts Community
- A Science Community
- Two Student Residence Life and Services Communities (North and South)
- A Student Family Housing Community
- A Health Affairs Community
- A Health Research Community
- An Athletics and Visitors' Complex

The details of each of these groupings were worked out during formal and informal design review processes.

DESIGN REVIEW

New campus buildings and facilities were reviewed according to two basic types of metrics: those related to the project design process and those related to the project's impacts. *Design metrics* assessed the function and appearance of a proposal in terms of its ability to satisfy program needs and its compatibility with existing campus structures. *Impact metrics* assessed the effect of the proposed design on Town neighborhoods and services. While review processes for the two types of measures overlapped at times, design metrics were applied primarily by intra-campus procedures, and impact metrics were applied primarily by extra-campus, or Town, procedures. As with all impact assessment techniques, metric application involved both objective and subjective assessments.

Intra-Campus

FACILITIES PLANNNG

DESIGN REVIEW BOARD

CHANCELLOR'S BUILDINGS & GROUNDS

TRUSTEE'S BUILDINGS & GROUNDS

BOARD OF TRUSTEES

Extra-Campus

TOWN PLANNNG

TOWN MANAGER

TOWN BOARDS & COMMITTEES

TOWN COUNCIL

4-2. Project Review and Approval Process

Intra-Campus Reviews

Intra-campus reviews were done by the Facilities Planning staff, the Design Review Board, the Chancellor's Buildings and Grounds Committee, the Buildings and Grounds Committee of the University's Board of Trustees, and finally by the full Board of Trustees. The Facilities Planning staff and the Design Review Board were professional designers and planners who analyzed the proposed project in terms of "good design" criteria, as specified in the Design Guidelines in the Master Plan and enhanced by professional judgment. The Chancellor's Buildings and Grounds Committee members were University faculty and staff who analyzed the proposed project from their perspectives as representatives of the broader campus community. Lastly, the Trustees' Buildings and Grounds Committee and the Board of Trustees members had been appointed by the North Carolina General Assembly; they decided whether or not to approve the project based on their judgments about its "fit" with the campus and the University's mission.

During the dynamic decade of development at UNC, the numbers of projects and their associated reviews grew exponentially. As many as fifty-one projects were under consideration at any one time. The University's Facilities Planning staff was inundated with the coordination and reviewof proposed projects. To augment the staff, Chancellor Moeser appointed a Design Review Board. Made up of experienced architects, planners, and designers, this small group met with every architect selected for design of a University project from the start of site selection and project planning through the completion of project design. In informal peer reviews, design concepts and decisions were critiqued and alternative solutions were explored. This process proved to be very effective in encouraging project architects to improve, simplify, and refine their designs, as well as in ensuring that the final plans were compatible with the other buildings in the campus neighborhood.

In one illustrative example, Design Review Board evaluations of the Science Complex project played a major role in determining its final design. Conceived as a replacement for the obsolete and unsafe 76-year old Venable chemistry lab building, as well as a needed addition to science

DESIGNING PROJECTS 53

PETE ANDERSON, DESIGN REVIEWER

To commodity, firmness, and delight—the time-tested elements of a good building as set forth by Vitruvius (Morgan, 1914), a Roman architect, a couple of thousand years ago—Pete Anderson would add three more. As a member of UNC's Design Review team, Anderson sees his role as to bring out the sense of place, time and memory in every design that crosses his desk.

Place, meaning how the building fits into the context of a campus; time, meaning how it reflects the age in which it is built; and, perhaps most elusively, memory—the role of good architecture in "creating a fondness for a place."

"Adding these very subjective requirements to the basic elements is the job of the design review board," says Anderson, who was campus architect at the University of Virginia from 1995 to 2003. "Our basic idea is that good architects will bring good ideas, and what the board will do is help make them even better."

Just how easy that improvement comes rests heavily on the architect involved. Anderson describes designing a building as an iterative process, and one that must reflect the needs and interests of many different audiences: administrators, faculty, students and residents, to name a few. A promising initial design can be wasted if the architect isn't skilled at listening and responding to those needs. "Some architects are adept at dealing with large groups of people, drawing from them their ideas and drawing from all of that a good building," Anderson says.

Anderson puts architect Bill Wilson, who designed the Science Complex, squarely in that camp. When working with Wilson, he says, "It was always a two-way street. We would ask questions, he would bring us well-thought-out alternatives, and we would discuss and choose one."

At one point, the design team's involvement became hands-on. To work through big questions about the massing and siting of the second and third buildings, as well as how to best connect them via courtyards, Anderson and his colleagues spent a day at Wilson's office, building and rebuilding project models. "We would literally shove models around until we got a pattern that we liked," he says.

Wilson, the architect, found the review panel to be highly effective in vetting ideas that flowed to and from UNC's Board of Trustees, which was heavily involved in the design process. He says the group can also lend continuity and stewardship to the University's long-term building plans. "I recommend it to other universities," Wilson says of the design review process. "It's not typical, but it should be."

The new baseball stadium, completed in 2009, is another design on which Anderson says the Design Review team had a big impact. The architecture firm hired by UNC specialized in stadiums, he says, and as a result focused first and foremost on functionality: getting the sight lines right, the circulation right, and the dugouts right, for example. "What we were able to do there was to build on those parts and make them into a building that has some elegance and grace to it," he says. "The design was not all that it might be, and we were able to coach the architects along."

Of course, not all architects take coaching well. Some of the architects the team met with "really did not care at all" about the feedback they heard, he says. "They say, 'This is what we do, and this is what we're going to do for you.'"

In those situations, Anderson says, the Design Review team can only do so much. They do not hire or fire the architects, and they cannot force them to take their advice. "When all goes well, it is rewarding," Anderson says. "Then we get the architect who doesn't listen and doesn't work well with others. The best we can do is keep the building from being as bad as it might be. We can sand off the rough edges."

Regardless of the architect involved, Anderson says that simplicity is the common thread that runs through the Design Review team's counsel. "Think about what's around you and keep it simple," he tells architects. "A complexity will develop in a building as you mine it further and further."

education and research facilities, this multi-building complex was allocated a key site on the south end of the central campus. The site adjoins Wilson Library and Dey Hall on the east, the Kenan and Morehead Labs on the south, Carroll Hall on the north, and the ROTC Building on the west. As built, the Complex houses classrooms, offices, labs, and a library for the Departments of Marine Sciences, Chemistry, Physics, and Computer Science. It features a large interior courtyard, a major pedestrian walk linking to Polk Place, and bridges connecting the various buildings.

Wilson Architects, primary designers of the Science Complex, embraced the spirit of the design review process. They took a very collaborative approach, bringing all of the UNC stakeholders together in a participatory group. According to the UNC project manager, Peter Krawchyk, the principal architects were present at two days of meetings every month during the several years of the project design process. They met with the Design Review Board numerous times to discuss layout and architecture issues. Working from scale drawings and architectural models, the building architects and the reviewers analyzed countless alternatives before arriving at the final solution. During a visit to the architect's office in Boston to study the latest massing model, a major wing of the building was re-oriented in response to review comments, and many revisions to architectural details flowed from review suggestions.

Wilson Architects also met many times with a committee of faculty and staff from the sciences in order to arrive at the final program for the buildings. Over the course of many meetings and negotiations, this committee, led by Physics Professor Tom Clegg, arrived at a proposed allocation and arrangement of the interior spaces of the buildings. They also worked with the architects on revised space decisions as budgetary constraints became clear when the actual construction costs were known.

As built up to 2011, Phase II of the Science Complex includes Caudill Laboratories, New Venable Hall, Murray Hall (the easternmost wing of New Venable), Chapman Hall, and Brooks Hall, an addition to Computer Sciences, as well as a temporary parking lot. When the proposed Phase III is completed, the Science Complex will include two future buildings on the west side, facing a large landscaped commons area where the temporary parking lot is located. The new courtyard will add a significant open space anchoring the science area. Potential uses of space beneath the courtyard include both offices and parking.

Extra-Campus Reviews

Extra-campus or external reviews were coordinated by the Town's Planning Staff and Town Manager's Office, and then proceeded through the Town advisory committees to the Town Council. These reviews tended to focus on the community impacts of the proposed projects. They were guided by the Town zoning regulations, embodied in its Land Use Management Ordinance, as well as by judgments and citizen input derived from public hearings.

BILL WILSON, ARCHITECT

Of all the photos of UNC's campus that architect Bill Wilson has at hand, it is an image of an empty lot that he refers back to most often. That lot is—was—the last free building site on Polk Place; for him, it is a reminder of how precious space is on a campus that is both established and growing fast.

"There was a lot of electricity around that site, a lot of concern," says Wilson, whose Boston-based firm designed the five buildings—New Venable, Murray, Caudill, Brooks and Chapman—that comprise UNC's science complex. "You have to make sure that when you're using a site like that, you use it well."

Using it well, he says, started with finding out exactly what the science complex would be used for. Wilson held over a hundred meetings with UNC faculty and staff—grilling them on size, focus, teaching and research loads, among other topics—and then asking them what the answers to those same questions would be 25 years from now. "It was rethinking physics, chemistry, marine science," he says. "Architecture was the reason to ask the questions, but it was really academic planning."

The planning process was often revealing. For example, when discussing the 143,000-square-foot old Venable building that would be razed to make way for a replacement, Wilson found that almost everyone claimed at least a little bit of space there. "It was like a giant garage," he says, describing Venable's mishmash of labs, offices, libraries, and storage. "I bet only two or three people on campus actually knew what was in that building."

Planning determined how much space was needed; the next step was deciding what it should look like. Again, Wilson listened first, but this time it was to the history and natural power of the setting. He notes the primacy of landscape over buildings on UNC's campus. "The starting point is a series of quality outdoor spaces all linked together," he says of his design. "The buildings are the walls of the spaces. You're creating outdoor rooms."

Those rooms—a series of linked courtyards—and the buildings that surround them, were sited on 15-foot intervals along the natural fall of the land from Cameron Avenue to South Road. The lowest level, at South Road, is for building services (parking and loading). The second level is even with the walkway from Wilson Library, the third is Gardner, and the fourth is Phillips, where physics and astronomy are housed. "It just fit so well. The grades worked out," Wilson says. "People won't even know they are climbing up 60 feet."

To create the buildings themselves, Wilson drew on architectural language from other campus buildings, and from history books. Brickwork and vertical windows match those of UNC's oldest buildings; overhanging slate roofs and chimneys on both ends are a nod to traditional North Carolina design. The underlying philosophy might best be described as a sort of informal elegance. "Chapel Hill has a brand," Wilson says. "What we were trying to do was use traditional architecture to express that brand."

While the building exteriors are meant to stand the test of time, Wilson made sure that the interiors could change and grow with the researchers who worked there. The architect built in responsiveness by using a modular approach. Each building consists of 22-by-30 foot units of space within which the services overhead and in the walls—air, gas, water, exhaust vents, and so on—are a repeated pattern. The modules come in different "flavors" to meet the differing needs of faculty. Some have lots of electricity, others are heavy on plumbing and fume hoods, still others are designed to be extremely quiet. "You're not customizing. You're really giving the University a generic system with small variations," he says. "It is very economical to build it, and it is easy to manage and reassign space."

The ultimate goal of his designs, he says, are buildings that someone will choose to renovate, rather than raze, 40 years down the line. "We think of the shell as robust, and the interior as changing," he says. "The building wants to be able to respond over time."

Time will also bring one more "outdoor room" to the campus: a vast new quad, with the dimensions of Polk Place, that will be formed behind Murray Hall when the old ROTC building gives way to its replacement. "You can't feel it yet," Wilson says of the quad that he has designed. "The big payoff has not been achieved."

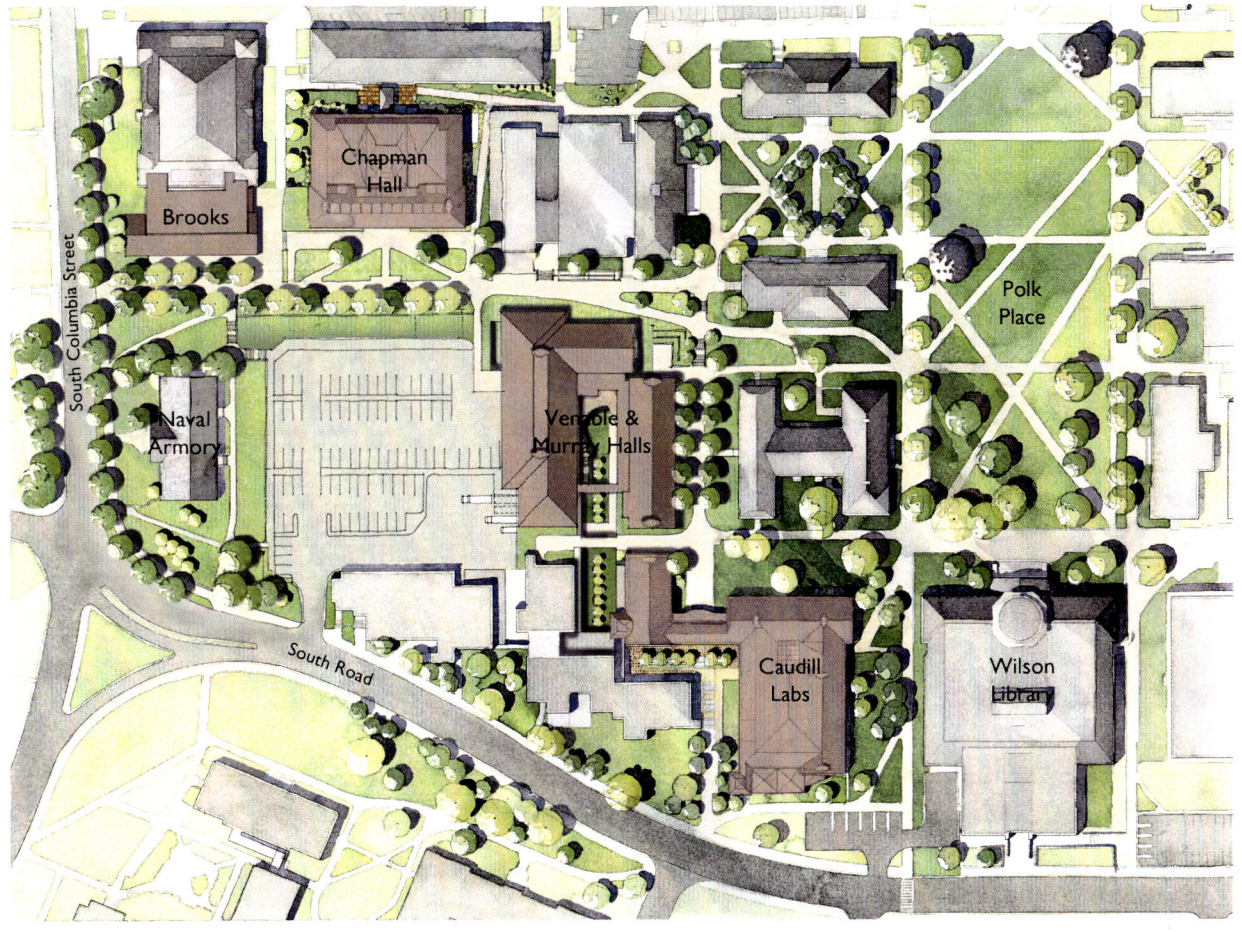

4-3. Plan of Science Complex, Phase II. Source: Wilson Architects

While town/gown issues over university land use and development are widespread around the country, the University of North Carolina at Chapel Hill is one of a limited number of U.S. universities whose land use and development is regulated by its host community (Sungu-Eryilmaz 2009). Public universities are only under local zoning control in 11 states, and only the states of North Carolina, South Carolina, Vermont and Washington have no special university zoning, forcing university property to fall under the various zoning districts with their various restrictions. Jonathan Howes, a former mayor of Chapel Hill, has termed this "concurrent jurisdiction" over campus plans. Not only is the University subject to the local zoning ordinance, but the local planning department and elected officials have tended to scrutinize its proposals with extra diligence, and town residents have tended to resist its efforts to expand beyond its existing boundaries. Campaigns of those seeking election to the Chapel Hill Town Council have often highlighted the willingness of the office-seeker to favor neighborhood interests over those of the University.

Adoption of a new zoning district, the Office-Institutional-4 District, in 2001, removed the focus of external reviews from individual buildings

DESIGNING PROJECTS 57

> ...the 2001 Development Plan was hotly debated by Chapel Hill citizens and elected officials.

and placed it on the overall Development Plan, as discussed in Chapter 3. According to the Land Use Management Ordinance, the purpose of the OI-4 District is to "establish procedural and substantive standards for the town council's review and approval of development on large tracts of land where the predominant use is to be college, university, hospital ... and related functions." The objective is to "allow for growth and development while protecting the larger community, nearby neighborhoods, and the environment from impacts accompanying major new development." A key feature is the preparation of a development plan that would "allow the property owner, immediate neighbors, and the larger community to understand specifically what levels of development are being proposed, and what impacts would likely accompany the development, so that mitigation measures can be designed and implemented."

Because it embraced a ten-year swath of campus growth proposals of unprecedented magnitude, the 2001 Development Plan was hotly debated by Chapel Hill citizens and elected officials. At one point, when public opinion was centered on the negative impacts, it seemed that the Town might reject the plan. Adding fuel to the fire, a powerful state senator, Tony Rand, introduced a bill in the North Carolina General Assembly in 2001 that would strip Chapel Hill of its zoning control over the campus. While this bill was eventually withdrawn, it cast a threat over the issue of how far the Town could go in regulating a State institution, such as UNC. When the Town Council ultimately voted to approve the Development Plan, one Council member remarked that he was joining the favorable vote only because he felt like he "had a gun to his head."

Despite approval of the Development Plan, some project designs continued to generate town/gown controversy. For example, residents of the neighboring Gimghoul subdivision, calling themselves the "Coalition of Neighbors Near Campus," vehemently opposed construction of the North Campus Parking Deck and Chiller Plant. Since the facility adjoined the Old Chapel Hill Cemetery to the south, a number of historic preservation advocates also joined the opposition. This support facility added needed parking for the Paul Green Theater and nearby academic buildings and provided chilled water for air conditioning of central campus buildings. The project also provided for the renewal of the "front yard" of Cobb Dormitory with new tennis courts and landscaping.

Opponents enlisted members of the Town Council, who threatened to block the structure, citing issues of traffic congestion on Country Club Road due to parking deck traffic, safety to pedestrians from the Gimghoul neighborhood, and intrusions on the historic cemetery. In response, the University modified the road pattern to include a second access point, added a traffic signal at the Country Club Road entry, decreased the size and limited the height of the building, and increased the landscape buffer next to the cemetery. The resulting structure was designed to look more like a campus building than a utility facility.

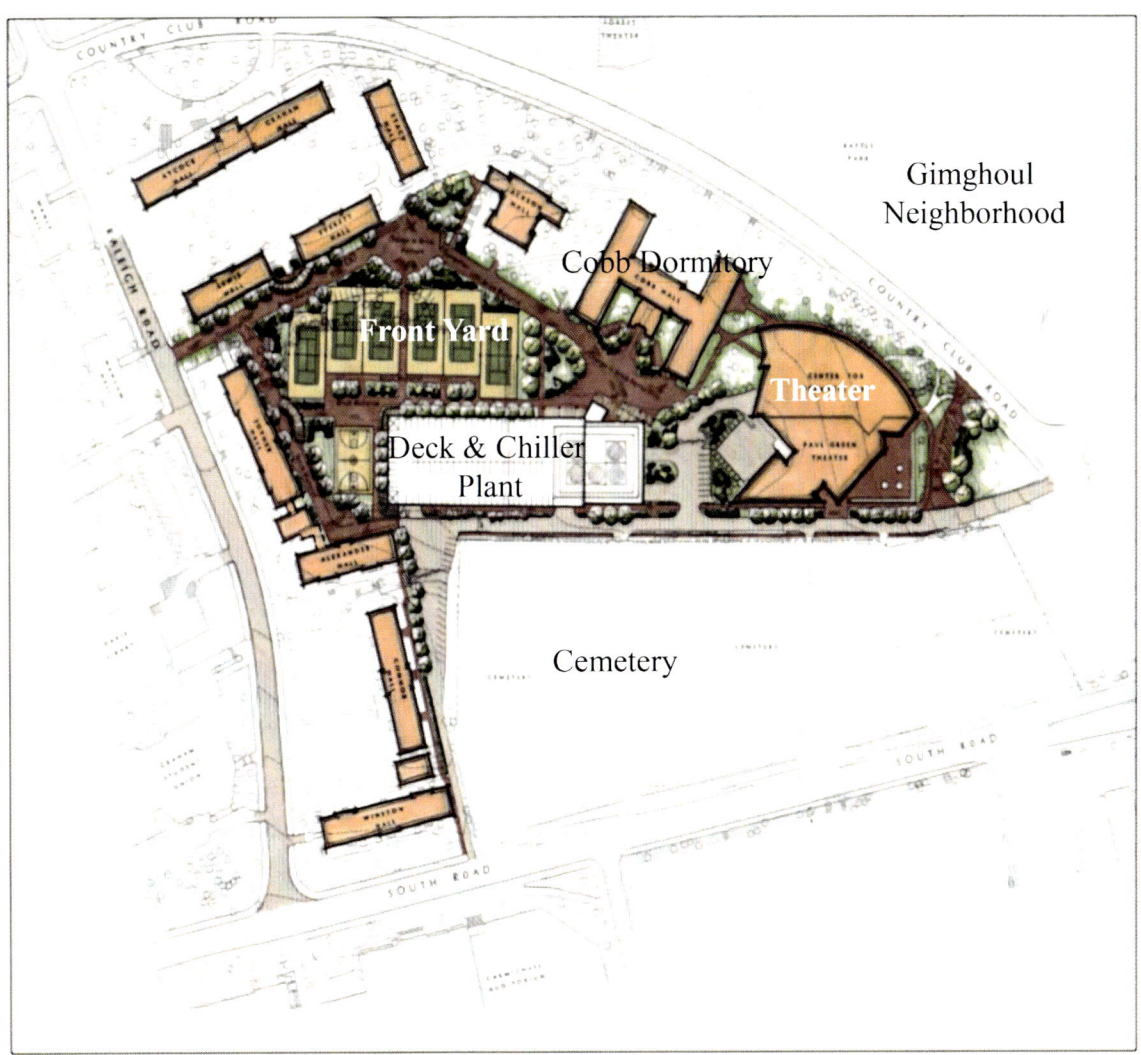

4-4. Plan of Cobb Parking Deck and Adjacent Area. Source: UNC Facilities Planning & Construction

The Chancellor's Buildings and Grounds Committee strongly supported the design of the North Campus Deck and Chiller and recommended it to the Chancellor for approval. He backed it with the Trustees, who also approved it. However, only after University Trustees negotiated site planning changes and cemetery improvement funding with the leaders of the opposition from the Town Council (including promising to withdraw support for the planned widening to four lanes of far-away South Columbia Street, the key access route to the University hospital from the south—an issue unrelated to the Parking Deck and Chiller Plant, but one that neighborhood advocates had long demanded), did the Council accept the project on a split vote. Although the project was approved, in the ensuing 2003 Town election the opponents threw their support behind three candidates for the Council who promised to control the "campus building explosion" (Shapard 2003).

DESIGNING PROJECTS

4-5. Cobb Tennis Courts and Parking Deck. Source: Affiliated Engineers, Inc.

LESSONS FOR PROJECT DESIGN

Siting and design issues for campus projects can be very controversial. Because the UNC campus has been surrounded on three sides by designated historic neighborhoods, any proposal to place a new building or facility near the edge of the campus has been singled out for aggressive opposition. Because the historic center of the campus is recognized as a key element in its charm and beauty, any architectural design that did not appear to be compatible with the existing environment was slated for serious questioning.

By devoting substantial resources and effort to both intra-campus and extra-campus reviews, UNC managed to grow and develop in a sustainable fashion. The dynamic decade demanded extraordinary efforts to keep development from being derailed by pushback.

Important lessons learned during project design included:

- Augmenting campus architectural staff with a small professional Design Review Board paid large dividends through regular monthly design critiques with architects hired to design new buildings, in order to maintain an overall perspective on the cumulative effect of projects under design. Buildings that emerged from the Design Review Board's critiques with their rough edges removed also were more likely to pass review by the Chancellor's Buildings and Grounds Committee and the University Trustees.

- The Trustee's Buildings and Grounds Committee was particularly senstive to issues of design compatibility and architectural style. Modern designs required extra education about their merits and fit by the staff and the building architects.
- Adopting a new zoning district for the University that allowed for approval of the 10-year Development Plan, as opposed to separate Council votes on each building, was an effective way to deal with public participation in a coordinated fashion. However, for some controversial projects, navigating the rocks and shoals of Chapel Hill's approval process took an extraordinary amount of effort by University officials in order to avoid being turned down by the Town Council.
- Fallout from controversial campus projects and plans, even when ultimately approved, could influence subsequent town elections and political deliberations for many years in the future.

According to a study of the issues of town/gown collaboration in the United States, "Successful collaboration requires a sufficient investment of time and resources from each stakeholder to create lasting change founded on ongoing communication and long-term relationships. These efforts can generate good will in the community and support in the public sector, as well as a sense of cohesion and cooperation within the university itself. By acknowledging each other's concerns and constraints, and the costs and benefits inherent in any long-term working relationship, all parties can look to the future as a win-win opportunity for positive growth and change" (Sungu-Eryilmaz 2009).

Any university campus that plans a sizeable development program would be well advised to follow the UNC model of intra-campus and extra-campus design reviews. Investing in careful deliberations throughout the design process, while treating all stakeholders with respect, can pay large dividends in the form of fewer delays and better long-term relationships.

CHAPTER 5

Preserving the Historic Campus
BUILDINGS AND LANDSCAPES

The secret to the charm and beauty of the UNC North Campus is its seamless integration of new buildings into the existing landscape. Tree-shaded commons areas are defined by low stone walls and flanked by historic buildings, whose scale and architectural features define a design palette used to ensure the compatibility of new projects. Behind this award-winning environment lies a careful process devoted to preserving both historic buildings and the landscape that embraces them.

The sustainability challenge for preservation during the massive development surge of the dynamic decade was to elevate concern for UNC's historic environment to a level equal to that expressed for its planned new buildings. Not only did the valuable historic resources of the campus have to be protected from bulldozers and construction crews, they also had to be protected from well meaning, but potentially destructive, plans for new facilities and structures. That is, there had to be a preservation ethos built into master planning from the start, to assert and protect the priceless value of UNC's 200-year old mix of historic buildings and landscapes. If historic preservation was going to be able to hold its own during the heady growth days, it needed its own champion, its own plan, and its own design guidelines. Fortunately, campus leaders and planners recognized that a sustainable campus was one that not only valued the future but also valued the past.

HISTORIC BUILDING PRESERVATION

At the start of the dynamic decade, Chancellor James Moeser realized that the University needed to plan for its older buildings as well as its newer

5-1. Students Enjoying McCorkle Place. Source: Dan Sears, UNC

ones. In 2002, he initiated a new post for a Campus Historic Preservation Manager. Paul Hardin Kapp, an experienced preservation architect, was recruited to fill this post. Kapp's first act was to compile a systematic survey to document the historic resources of the campus. The 2003 Historic Preservation Survey identified and described "historic buildings, monuments, and landscape features that have contributed to the history and the sense of architectural and cultural place of the oldest state university in the United States" (Kapp 2003).

It is impossible to overstate the impact of historic preservation in sustaining the campus during the dynamic decade of development. UNC's North Campus is a treasure-trove of historic buildings. With the completion of the 2003 Historic Preservation Survey, the University gained a professionally-prepared tool to educate and guide designers, building users, maintenance staff, and the community about the significance of their architectural inheritance for the first time in its history. This critical new tool provided foundational knowledge for the UNC Facilities Planning Department's Historic Preservation Program.

Of the 84 buildings surveyed in the 2003 Historic Preservation Survey, 32 were listed as National Historic Buildings, though some additional older buildings met some of the criteria for designation. Of those listed, 8 were completely renovated and 3 received exterior renovation. In addition, 5 of the unlisted older buildings were completely renovated and 1

PAUL KAPP, HISTORIC PRESERVATION ARCHITECT

When Paul Kapp signed on as UNC's Historic Preservation Manager in 2002, he was looking for a few good buildings to save. He was, after all, an architect and an expert in historic preservation. What he soon decided, however, was that the most precious parts of UNC's campus were not always to be found in its bricks and mortar.

While UNC has standouts like Old East and South Building, Kapp says, most of its other buildings "are not what architectural historians get all in a hot fever about," Kapp says. The real star, he says, is the "connective tissue" of campus—its quadrangles, stone walls, brick walks and magisterial trees.

"When you go to Polk Place, for example, the buildings were meant to be more on the periphery. Those are not 'look-at-me' historic buildings. They are meant to help define that space of the great rock walls and brick walks and oaks and maples. It's all one thing."

Which isn't to say that there weren't buildings that were worthy—and in dire need—of help. Kapp immediately encountered a laundry list of deferred maintenance throughout the campus. A number of buildings, many of them historic in nature, hadn't been upgraded or otherwise touched in decades. His first priority was to evaluate all the buildings, identify what was historic, and what needed to be done. From that survey, he created a five-year maintenance plan.

The restoration and renovation process of historic buildings was constrained by the twin realities of working with public money, and of working on a living, rapidly growing campus. The year 2000 bond issue, source of the biggest pool of renovation money, was earmarked for buildings that had teaching functions. Work on research, office and administration buildings like Battle-Vance-Pettigrew was bumped down the list in favor of classroom buildings like Murphey Hall. "You can't just restore a building because it is a nice thing to do," Kapp says. "You're talking about taxpayer dollars here."

At the same time, any renovation work had to be guided first by the notion that these buildings were meant to be used first, and admired second. "Historic buildings on campus need to be repurposed," Kapp says. "You can't keep up museum pieces."

The utility argument, in fact, was what helped Kapp make the case for the renovation of the long-neglected Campus Y building, which had so many rooms closed off or condemned that very few square feet of usable space remained. Kapp was able to show that the building had 10,000 square feet to offer, including rooms that could serve the teaching mission of the University, a compelling argument for "the potential that was underneath all the junk."

"The way to save the Y was to say, 'A rock's throw from South Building, we have all this space that is just sitting there,'" Kapp recalls. " 'We can use it.'"

Other historic buildings, on the other hand, flunked the utility test. West House was a 1,100-square-foot 1935 brick building that looked, Kapp says, like a "Jeffersonian pavilion with a single-wide trailer crashed into the side of it."

While many on campus were captivated by West House's odd charm, Kapp found that renovating the structure didn't make sense, and relocating it was too expensive. "You couldn't teach in it," he says of the building, which was torn down in 2006 to make way for the Arts Common. "Put an addition on it and you really would have lost its quirky significance."

While the fate of the buildings took up much of his time, Kapp also made every effort to preserve that "connective tissue"—the landscape of the campus itself—by securing a campus preservation grant from the Getty Trust Campus Heritage program that supported the development of the UNC Historic Framework Plan.

"When I came into the position, I was looking for important buildings," says Kapp, who is now an associate professor at University of Illinois at Urbana-Champaign. "I left with a different perspective, which is that the most important aspect of UNC is the historic landscape."

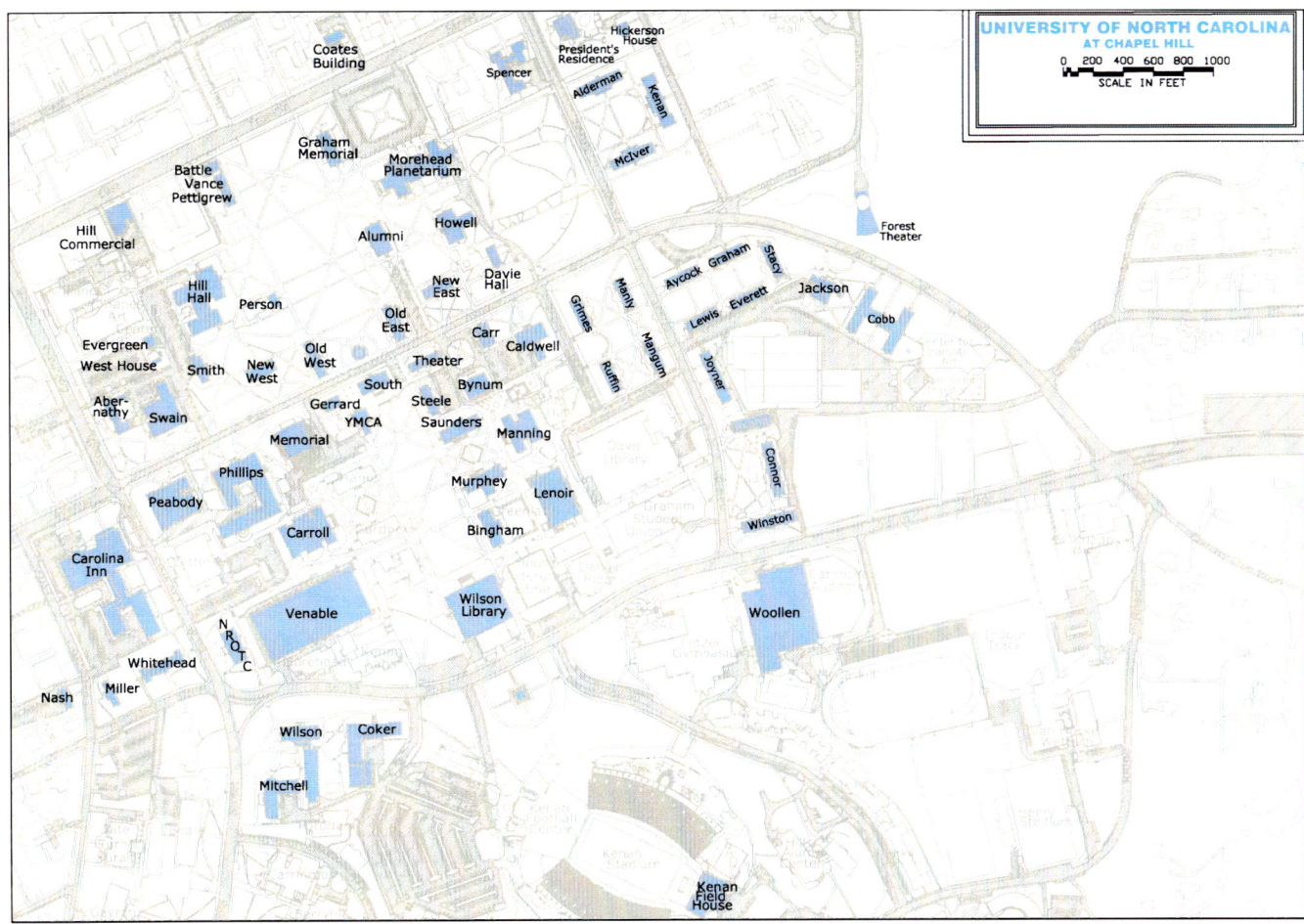

5-2. UNC's Historic Buildings Map. Source: UNC Facilities Planning & Construction

was partially renovated. The 2003 Historic Preservation Survey also provided critical input to decisions about which historic buildings merited preservation and which could be taken down to make room for new replacement buildings.

The Historic Preservation Survey recognized that the campus was not a static entity to be preserved intact, as a Colonial Williamsburg or an Old Salem theme park, but rather a living and dynamic environment that "must continue to change, grow, and evolve in order to meet its ongoing mission and challenge." However, it also recognized that some campus buildings are architecturally and historically vital to the history and significance of the campus. The Survey worked within the framework of the 2001 Campus Master Plan, which extols the character of its landmark spaces in McCorkle Place and Polk Place, but also marks some older buildings for demolition. The historic preservation program took responsibility for recommending to the Chancellor actions to carry out those life and death decisions for the older building stock, including recommendations on the expensive but important upgrading and repurposing of these historic treasures.

PRESERVING THE HISTORIC CAMPUS

5-3. Old Well and Old East.
Source: UNC Facilities Planning
& Construction

Historic Campus Precincts

In order to place individual buildings within the historical chronology of campus development, the Survey mapped and discussed the architecture of significant campus development periods by precincts. The Early Republic Precinct from 1795 to 1798 reviewed the condition of the original four campus buildings: Old East, a National Historic Landmark, the first building on a public university campus in the U.S., whose cornerstone was laid in 1793; Old West; Person Hall; and South Building. The exteriors of these four Federal style buildings still retained some aspects of their original design although their interiors had been largely replaced.

The Antebellum Precinct from 1837 to 1861 included the high-style buildings that expressed the value of the University before the Civil War. These included two buildings restored as performance spaces: the Playmakers Theatre, a National Historic Landmark designed by Alexander Jackson Davis, and Gerard Hall. New East and New West were also included in this Precinct. The Survey found their exteriors still reflective of their original designs, although in need of major restoration along with their interiors.

5-4. Playmakers Theatre.
Source: Dan Sears, UNC

The Pre-World War I Precinct from 1891 to 1917 contained mostly dormitories and classroom buildings, except for the Campus YMCA and Bynum Hall, a gymnasium. Almost all of these buildings were designed by Frank Milburn and Milburn and Heister. Surrounding the original building cluster, they extended the campus along the Cameron Avenue axis. They freely mixed architectural styles, ranging from the French Neoclassical style of Hill Hall (originally the Carnegie Library,) to the Jacobethan style of Battle, Vance, and Pettigrew Dormitories. Many of them contained distinctive mass-produced architectural elements of their era (for example, stamped metal cornices and shingles) which could be preserved to maintain the architectural styles.

The Pre-World War II/Colonial Revival and Neoclassical Buildings Precinct from 1921 to 1940 included the creation of Polk Place by the architectural firm of McKim, Mead, and White, with its Colonial Revival style buildings defining formal quadrangles. This stylistic unification set the tone of the physical character of the campus and extended it south to Wilson Library, the Bell Tower, and Kenan Stadium.

5-5. Hill Hall, Originally the Carnegie Library. Source: Dan Sears, UNC

5-6. Wilson Library. Source: Dan Sears, UNC

5-7. South Building. Source: UNC Facilities Planning & Construction

Determining Historic Significance

The Survey documented some ninety buildings and monuments. Historic determination criteria were based on whether the resource was:

- At least fifty years old.
- Associated with events or persons that influenced the history of the University, State, or Nation.
- An embodiment of distinctive characteristics of type, period, construction type, and style that define the historic campus.
- Able to yield potential archeology that is significant to the history of the University.

Each building was described in a table listing the year it was built, condition, style of architecture, architect, and whether it is listed on the National Register for Historic Places, as well as an assessment of its level of historic significance. Level (3), the highest level of historic significance, was when the complete building—exterior and interior—was historically and architecturally significant. Level (2) was when the exterior and some interior spaces were historically significant. Level (1) was when only the exterior of the building was of historic significance.

Buildings were further described in a narrative that identifies the important features of the resource that should be preserved. Significant elements were discussed in terms of material, craftsmanship, and style, along with material failures and decayed elements. Issues of deficiencies or critical maintenance were highlighted. Many of the buildings had served a succession of uses. For example, before it became home to the Chancellor's office, South Building originally contained dormitories and the Dialectic and Philanthropic halls.

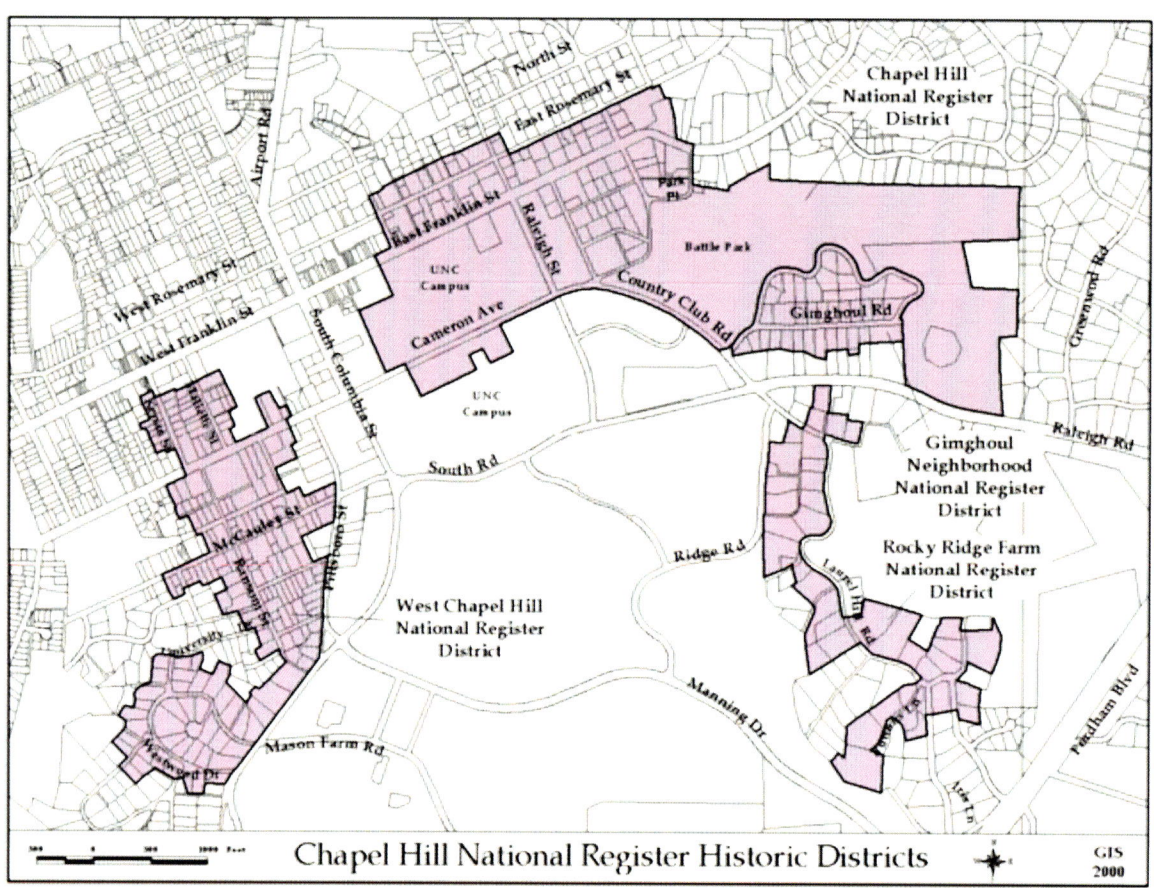

5-8. National Register Historic Districts Surrounding the UNC Campus. Source: 2003 Historic Preservation Survey

All proposed historic building renovation was required to conform to the *Secretary of Interior Standards for Rehabilitation.* (http://www.hpo.ncdcr.gov/standard.htm.) Furthermore, the campus was surrounded on three sides by a combination of National and Local Historic Districts, which required additional standards. The Chapel Hill Historic Districts—Gimghoul, Franklin/Rosemary, and Cameron/McCauley—were included within the more extensive National Districts, some of which extended into the UNC campus. All new capital construction projects with a potential impact on adjacent local historic districts were subject to review and approval by the Historic District Commission of the Town of Chapel Hill, a citizen group staffed by the Town's Planning Department.

As historic buildings were slated for renovation, their occupants had to be temporarily relocated, leading to a need for available "swing space" during the construction period. Thus, the campus planners needed to recognize the domino effect of each preservation decision. They also had to contend with the public relations issues that arose when venerable old structures were slated for demolition.

The Historic Preservation Decision-making Process

Despite an overwhelming rate of success, all historic preservation initiatives did not run smoothly. For example, two preservation decisions during the dynamic decade prompted major public outcries. One—the Campus Y Building—resulted in preserving the structure. The other—West House—resulted in demolishing the structure. Together they illustrate the importance of historic preservation planning that is strong enough to provide objective data that will stand up during controversial decisions.

The Campus Y's unique Collegiate Gothic Revival architecture set it apart from its Federal style neighbors, such as South Building. Built in 1907, it was designed for use as a student union and chapel. The noted author, Thomas Wolfe, roomed on the third floor when he was a student at the University, and the Y served many generations of students as their headquarters for social justice projects. Slated for demolition prior to the 2001 Master Plan, it was poorly maintained. The chapel had been turned into a snack bar, and the second story had been condemned as unsafe for occupancy. But the exterior was renovated in 2001 and the Survey rated the building as historically significant. Meanwhile, a preservation advocacy group clamored for its preservation and offered to raise funds for the work. Private donors put up $1.5 million on top of the University funding of $750,000, and a splendid restoration project was completed in 2007. The dropped ceiling in the chapel was removed to open the tall windows and turn this high-ceilinged space into a beautiful faculty-student lounge and meeting room.

The West House story took a different turn. This little 1,141 square foot brick building was built in 1935 as a private residence for a textile magnate's sons and their friends. It was used for military training in World War II, and at various times housed the Computer Science Department, the Institute for the Arts and Humanities, and the International Studies curriculum. Its main visual feature was a serpentine brick wall surrounding a small garden. Its historical significance was rated as one (1), how-

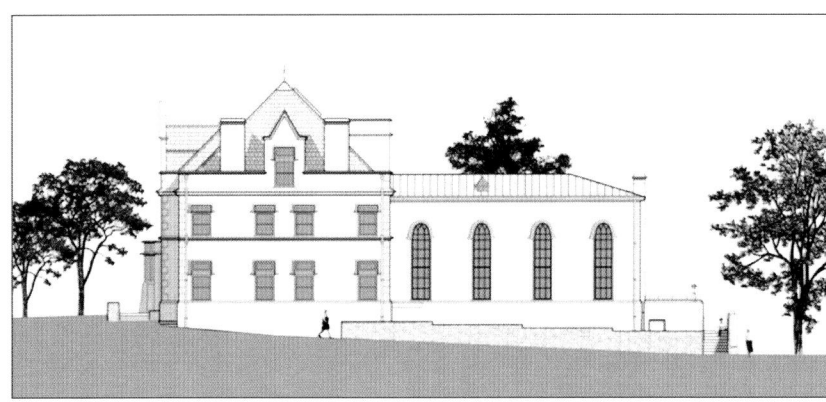

5-9. Rendering of Campus YMCA. Source: UNC Facilities Planning & Construction

5-10. West House. Source: UNC Facilities Planning & Construction

5-11. Murphey Hall. Source: UNC Facilities Planning & Construction

ever, and it would have had to be completely gutted in order to be useable. Scheduled to be demolished to make room for the proposed new UNC arts commons, an expanded area of visual and performing arts facilities adjacent to the Hanes Art Center, it became the focus of an ardent preservation campaign led by a campus librarian. Despite attracting support from a member of the Chapel Hill Town Council and the State Senator from the area, West House was taken down in 2006.

A more common story is that of the renovation of Murphey Hall, a Colonial Revival building constructed in 1924 and one of the first to be located on Polk Place next to Saunders Hall and Manning Hall. The Survey found Murphey to be in excellent condition with a historically significant exterior and some interior spaces. Its interior renovation had restored the original maple flooring and enhanced the classrooms and offices.

A final tale is that of the Spencer Love House, a Queen Anne-style residence by an unknown architect. Built in 1885 by Professor James Lee Love as a home for himself and his wife, June Spencer, this single story house sits on the corner of Franklin Street and Battle Lane, where it adjoins the Chapel Hill Historic District. With its wraparound porch and distinctive gables, it was a long-time Chapel Hill landmark. The Survey found it in fair condition, needing work on its wood siding, roof, and windows. However, to justify the needed investment in renovation, it needed to be converted to a University center, as opposed to continuing as a residence. But conversion required considerable collaboration with the Chapel Hill preservation community, who insisted that its future use maintain its residential character. After many meetings and discussions, agreement was reached. The house would be extensively renovated to become the home of the Center for the Study of the American South, a fitting use for a Historic District neighbor.

5-12. Spencer Love House.
Source: UNC Facilities Planning & Construction

> "My first impression of Chapel Hill was trees. My last impression is trees."
> —*Robert House, former UNC Chancellor*

LANDSCAPE PRESERVATION

During the dynamic decade of campus development, landscape preservation planning proceeded in parallel with the master planning process. Two major landscape preservation events shaped the UNC approach. First, the Task Force on Landscape Heritage and Plant Diversity issued its *Final Report* in 2005. That report presented a vision for the present and future campus, defined protection measures for heritage trees and landmark spaces, and established landscape design guidelines to be followed in all project proposals. Second, the Historic Landscape Framework Plan was published in 2008, the fruit of a study to preserve and enhance the University's majestic tree landscape. That study, entitled *The Dignity of Restraint*, set forth a series of guiding principles, along with priorities for five landmark campus sites: McCorkle Place, Polk Place, the Bell Tower Formal Garden, Kenan Woods, and the Forest Theatre.

Task Force on Landscape Heritage and Plant Diversity

Concerned about losing important trees to the construction of new buildings under the campus master plan, Chancellor James Moeser appointed a task force in 2003 to devise criteria and guidelines for the preservation, protection, and development of Carolina's landscape plantings. Their report aimed to provide guidelines for decision makers to:

- Identify heritage trees and groves, significant trees and landscapes, and landmark spaces,
- Guide the siting of new buildings before designs are approved,
- Ensure sound design of new and renovated landscapes, and
- Protect significant existing trees and shrubs during construction.

The Task Force looked back 200 years to the founding of the University and ahead 100 years to its long-range future. Their vision was "a landscape that will be as beautiful at the University's tricentennial in 2093 as it was at the bicentennial in 1993." Their 2005 report stated (pages 1–11):

"… we imagine a university community that will continue to value Carolina's deep roots in the natural world—a community that will consciously safeguard its irreplaceable legacy of trees, rock walls, and brick paths on a hilltop site carved out of the ancient forest."

The principal feature of the campus landscape—mature individual trees in a park-like setting, along with scattered tracts of remnant forest—has survived from the 18th century to the 21st century. The large trees are so commanding that the landscape is an equal partner with campus buildings in creating the signature UNC appearance. The trees unite buildings of diverse architectural styles into a unified whole, create an atmosphere of calm and closeness to nature and the past, and provide outdoor rooms for study and recreation.

What is it about the Carolina landscape, besides trees, that creates its

5-13. Coker Arboretum.
Source: Dan Sears, UNC

signature appearance? The Task Force identified a unique combination of elements, including:

- A hilltop setting with sheltering woods, including Battle Park, the Coker Pinetum, and smaller pockets of the original forest,
- Natural slopes, untouched by bulldozers and criss-crossed by pedestrian-determined pathways and brick walks,
- Low walls of native stone that define boundaries and offer sitting places, and
- Campus beautification that values gardens designed by great botanists like Professor William Chambers Coker, who transformed a boggy pasture into the Coker Arboretum, a place for teaching and enjoyment.

The original quadrangle, now called McCorkle Place, was called "The Grove" in recognition of the fact that the University and its trees were almost synonymous. Thomas Wolfe, the famous author who was an undergraduate at UNC, described a fictional version of the University in *Look Homeward Angel*: "The central campus sloped back and up over a broad area of rich turf, groved with magnificent ancient trees." University Students, faculty, staff, and visitors alike continue to be struck by the beauty of the remaining hilltop deciduous forest. During a 1996 radio broadcast of "A Prairie Home Companion" from Carmichael Auditorium, Garrison Keillor described the area as "... forest country down here. Beautiful trees all around. These are woodland people down here."

In order to preserve, protect, and carry forward this unique environment, the Task Force defined two landscape categories and procedures for designation and protection: 1) heritage trees and 2) landmark spaces. *Heritage trees* are defined as individual campus trees that have developed exceptional historical, cultural, or aesthetic value because of their age, descent, legendary stature, contribution to the diversity of the campus landscape, exemplary representation of genus or species, rarity, or association with an important event or person. *Landmark spaces* are defined as spaces recognized in significant campus publications, such as Archibald Henderson's *The Campus of the First State University* (1949), or by the Task Force, following the same criteria as heritage trees. McCorkle Place, the original Grove, is one of several designated landmark spaces.

By designating a tree as "heritage" or a space as "landmark," UNC committed to significant preservation efforts: appointed officials would monitor the status of all such trees and spaces, review any proposed changes, and enforce appropriate protection measures. Should something have to be removed, suitable replacements would be provided. The Task Force Report included comprehensive lists and location maps of all designated heritage trees and landmark spaces. Rather than specifying a one-size-fits-all approach, the report proposed landscape characteristics and guidelines for each of three campus districts: North, Southwest, and Southeast.

The Task Force Report laid out guidelines for landscape designers working on campus construction projects, building renovations, and road improvements or utility projects. They must respect and enhance existing landmark spaces and heritage trees, as well as existing topography, rock outcroppings, and natural systems. Displaced trees should be replanted and maximum infiltration of stormwater into the soil should be accomplished. A safe overall environment should be achieved, with adequate lighting, safe pedestrian paths, and well-marked routes. Building entrances should be clearly defined, remnant forests retained, and shade trees provided along the edges of open spaces. Each proposed project must include a survey, utility impact mitigation plan, tree protection plan, and pedestrian circulation plan to fit with the Campus Master Plan pedestrian network.

The Task Force report was an important influence on campus design projects during the second half of the dynamic decade. Its guidelines ensured that the result of the major building boom would protect the historic landscape fabric, a critical feature of sustainable campus development. A second report, *The Dignity of Restraint: A Study to Preserve and Enhance the University of North Carolina's Majestic Tree Landscape* (Hoerr Schaudt Landscape Architects. 2008), built on this foundation and developed principles and recommendations for the Historic Landscape

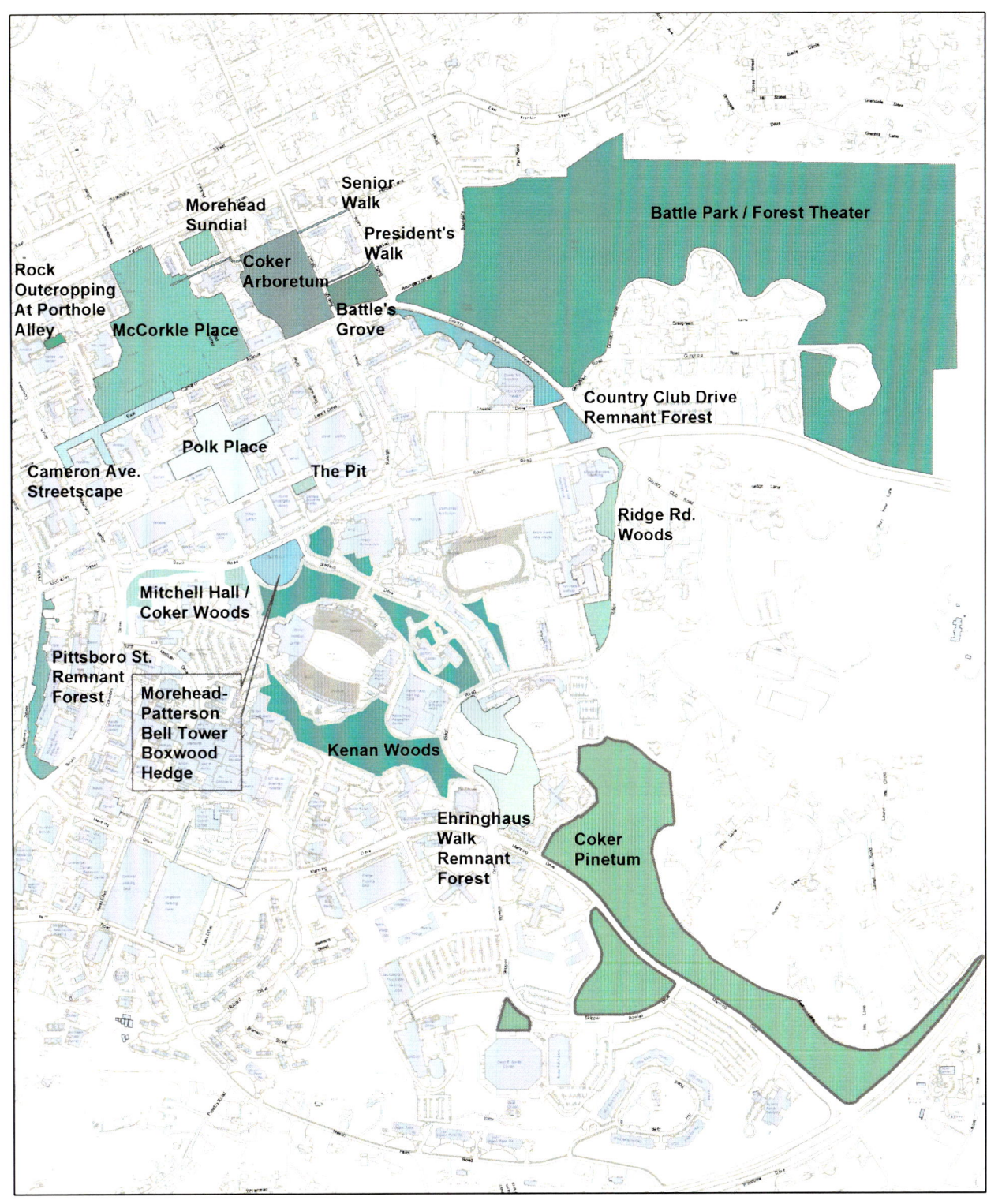

5-14. Map of UNC's Landmark Spaces. Source: UNC Task Force on Landscape Heritage & Plant Diversity

> "The jury admired the attributes of the historic campus and the designers' sensitive touch on it: 'the diversity of site types, from historical to towers, is achingly beautiful. The level of planning is perfect. It takes the approach of knitting the campus together. They aren't trying to do more than they need to do.'"
>
> —*ASLA 2011, Professional Award for "The Dignity of Restraint"*

Framework Plan, focusing on five landmark sites. The thinking in this Framework Plan then influenced proposed project plans for areas such as the Bell Tower and the Kenan Stadium Woods.

The Dignity of Restraint

The Study to Preserve and Enhance the University's Majestic Tree Landscape was carried out by a team of consultants and UNC staff and faculty. It included the renowned horticulturalist Mike Dirr, founder of the cultural landscape foundation Charles Birnbaum, and urban arborist James Urban. Underwritten by the Campus Heritage Grant Program of the Getty Foundation, the study analyzed five landmark sites in the historic core of the campus: McCorkle Place, Polk Place, the Morehead-Patterson Bell Tower Formal Garden, Kenan Stadium Woods, and the Forest Theatre. Led by landscape architect Peter Schaudt, it recommended specific preservation actions for each site. In 2011, Hoerr Schaudt received a Professional Award from the American Society of Landscape Archiects for the report.

After tracing the evolution of the landscape through five periods from 1793 to the present, the study laid out a series of guiding principles:

- New Foundations—integrate cultural, scenic, and natural values into the UNC decision process, which previously focused on buildings and architecture.
- Quest for Dignity—consider the impact on the whole to safeguard and manage the cultural, scenic, and natural values of the campus landscape, which has been impacted by evolutionary changes such as overgrown vegetation and addition of out-of-character elements.
- Recognition for Uniqueness—balance the site-specific design requirements of historic landscape features while understanding this space within the context of the larger campus framework, by emphasizing the individual character-defining features and relationships of spaces that define the Picturesque McCorkle Place as compared with the City Beautiful/Beaux Arts Polk Place.
- Integration of Civic Intent—retain and honor the civic ambition of patronage while insuring its careful integration into the larger cultural landscape, so that features such as the Bell Tower are linked to surrounding areas such as Kenan Woods.
- Respect and Honor the Legacy—preserve and reveal character-defining features and relationships that are historically significant while accommodating change through actions such as pursuing National Register of Historic Places designation for the Forest Theatre or transforming the setting of the Old Well.

The study applied these principles to each of the five landmark sites through proposed design interventions. In McCorkle Place, new trees would be planted to replace the aging canopy trees, and foundation and

PETER SCHAUDT, LANDSCAPE ARCHITECT

Look at many of the country's most distinguished campuses, and you see the legacy of high design: the master planning of Frederick Law Olmstead at Stanford or the University of Chicago, for example. But the legacy at UNC's campus, says Peter Schaudt FASLA of Hoerr Schaudt Landscape Architects, has its roots in botany.

It's a legacy that reflects the natural power of the original site—a forest that, even in 1789, was called ancient; and the heavy influence of UNC's own master botanist, William Coker, who worked to beautify the campus over the first half of the 20th century. "Very little was done by landscape professionals," Schaudt says of the campus. "What's amazing is that this place just kind of evolved through botany."

The evolutionary nature of campus design here offered a challenge to Schaudt and his firm as they created a restoration plan. Many of the campuses that he has worked on are tied together by architecture or other elements, like the sameness of the buildings at the University of Illinois. When he looked at each of the five sites he was contracted to work on at UNC— McCorkle Place, Polk Place, the Bell Tower Formal Garden, Kenan Woods, and the Forest Theatre—he found five distinct styles.

Big trees and meandering pathways make McCorkle, for example, a textbook example of the picturesque period. With its grand, McKim, Mead, and White library dominating one end, Schaudt says, Polk Place was classic Beaux-Arts. Look at them all together, he says, and "the only unifying element really is the tree canopy."

In the 2008 plan for the landscape, entitled *The Dignity of Restraint*, Schaudt and the project team didn't try to fight this mish-mash of styles. "In most campus master plans, there's this desire to unify things," he says. "But in this case, we decided to celebrate those differences."

In many areas, the celebration meant returning to the simplicity of the original design: addition by subtraction of overgrowth and additions that had cropped up over the decades. At the Bell Tower, the boxwood had grown so high that it created a "no man's land" between it and the structure. The team recommended that it be replaced by grass terracing to create a space that is more open to the street and accessible to people. "The Bell Tower was a very simple, strong, surgical move," he says.

At Polk Place and the courtyards surrounding it, the team's recommendation was to reclaim open space by removing lights and flagpoles from the center, and "erasing" the raised planters in the smaller quads on either side. "If you look at early photos (of those areas), there is a beautiful simplicity to the trees and the paths," Schaudt says.

In the woods surrounding Kenan Stadium, which had grown stagnant and unhealthy under the pressure of tens of thousands of game-day pedestrians, the team proposed to remove the utility boxes, shelters and other features that intruded on the forest floor, and draw foot traffic away via wider walkways and picnic areas. At the same time, they recommended planting a greater diversity of tree species to recreate a healthy forest.

The importance of replanting was a key theme across all five sites. The landscape architects developed a system to ensure continuity as old trees died off. Each lost tree would be replaced by two: a fast-growing tulip poplar to help plug the hole over the next 20 years or so, and a slow-growing oak to grow up and into its role as the long-term replacement. "They were replanting, but not in a systematic, planned way. It was more reactionary," Schaudt says. "You need to constantly replenish your resource."

It is that arboreal resource—"the only unifying element"—that Schaudt returns to again and again when talking about naturalistic beauty of UNC. "Nothing looks engineered," he says, describing Polk Place and its ancient trees, which he calls the "heart and soul" of campus. "The beautiful thing about that space is that it was never designed by an architect."

screening planting would be redesigned to maintain the 19th century character while screening parking and service areas. Dignity would be returned by removing, limiting, and/or strategically locating site furnishings. The most dramatic proposal would extend the brick paving of the Old Well plaza across Cameron Avenue, linking it to South Building and Polk Place to the south so as to create a more important pedestrian plaza.

For Polk Place, similar types of strategies were recommended, with adjustments for its particular landscape features, such as the soil compaction that was affecting the health of the trees. A special recommendation for Polk Place was to restore the side quads leading to Manning Hall on the east and Carroll Hall on the west by "erasing" the raised stone planter walls that had been introduced into the formerly open lawn quads. These raised beds were out of character with the Beaux Arts buildings and landscape; removing them would restore the uninterrupted ground plane and keep the central lawn panel open. Seating areas would be maintained by locating benches along the edges of the quad near building entrances.

For the Morehead-Patterson Bell Tower, a modern interpretation of an Italian Romanesque campanile, the recommended design strategy was to make it a destination place and reintegrate it into the surrounding campus. The current use of the area was limited by lack of access and visibility. Visibility and accessibility would be increased by remov-

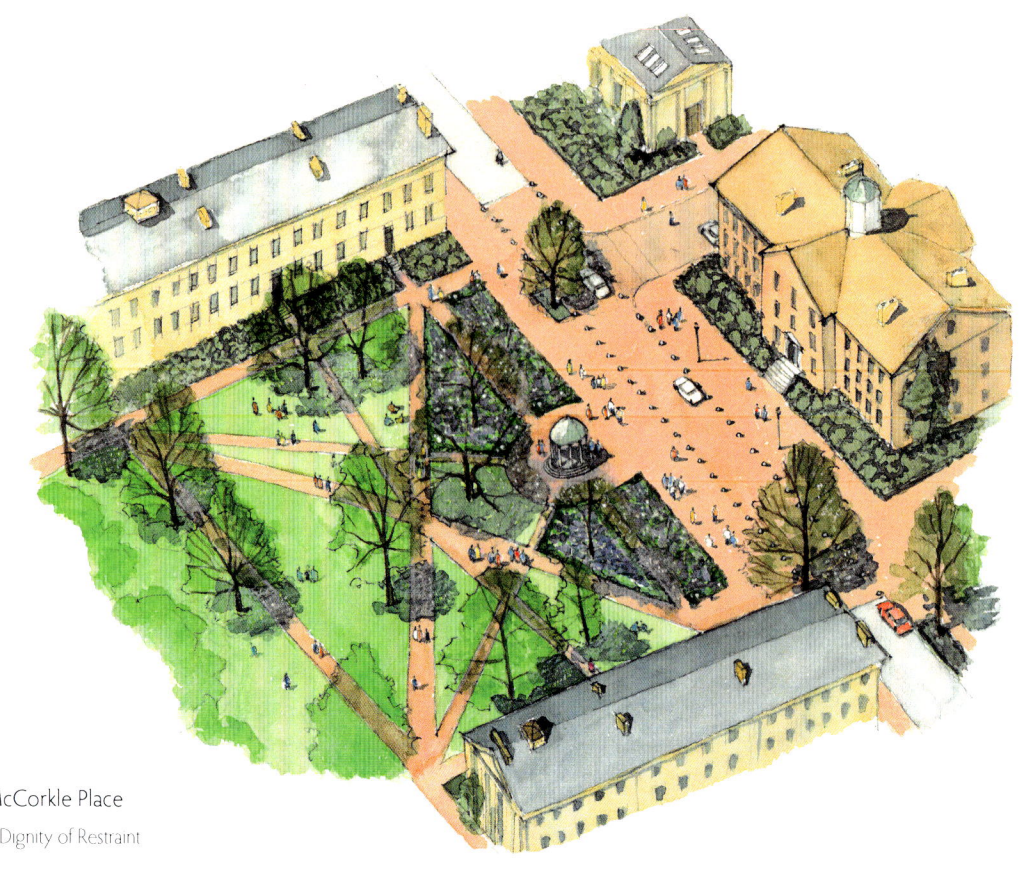

5-15. Potential McCorkle Place Extension. Source: Dignity of Restraint

5-16.
Restored
Manning Hall
Side Quad.
Source: Dignity
of Restraint

5-17.
Possible
Bell Tower
Integration.
Source: Dignity
of Restraint

ing the boxwood hedge on the north side facing South Road and replacing it with a stepped grassed terrace with limestone risers. At the same time, new ramps and walkways would be added and the boxwood hedge on the other three sides would be trimmed down to open views into the space. Connections from Wilson Library would be created by planting evergreen trees in the existing planting beds there. Finally, an engraved limestone memorial bench would be located around the south edges of the Bell Tower space as a way to accommodate future campus memorials.

For Kenan Woods, the forest surrounding Kenan Stadium, the master plan for expansion of the stadium emphasized woodland conservation and regeneration. Utility boxes, shelters, plazas, and parking areas impinged on the forest floor, and game-day crowds and tail gating had limited the opportunity for forest regeneration. The recommended strategy was to institute forest management, including phased replanting of

5-18. Kenan Woods Opportunities. Source: Dignity of Restraint

fenced woodland patches, and to control pedestrian traffic through creating pathways and gathering spaces defined by low stone walls to channelize visitor traffic into desired routes and destinations, rather than to let it spread haphazardly throughout the woods.

For the Forest Theatre, the outdoor theatre in Battle Park, the proposal centered on rehabilitating the existing theatre and its infrastructure, while pursuing National Register of Historic Places designation. In addition, a primeval forest management strategy would add native trees and screening materials. To increase visibility and accessibility, new public gathering spaces, reconfigured parking areas, and enhanced entry points into the site would be created.

PRESERVATION LESSONS FOR SUSTAINABILITY

Historic landscape preservation goes hand-in-hand with historic building preservation. Both are important elements of the planning initiatives that sustained the campus during the dynamic decade of development. Without them, UNC's new projects would not have succeeded as well in their integration into the campus fabric and *zeitgeist*—its distinctive spirit.

Campus sustainability demands that planners protect and enhance the historic resources that form the foundation of the university. It is not enough to project and meet future needs. To lose the soul of a campus in a flurry of new construction would be a catastrophe.

To build the case for preservation of historic buildings and landscapes, a systematic analysis of their condition and value must be conducted. Sustaining these irreplaceable resources requires careful surveys by professionals experienced in historic architecture and landscape architecture. To ensure that they will be followed, the findings and recommendations of these studies should be published and widely circulated within the university community. Furthermore, these findings should be written into design guidelines for all new development projects.

For a university campus, the long-term value of preservation is embedded in the concept of "adaptive reuse." The external appearance of the historic buildings is preserved, while their interior functions are adapted over time to meet the changing needs and educational mission of the institution. The essential character of the historic landscapes is preserved, while their functions are adapted to respond to contemporary use patterns. This fits the definition of campus sustainability: creating continuity between the past and the present, while maintaining the flexibility needed to satisfy future needs.

A serious preservation program requires resources and time. To be successful, it must be initiated in parallel with master planning for new projects, and it must be supported by university decision-makers and staff at all levels. Preservation's benefits far outweigh its costs, and true campus sustainability cannot be achieved without it.

> For a universtiy campus, the long-term value of preservation is embedded in the concept of "adaptive reuse."

5-19. Forest Theatre Potential.
Source: Dignity of Restraint

Important historic preservation sustainability lessons were:

- Conduct a careful study of the historic resources of the campus prior to large-scale reconstruction efforts and disseminate and document the findings as guides to future campus planning and development.
- Incorporate historic preservation criteria and standards into the campus master plan and design guidelines and require that they be followed in all new projects that involve historic areas.
- Instill an ethic of sustainability into campus decision-making so that adaptive reuse of historic structures is actively considered in development planning and programming.

CHAPTER 6

Enhancing the Historic North Campus

Adding a raft of new projects to the UNC campus during a ten-year span, while preserving the historic buildings and landscapes, marked a critical turning point in the life of the University. If not done with sensitivity and care, the new development could have damaged or destroyed the work of two centuries of thoughtful planning and intelligent growth. This was a particular danger for the historic North Campus, where the mellow beauty of the historic environment was well established, while new development on the South Campus was more of an opportunity to link disparate areas and to begin to build networks of buildings, open spaces, and circulation paths.

The sustainability challenge for design of new projects on the North Campus was to expand and modernize its traditional arts, sciences, and student living facilities without running rampant over its historic architecture and landscapes. This was demanding because many of these functions were housed in older, sometimes obsolete buildings, such as old Venable, the chemistry building that was torn down to make way for the new Science Complex. Yet, if the University was not to lose its edge in its outstanding scientific research, it badly needed new labs and teaching facilities. If it was not to lose its edge in the performing arts, it badly needed new performance and teaching venues. If it was not to lose its edge as a desirable place for student life, it badly needed to update its dormitories and recreation areas. And it needed to do all of this while at the same time attacking its overdue needs for green buildings and sustainable landscapes.

Well aware of this challenge, the Master Plan demanded a high order

> The sustainability challenge... on the North Campus was to expand and modernize... without running rampant over its historic architecture and landmarks.

of design sensitivity. The genius of the master planning process stemmed from establishing two fundamental design values:

- Respect for the existing campus environment, implemented through requirements that any new project maintains compatibility with the historic architecture; and
- Community building implemented through conscious place-making efforts that visualized individual new buildings as opportunities to create activity-based campus neighborhoods or precincts.

The Master Plan and the Development Plan formulated and implemented these values and they guided ten years of ensuing project design and construction.

In order to respect the existing environment, new buildings and facilities were surgically inserted into the historic campus fabric. At the same time, their architecture was required to follow design guidelines based on compatibility with predominant historic styles and details. Constructing and renovating some six million square feet of development in one frenetic decade might have torn asunder the UNC campus. Indeed, there was considerable temporary inconvenience as construction crews and cranes took over parts of the landscape. When each project was complete, however, the campus beauty was reasserted, integrating a panoply of handsome and compatible new structures into the historic framework.

This chapter takes up the three major new North Campus communities developed by the implementation of the Master Plan: the Science Community, the Arts Community, and the North Student Residence Life and Services Community. The stories of the development of these com-

6-1. Old Venable. Source: UNC Facilities Planning & Construction.

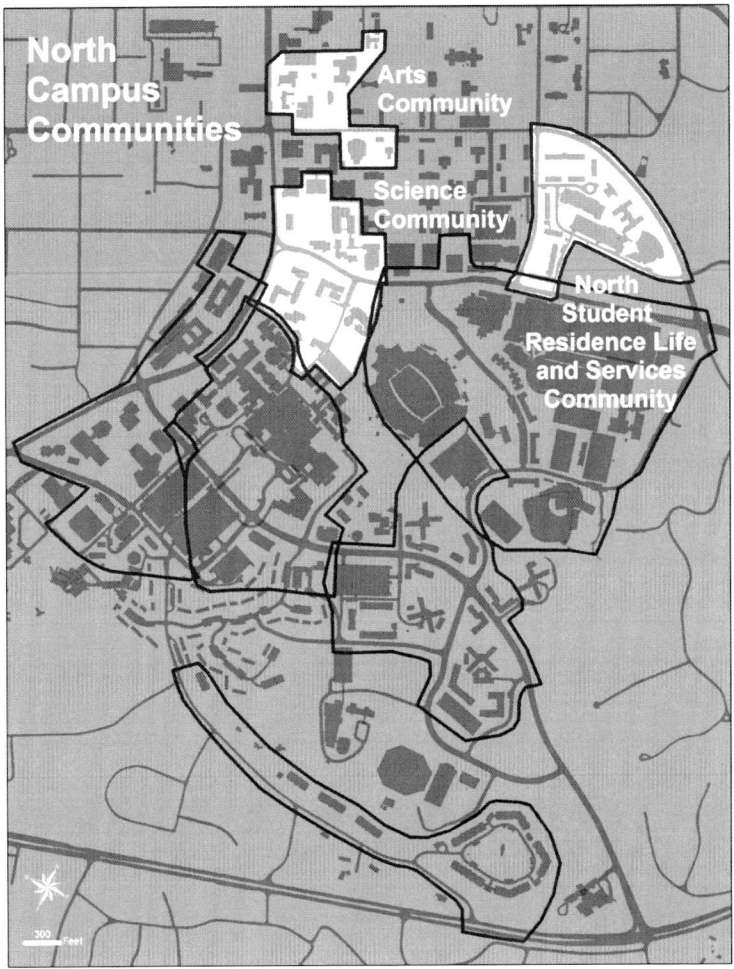

6-2. The Three Major North Campus Communities. Source: UNC Engineering and Information Services

munities are told not only in terms of the building construction, but also in terms of interviews with the some of the key actors involved. Details of square footage, cost, and architect for each project are provided in the Appendix at the end of the book. The following two chapters take up the Southeast and Southwest Campus communities.

MODERNIZING THE SCIENCE COMMUNITY

The Science Community includes a number of buildings located in three separately designed projects:

- The *Science Complex* north of South Road, including Caudill Laboratories, New Venable Hall (a replacement for the old Venable), Murray Hall, Chapman Hall (an addition to Phillips Hall), and Brooks Computer Science (an addition to Sitterson Hall);
- The *Bell Tower Lot Complex* south of South Road, including the new Genomic Sciences building, a parking deck, and a commons garden ("Central Park");

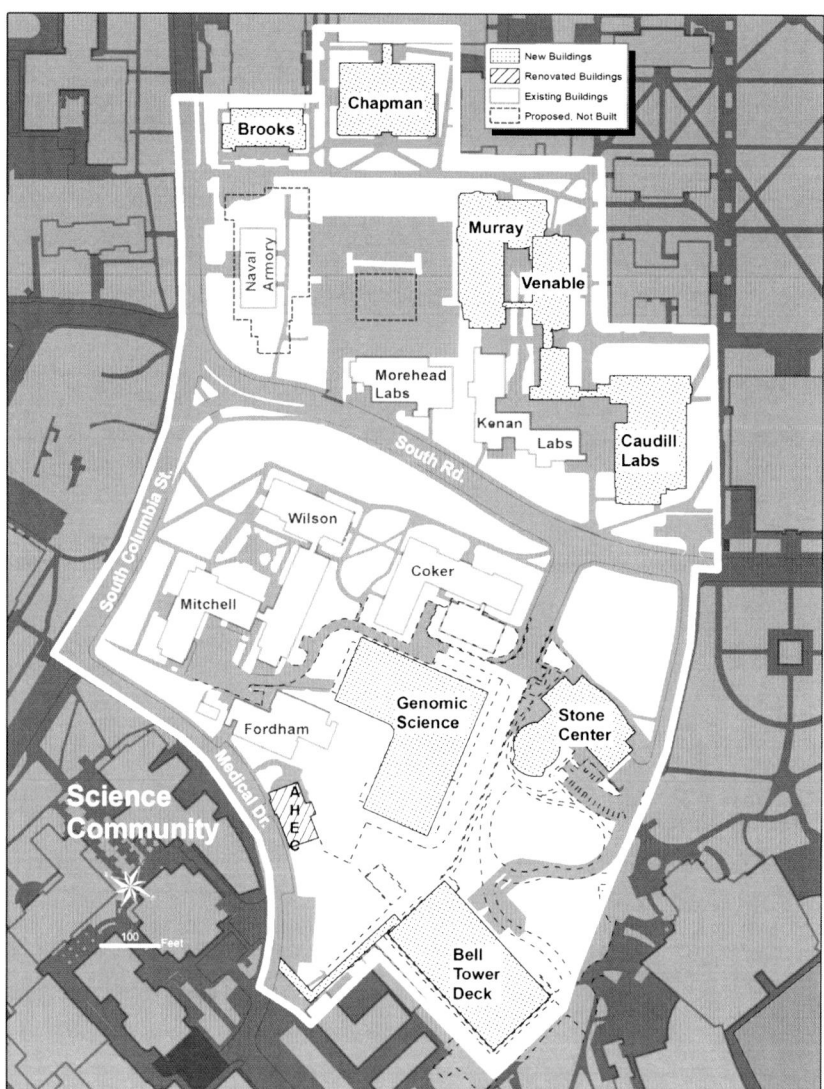

6-3. Science Community Map.
Source: UNC Engineering and Information Services

- The *Sonja Haynes Stone Center for Black Culture and History*, whose location in the Bell Tower area south of South Road was approved by Board of Trustees in 1993 prior to the 2001 Master Plan, but whose construction did not take place until the dynamic decade of 2001 to 2011.

Geography unites these projects, whose adjacent sites share access roads and parking, even though their functions differ. The design challenge was to build on these basic relationships to create an attractive and effective community through placement of building masses, pathways, and open spaces.

The Science Community occupies major sites on each side of South Road, and, in this way, helps link the North and South Campuses. On the north side, the Science Complex site fits between Wilson Library on the east and the Naval Armory (ROTC) Building (planned to be replaced in future development) on the west. On the south side, the Genomic Sciences, parking, and Central Park site occupies the former Bell Tower Parking lot, which is a large bowl adjacent to the Football Center on the east and Coker and Fordham Halls on the west. The Stone Center for Black Culture and History, completed in 2004, lies between the two science sites in a small grove of trees. By designing the new buildings and open spaces together, two outdoor rooms were created: one within the Science Complex on the north and one within the Bell Tower Complex on the south.

Science Complex

The designers of the Science Complex faced a complicated challenge. The task included demolishing a large and obsolete chemistry classroom and lab building (old Venable) and replacing it with modern teaching and research facilities while simultaneously providing new space for three other science programs. All of this was to be completed on a site with challenging topography located among existing historic buildings, adjacent to the major green axis of the North Campus, and along an important east-west connector road. While solving all these design problems, the design team had to work closely with an interdisciplinary group of science faculty who were developing the building programs while trying to stay within feasible budget limitations.

The Science Complex represents the fruition of a long-standing dream of the UNC physical sciences departments to upgrade and unite their research and teaching spaces. Previously located in scattered buildings with inadequate laboratory facilities, these departments had been hampered by physical constraints that limited their ability to conduct top-level research and to recruit top-level faculty. Because of these departments' large contribution to the University's reputation, they were able to make a convincing argument to University priority-setters for adding new science facilities. They started making their case in the 1990s, prior to the 2001 Master Planning process, and continued advocating for an improved and unified science complex throughout the process.

First, the science faculty had to generate support for a building site of adequate size located in proximity to the existing science area. Their chosen site on the North Campus, adjacent to the Chemistry, Physics, and Computer Science departments, ran into fierce competition from a campus group demanding this site for the location of the proposed Black Cultural Center. Even though the Black Cultural Center would be a much smaller building, its advocates believed that a location north of South Road would be symbolically important in recognition of their cause. After an intensive site study that included a consultant recommendation in favor of an adjacent southern site by Harvey Gantt, a noted architect-planner from Charlotte, the Trustees decided to place the Black Cultural Center on the south side of South Road, awarding the larger North Campus site to the sciences.

Next, the science faculty had to generate consensus amongst themselves about their individual and group space needs and the desired proximities of their functions. Led by Physics professor Tom Clegg, they went through an intensive planning process, working together and with the campus planning team to prepare a program statement for their new building needs. The process required many sessions to arrive at consensus on how to balance their needs with the available site space, budgets, and feasible building envelopes.

The science faculty planning team requested that the new projects should be designed to facilitate interdisciplinary collaboration. They asked for clear and convenient connections among the buildings and departments to facilitate communication and interchange among the scientific disciplines. This led the designers to lay out an interlocking complex of individual buildings connected by proximity, surface walks and outdoor common spaces, views, and upper-level bridges.

Though differing in massing and interior arrangement, the Science Complex buildings share a common architectural vocabulary that visually demonstrates their common functions of scientific research and education. For example, the design of the new Caudill Laboratories building, carefully sited on a former open space adjacent to Wilson Library, incorporates brick and limestone, as well as windows scaled to be consistent with traditional campus structures. However, its transparent nature clearly signifies a modern science facility.

The site designated in the Master Plan for the Science Complex initially extended to South Columbia Street and included new areas to be

6-4. Caudill Laboratories. Source Wilson Architects, Photographer Anton Grassl

TOM CLEGG, SCIENCE PLANNING TEAM LEADER

It is fair to say that the design and construction of UNC's science campus wasn't any more complicated than Tom Clegg's day job. It is also important to note that Clegg, who led the science faculty's planning team for the project, is a professor of physics who studies intense spin-polarized ion beams and gaseous polarized targets.

"It took a lot of work and a lot of meetings," says Clegg, who engaged more than 100 scientists across campus in the process that helped shape the Brooks, Caudill, Chapman, Murray and Venable buildings. "But we were so desperately in need of this space that the only thing we could do was to lock arms together and to do it."

Bruce Carney, a distinguished professor of physics and astronomy and now the provost, also recalls that sense of common purpose. "We all knew that the departments were compressed," Carney says. "We didn't have enough quality laboratory space, or room for students. Old Venable is fondly remembered, but it was frankly hampering chemistry's ability to keep up with changing practices in the field."

Driven by these concerns, the science departments were meeting and planning long before there was any money to build. "We talked about how might we build a more coherent science complex and help the departments work better together," Carney says. "We began sketching out what sort of things we thought we really needed with a 25-year horizon."

As soon as the shovels hit the ground, the scientists learned how flexible the best-laid plans would have to be. The construction of Phase I turned into an informal master class on construction management: unexpected roadblocks and opportunities, doors slammed shut in one direction and springing open in another.

First, the design of the building ran headlong into the state building codes. The original Caudill Hall concept included a four-story atrium. However, the NC Department of Insurance code interpretation limited the height to two stories. Later, planned basement-level connections—running between Phillips and Chapman, Chapman and Brooks—had to be shelved as construction moved forward and costs mounted. "You never have enough money to do everything you want to do," Clegg says, adding that it would have taken roughly a half-million dollars to finish the connections.

Unforeseen expense also cropped up despite the countless hours of planning and budgeting. Money was set aside to move the Department of Marine Sciences into Chapman Hall, its temporary home for two years while Venable was completed. Also not anticipated was the magnitude of refitting Chapman for the use of the next occupants, the astronomy and math departments.

To compound the problem, Carney recalls, the cost of materials was on the rise. "Every time we calculated costs per square foot, they were going up," he says. "And the demands on the buildings were pretty significant."

But the fluid nature of the construction process also brought opportunities. Chapman's basement floor, for example, was originally designed to be a half-floor—unusable space. When contractors discovered that they would have to excavate more than they had planned, however, Clegg and his colleagues quickly authorized $200,000 to pour a slab of concrete in the basement instead of graveling it, thus claiming an additional 10,000 square feet of space. That space would eventually become a fluid dynamics lab, complete with a 120-foot big wave tank, shared by the math and marine science departments.

The building team was also quick to learn from earlier challenges. The designs of the last buildings in the complex, Murray and Venable, are U-shaped and open to the south to provide the light-filled interior that regulators ruled out in Chapman. And the departments whose homes were built later were able to more precisely estimate the construction costs that lay ahead.

"I think the chemists and marine scientists are absolutely delighted (with their buildings)," Clegg says. "In having Murray and Venable at the end of process, they benefited from the learning that went on in earlier stages. They also maintained sufficient resources to get exactly what they wanted."

Regardless of the bumps in the road, Clegg says, the complex is paying dividends. The vibration-free space built in Chapman allows microscopes used in nanoscience to perform up to specifications, meaning better results; the roof of the building has an observation deck for teaching introductory astronomy classes. The end result, he says, is spaces that allow for better science and better teaching.

gained by demolishing not only the old Venable Chemistry building, but also the Naval Armory Building on the corner of South Road and South Columbia. It was to be linked back to Wilson Library and Polk Place via an east-west pedestrian walkway. Preliminary site planning alternatives considered locating an underground library or parking facility in the low area east of the New Venable Hall, with a landscaped commons above it, framed by two new academic buildings. This underground facility and the two buildings were not realized during the dynamic decade, due to lack of funding, though the buildings remain on the site plan for possible future development. However, improved east-west pedestrian connections were achieved through walkway enhancements.

The portion of the Science Complex built during the dynamic decade includes five new buildings with a total of almost 500,000 square feet at a cost of over $250 million (Appendix A). The lead firm for the architectural and site planning work was Wilson Architects of Boston. This design was the product of intensive review and discussion about everything from the small details of window frames and handrails to major questions about tying the buildings back into Polk Place circulation and viewpoints. The remarkable thing about this process was its collaborative nature, as ideas flowed freely and many alternatives were tested.

Bell Tower Lot Complex

The master planners visualized the Bell Tower Complex as a physical link between the North and South Campuses, as an interdisciplinary link among the sciences, and as a link from the Arts and Sciences area to the Health Affairs area. The design challenge for redevelopment of the Bell Tower surface parking lot was to turn this strategic but under-utilized space from an asphalt-covered automobile storage area into a higher intensity location for the emerging science of genomics, while moving the parking into a deck, creating a new green commons, respecting the previously planned Stone Center, and ensuring good pedestrian connections to the Science Complex across South Road to the north and to the Health Affairs complex along Medical Drive to the south. A further complication for the project was the topography of the site, which was shaped like a bowl with a steep ridge on its south edge, and a historic stream that ran through the area. However, because the site did not host historic buildings, the architecture was free to reflect the contemporary thrust of genomic science.

The designers solved these problems by placing the new Genomic Science Building along the west side of the site with views into and access from Central Park, Kenan Woods, and the Bell Tower. They located a new commons space to serve as an outdoor room for Genomic Sciences, the adjacent Football Center, and the previously planned Stone Black Cultural Center. They placed the new parking deck so it served not only Genomic Sciences, but also Health Affairs buildings several stories

6-5. Rendering of Genomic Sciences Building. Source: UNC Facilities Planning & Construction

up from the Bell Tower lot and entrances to the Football Center for game days. The deck's elevator became the vertical circulation link connected by a bridge to existing buildings along Medical Drive.

Not all construction was completed during the dynamic decade, although design and approval decisions were made in that period. The Stone Center was finished in 2004, the parking deck was opened in 2010, and Genomic Sciences and Central Park are on schedule to open in 2012. The three major structures were built or started during the dynamic decade, totaling almost 572,000 square feet at a total cost of over $192 million (Appendix A). Lead architects for Genomic Sciences, the parking deck, and the Central Park were Skidmore, Owings, and Merrill, Chicago; the Stone Center was designed by The Freelon Group.

UPDATING THE ARTS COMMUNITY

The design challenge for planners of the Arts Community was straightforward: to reinvigorate the campus arts venues by replacing outmoded spaces, tying existing music, visual arts, and performance facilities together into an arts neighborhood, and increasing accessibility for patrons. In concept, the Arts Community was to consist of a cluster of new arts buildings adjacent to the Ackland Art Museum, the Hanes Art Center, and Hill Hall and an area of renovated historic buildings, including Memorial Hall, Gerrard Hall, and the Y Building connected by Cameron Avenue, as well as the new Hyde Hall on McCorkle Place.

The planners devised a bold strategy for creating an "arts commons" that attempted to meet the challenge of tying music and visual arts together around a new landscaped commons over an underground park-

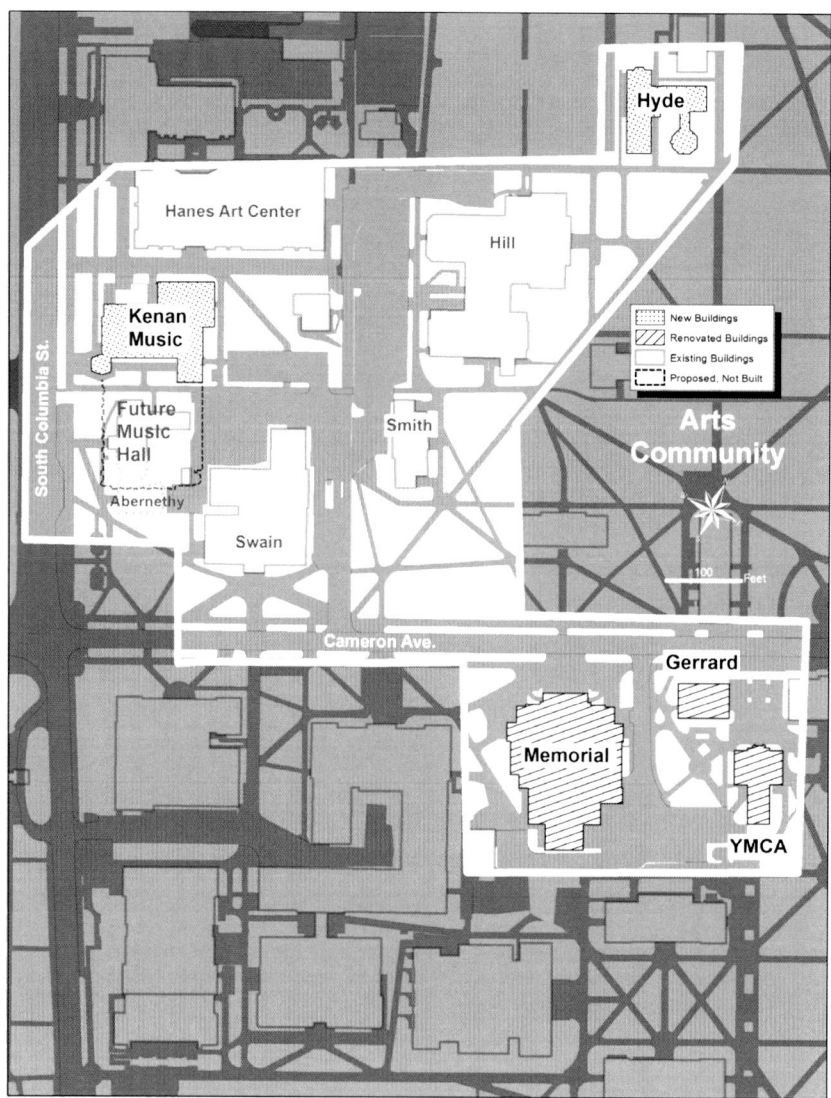

6-6. Arts Community Map.
Source: UNC Engineering and Information Services

ing facility. Its story is one of partial success; its bold vision was not fully realized.

The arts commons plan was to expand and modernize the existing music teaching and performance facilities and to connect them with the visual arts facilities through creation of a major new landscaped commons, along with expanded parking and pedestrian access. The vision was to replace the obsolete academic and performance spaces in the old Hill Hall with a new music building and to add a major expansion of the existing Ackland Art Museum. In order to open up space for the commons and new buildings, West House, Evergreen House, Abernathy, and the non-historic portions of Swain Hall and Hill Hall were proposed for removal. Since access to the proposed destination facilities would be badly constrained by the lack of visitor parking in this area of the campus, the plan proposed to add an underground parking deck beneath the commons.

Unlike the Science Community, which benefited from major federal grants as well as funding from the state bond issue, the arts initiative had to supplement the State monies with substantial private funds in order to realize its vision. Unfortunately, the full Arts Commons concept was derailed by economic factors. The underground parking proved to be too expensive to justify and the planned expansion of the Ackland Art Museum had to be shelved. Fortunately, a major donor came forward to fund the office, academic, and rehearsal portion of the new Kenan Music Building, leaving its planned performance hall for future construction.

The handsome Kenan Music Building thus became the sole survivor of the original Arts Commons scheme. By the end of the dynamic decade, the bold vision of the Arts Commons had shrunk to a portion of a single new building with an adjoining open plaza and surface parking, while the older buildings originally slated for removal, except for already-demolished West House, lived on. As constructed, however, the work that was done during the dynamic decade did not preclude a return to the grand vision, including completion of the Music Building and the underground parking, at some future date.

Renovation of the historic buildings of the Arts Community further east fared better. Substantial private funds were raised for complete reno-

6-7. Kenan Music Building. Source: G. David Hughes

TOM KENAN, PRIVATE DONOR

The William R. Kenan Jr. Charitable Trust has funded countless good works at UNC—professorships, scholarships, and fellowships by the score—but bricks-and-mortar projects aren't typically part of its mission. When UNC's construction of a new music building was endangered by lack of funding, however, the Trust was quick to answer the call.

"They were going to drop the whole case," says Kenan Trustee Thomas Kenan III. "We said, 'We can't let this happen.'"

The Trust would ultimately donate $4 million toward the $31 million project (some $19 million came from the 2000 bond referendum, and the remainder from University funds). The 100,000-square-foot building, which opened in 2008, features classrooms, studio space, a recording studio, and a rehearsal space large enough to hold the marching band.

"As a Trustee, I saw the need to strengthen the UNC music department," says Kenan, who credits former Chancellor James Moeser for making the arts a priority during the building campaign. "Hill Hall was antiquated and out of date for the 21st century."

Kenan's own interest in the arts dates back to a childhood of piano lessons ("I was not very accomplished") and learning to play clarinet ("Not very well"). In the 1970s, he joined the board of the North Carolina School of the Arts Foundation. "That experience really taught me more than I ever dreamed to know about music, dance, drama and later, film," he says. "That was really my launching pad."

Kenan and his colleagues at the Charitable Trust took a hands-off approach when it came to the design of the building. "We were shown the plans and everything, but we never tried to interject our feelings," he says.

When it came to the issue of how to help build a music program to match the new building, they again rolled up their sleeves. "If they're generous enough to put our name on the building, we've got to set up an endowment that will allow the University to attract top-notch musicians from all over the world," he recalls thinking at the time.

The result was another $4 million grant from the Kenan Charitable Trust to create 16 full music scholarships—tuition, room, board, and even a $6,000 stipend to study abroad—for undergraduates. The goal, Kenan says, was to create scholarships on the order of those offered by Juilliard or other distinguished arts conservatories. The first class enrolled in 2007; Kenan notes that the first four runners-up were so impressed by the facilities and program that they elected to come to Carolina despite not winning the scholarships.

"We felt that one was as important as the other," Kenan says. "The students are the heart of this new building, and they haven't disappointed."

Nor has the building itself. "Treated acoustical space elevates the listening process in our music performance and education classes," says Jim Ketch, a professor of jazz studies and trumpet. "The large rehearsal hall is attractive enough to host performances, and the acoustics favor many ensembles over the rather booming acoustics of Hill Hall Auditorium. Students also find the Kenan space attractive for their junior and senior recitals."

Ketch adds that the new space also improves the experience of his own performances. "I have performed many times in the new building in a jazz setting and find the acoustics for this music particularly good," he says. "We hear more clarity in performances of louder ensembles."

And, coupled with the 2005 renovation of Memorial Hall on campus, Chapel Hill students and residents now have access to art events worthy of a major metropolitan area. "Students can attend and hear world class musical events at affordable prices in Chapel Hill," Kenan says.

6-8. Renovated Memorial Hall on Opening Night. Source: Dan Sears, UNC

vations of, and additions to, the historic performance spaces at Memorial Hall and restoration of the interiors of the historic Y Building. Historic Gerrard Hall also benefited from both interior renovation and reintroduction of its historic south portico. One new building was added adjacent to McCorkle Place: Hyde Hall, home to the Institute for the Arts and Humanities, was started prior to the dynamic decade, but completed in 2002.

The cost of the Arts Community projects totaled some $36 million for new construction and almost $24 million for historic renovation. New space amounted to about 60,000 square feet and renovated space amounted to about 47,000 square feet (Appendix A).

COMBINING A TRADITIONAL RESIDENCE LIFE COMMUNITY AND SERVICES

The design challenge for the North Student Residence Life and Services Community was to modernize and renovate older residence halls and their required services in a part of the historic campus adjacent to an established residential neighborhood. The plan upgraded existing dormitory facilities, replaced an old potpourri of surface parking and tennis

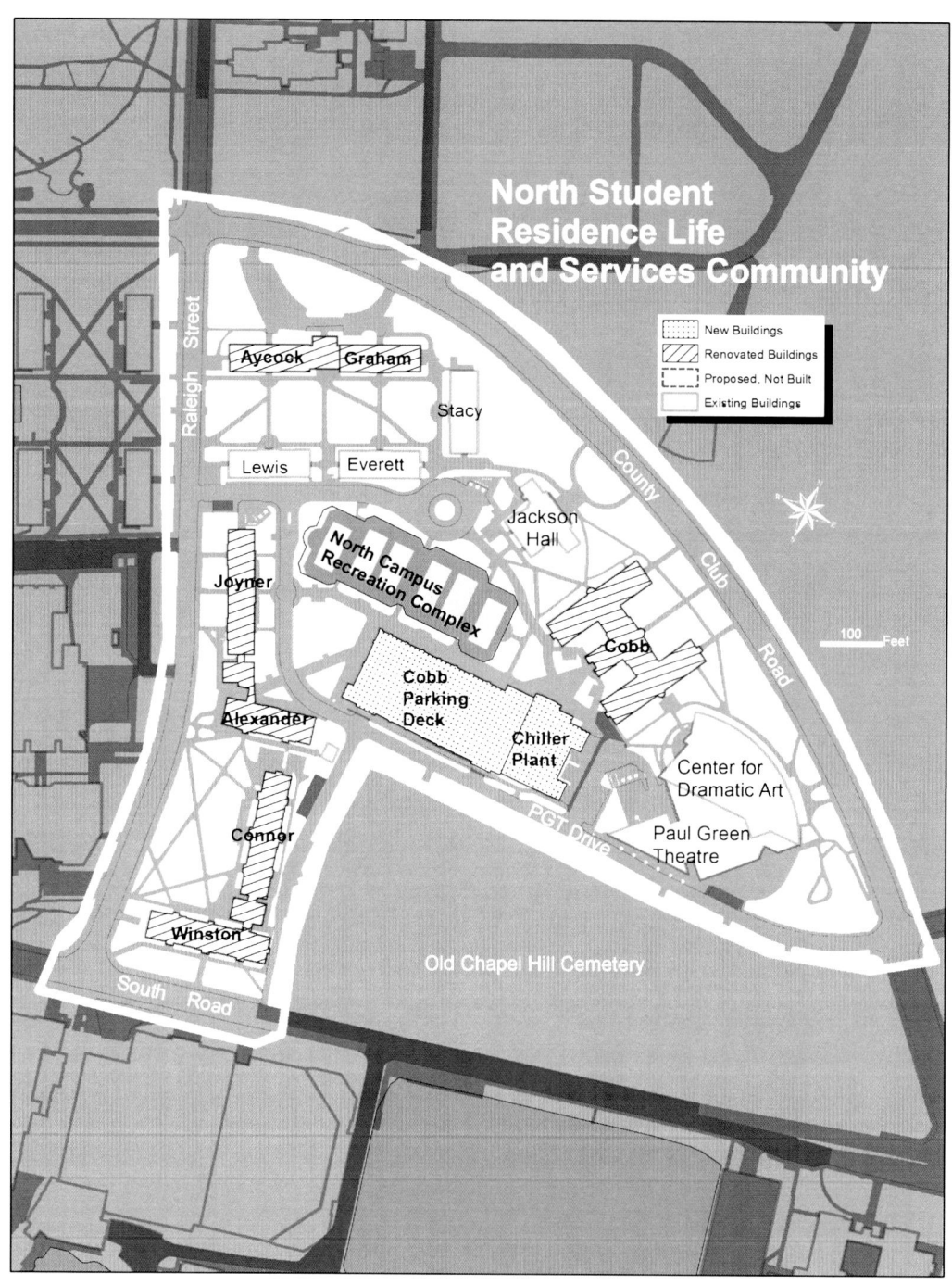

6-9. North Student Residence Life and Services Community. Source: UNC Engineering and Information Services

6-10. Renovated Cobb Residence Hall. Source: UNC Facilities Planning & Construction

and handball courts with a new landscaped "front yard" and recreation area for adjacent student housing residents, added a new parking deck and chiller plant, straightened out interior access drives, and made traffic signal improvements at the intersection between Country Club Road and Paul Green Theatre Drive. The new layout improved student access to recreation areas adjacent to their residence halls and cleaned up a formerly chaotic area of parking lots interspersed with outdoor playing courts, while meeting the need for new service facilities.

These place-making actions, along with renovations of student residence halls, significantly improved an existing historic area of student living. Pairs of older three- and four- story dorms, previously accessed only by stairways, were linked with new connecting buildings containing elevators and common rooms. Dormitory interiors were renovated and air conditioning was added. Cobb Residence Hall got a new entrance along with its elevator and common rooms.

While not a large project, one element, the proposed construction of the deck and chiller plant, generated a large community controversy. As described in Chapter 4, the proximity of this building to the Old Chapel Hill Cemetery aroused the ire of historic preservation advocates, and perceived impacts from traffic coming into the deck from Country Club Road aroused the ire of the adjacent historic Gimghoul neighborhood

ANNA WU, CAMPUS ARCHITECT

Even a sudden, crushing workload can have a silver lining. For Anna Wu, UNC's chief architect as it ramped up from a couple of capital projects a year to some 150 during the dynamic decade, that silver lining came in the form of a clarity of purpose: with so much work to do, there was no time for foot-dragging.

"I think the enormity of the program really drove us to make decisions and seek solutions," she says. "That was a different mindset from before."

Wu's observation doesn't downplay the magnitude of the crush. At the program's peak, Wu had 18 project managers on her staff, each one handling more than a dozen projects that ranged from relatively minor renovations and re-roofings to a $70 million Science Complex and the construction of a mile of walkable tunnel under the campus. "There were so many projects and so many moving parts," Wu recalls.

Making the parts move in concert was the baseline challenge, Wu says. Layered on top of that were a host of others: getting comfortable with a new construction manager-at-risk format, for example, or figuring out how to make the projects sustainable even as they were defining what that word meant. The University's master plan proved vital, Wu says, in encouraging and allowing her team to look at growth holistically rather than on a building-by-building basis. "While the Master Plan was conceptual, it still gave us a framework," she says. "During the design process, we drilled down."

Drilling down often meant finding ways for a project site to address multiple facets of the master plan. The master plan, for example, addressed enrollment growth and called for 3,000 new beds for students. With that in mind, Wu and her colleagues tailored plans for the Rams Head site to meet the increased need for services—dining, recreation and parking, for example. At the same time, they planned a green roof on the site's parking deck to address needs in the stormwater management plan. Meanwhile, the pedestrian network formed by the buildings themselves solved the University's overarching desire to connect North and South Campus in a more attractive and effective way.

"The planning process enabled us to make some real advances," she says. "We looked for every opportunity in terms of connecting projects."

As chief architect, Wu was the public face of those projects and often the first responder to community concerns and criticisms. The University's proposal to replace a parking lot behind Cobb residence hall with a combined parking deck and chiller plant, for example, faced fierce opposition from residents of the Gimghoul neighborhood across the street. "The neighborhood got really agitated even though we thought, probably naively, that converting that parking lot into a deck was cleaning up that area and would have no effect," she says. "Change is hard. People want to make sure that they aren't negatively impacted."

The Cobb controversy sparked the University to take a much more proactive approach to pitching its projects to the town. Wu and her staff now go to the Town Council twice a year to update them on existing and upcoming projects; they also reach out to the community and to the media, giving them advance notice of projects before they reach the public hearing stage. "We try to make sure people understand where we are institutionally," she says. "The Cobb issue was very reactive. It just makes it more stressful and antagonistic when you're doing it through a public hearing process."

Wu was also charged with presenting the plans to an entirely different but equally tough crowd: the Board of Trustees. There, she says, the value of context quickly became apparent. Certain projects, like the Science Complex, called for more traditional architecture because of their surroundings. Others, like the FedEx Global Education Center, were opportunities to push the stylistic envelope. "If you're looking for a building that matches UNC's global vision, do you want to put it in a Georgian building?" she says. "Different sites yield different approaches."

One of Wu's latest challenges has been establishing the design parameters for Carolina North, the 250-acre research campus planned for a site two miles north of town. In doing so, Wu transplanted a lesson learned on the main campus, where the landscape itself holds primacy over any single architectural style. The design guidelines for Carolina North, she says, are "landscape based," meaning that the landscape will determine building size and massing, and tie together the architecture for sites that will be developed over a 50-year time frame.

"Rather than trying to see into the future and anticipate what materials and innovations will be available, we're really betting the farm on the trees," she says.

residents. Despite the fact that the parking deck was needed to serve both academic users and patrons of the adjacent Paul Green Theatre, and that the chiller was needed to provide air conditioning to the north campus, the project hung in the balance until the University made a number of concessions, some unrelated to this project. The University paid for street improvements and new signal lights at the Country Club Road entrance to the campus. It also agreed to drop its support for four-laning South Columbia Street, an important access road to the UNC Hospitals, which was located several miles away from this community.

With fewer than 500,000 square feet of new construction in the parking deck/chiller plant and two new dormitory additions, as well as associated site and street improvements, the North Student Residence Life and Services Community was relatively small (Appendix A). However, adding even small University projects in an existing community with zoning control over development required a great deal of patient negotiation, as the University Architect discovered in this case. When politics entered the picture, the issues became even sharper and the rhetoric shriller. Only with firm University leaders and aware planners could these issues be surmounted in order to build the necessary campus facilities.

SUSTAINABILITY LESSONS FROM NORTH CAMPUS COMMUNITY DESIGN

Inserting new projects into a historic campus area takes considerable design and planning skill. If the existing architectural and open space fabric is to be sustained during growth periods, then care must be taken to build communities of new and old buildings. This is akin to the place-making skill of urban designers, who develop ensembles of structures, common areas, and circulation routes. For such places, the whole is greater than the sum of the parts.

Gaining approval for new projects may also require considerable negotiation skills, especially if the projects impact, or are perceived to impact, adjacent residential neighborhoods. Such neighborhood conflicts can take on a life of their own, powered by media reports of emotional citizen objections. If not successfully responded to, these disputes can prevent the construction of planned facilities and lead to lingering feelings of town/gown distrust. To head off such conflicts, the University planning staff, including its top managers, spent considerable time in conversations with community citizens, decision-makers, and staff. They proactively offered information about plans and projects, and responded to concerns, in order to enhance and sustain community understanding and trust.

Sustainability lessons that emerged from the pleasures and pains of UNC's North Campus place-making include:

- Design new buildings to be compatible with the existing architectural and open space context, in terms of form, appearance, and usage.
- Use the opportunity of new development to build communities that link adjacent buildings and create walkable mixed-use neighborhoods.
- Provide the community with continuous information about University plans and projects in order to create a transparent atmosphere and good working relationships.
- Anticipate the perceptions of potential opponents of new projects and be prepared to both amend and defend proposed designs.

CHAPTER 7

Recasting the Twentieth Century Southeast Campus

Much of the new development during the dynamic decade took place on the Southeast Campus, where new project design faced many challenges. Home to student housing, athletics, and support facilities, the Southeast Campus Community was a sprawling collection of large mid-twentieth century buildings without a central place. Although it contained Kenan Woods and the natural areas in the Pinetum, few parts of Southeast Campus contained an attractive outdoor common area. New projects that sought to turn this around were built at a human scale around central green spaces linked by landscaped walkways.

The sustainability challenge for Southeast Campus was to humanize this dense, fragmented, and auto-dominated area, while at the same time accommodating its continuing need to grow and protecting its precious environmental resources. Planners proposed a network of pedestrian paths and outdoor commons areas where people could move through a green landscape instead of always following cement sidewalks alongside busy streets. They sought to instill the design values of North Campus and to connect the two precincts to facilitate pedestrian movement between them. They realized the importance of managing the environmental resources and processes, including stormwater flows, in a sustainable fashion. On the other hand, fulfilling Chancellor Hooker's promise to provide a bed for every new undergraduate head required a surge in on-campus student housing, and the desire to modernize the popular athletic venues ensured constant requests for larger and more modern sports facilities.

7-1. The Twentieth Century Southeast Campus with New Projects. Source: UNC Facilities Planning & Construction

> The sustainability challenge for Southeast Campus was to humanize this dense, fragmented, and auto-dominated area…

Historically, the Southeast Campus had grown without an overall guiding plan. As each new construction appropriation was received from the state, new buildings sprouted. The result was a collection of diverse functions layered over the landscape and penetrated by busy roadways and parking areas. Stormwater runoff was consigned to underground pipes and little attention was paid to the natural environment. Rationalizing this unattractive and unsustainable land use pattern into working communities, while at the same time restoring the natural functions of the landscape, was a major planning and design task.

The Master Plan took up the challenge, laying the foundation for the rebirth of the Southeast Campus. The Plan visualized two major pedestrian axes springing from the end of Polk Place: one running southeast toward the undergraduate residence halls and one running southwest toward the Health Affairs area. New projects were used as levers to integrate land uses and facilities into communities. Natural systems were restored to create a greener and more sustainable environment.

Implementation of the Development Plan during the dynamic decade began a remarkable transformation of the Southeast Campus, including changes to Kenan Football Stadium and Boshamer Baseball Stadium approved under Modifications to the Development Plan. As built, the new Southeast Campus is home to three large and diverse groupings:

- A Student Residence Life and Services Community,
- A Student Family Housing Community, and
- An Athletic and Visitors Complex.

Much of the new development is along or adjacent to Manning Drive, and pedestrian paths and free bus routes link it internally and to North Campus.

The big story in the news media about Southeast Campus planning was the controversy over expansion of student family housing and campus access routes on the southern perimeter. The Mason Farm Road neighbors raised a major outcry that threatened to derail approval of the Development Plan. However, an equally important issue that did not receive much press coverage took place underground. To implement the Stormwater Master Plan, permeable surfaces were built into large proj-

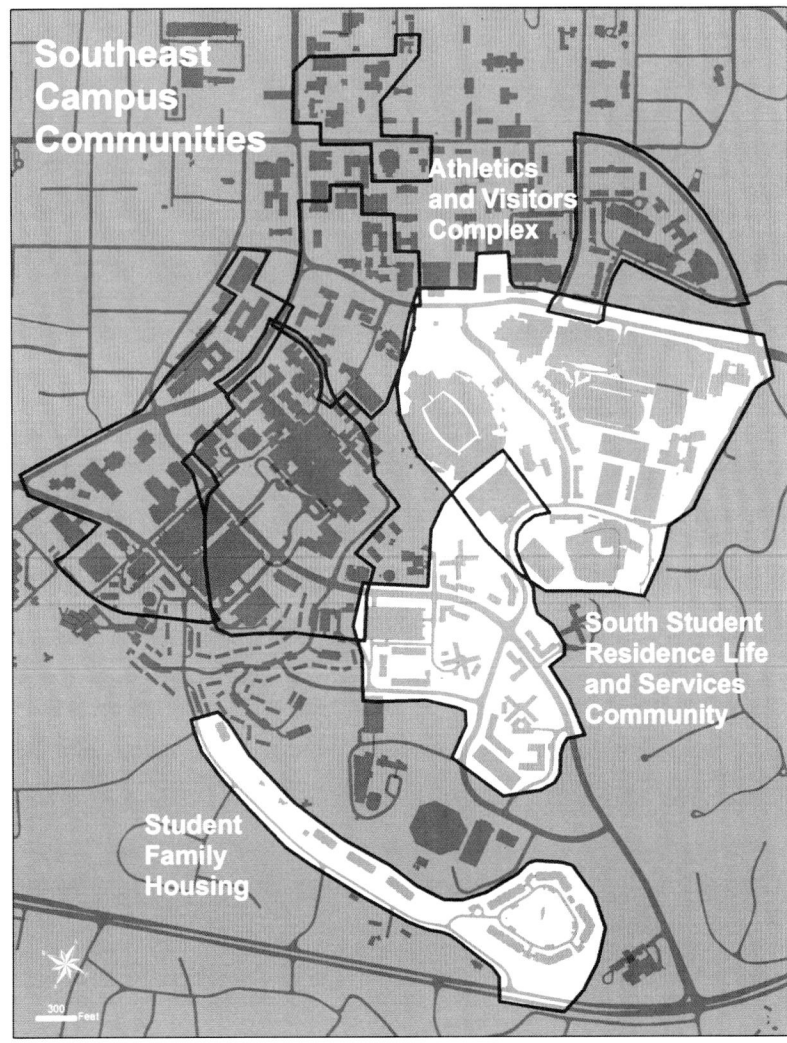

7-2. Southeast Campus Communities. Source: UNC Engineering and Information Services

RECASTING THE TWENTIETH CENTURY SOUTHEAST CAMPUS 105

7.3. Student Family Housing and Residence Halls on Southeast Campus. Source: Richard Tate, American Aerial Photos.

ects to allow infiltration of rain runoff into cistern storage areas below the Rams Head Center, the Hooker Field recreation area, and Ehringhaus Field. These projects resulted from the Impervious Surface Analysis that was included in the Development Plan.

REDEVELOPING A SIXTIES-STYLE STUDENT RESIDENCE LIFE COMMUNITY

Since the 1960s, undergraduate housing on Southeast Campus had been concentrated in four large high-rise residence halls—Morrison, Craige, Hinton James, and Ehringhaus. To the master planners, these ten-story buildings symbolized the problems inherited from previous eras of urban design on Southeast Campus. They saw them as huge "pinwheels" spinning by themselves in space, unconnected to the scale and texture of the older campus either three-dimensionally or at ground level. During the dynamic decade, student residents of Morrison financed the installation of solar panels on the roof of this ten-story residence hall to enhance its sustainability, but its architectural style remained inconsistent with the traditional Carolina image. To help bring the high-rise structures down to a human scale, the planners surrounded them with groups of new low-rise buildings.

New four-story residence halls—Horton, Koury, Hardin, and Craige North, each with its own small front commons and seminar rooms, were placed along Manning Drive in front of the older high-rise buildings. Two new clusters of four-story student apartments—Ram Village at Paul Hardin Drive and Ram Village at Williamson Drive, were placed behind them.

The Rams Head Center project was conceived to help solve the problem of the isolation of Southeast Campus residence halls and to bring student services closer to living areas. It added new eating, shopping, and recreation facilities within easy walking distance of the residence hall concentrations in order to create a more complete student housing and services community. A new Chase Dining Hall, convenience store, and recreation center sit atop a 700-space, 3-story parking deck that includes

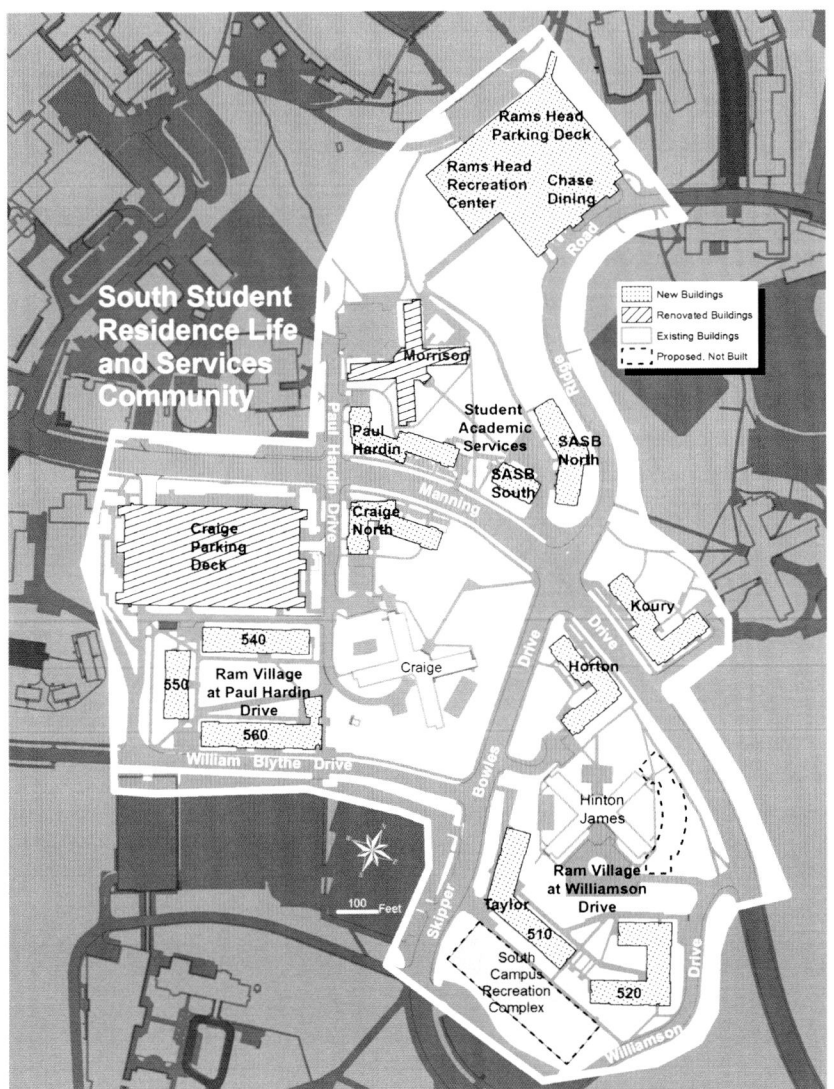

7-4. South Student Residence Life and Services Community.
Source: UNC Engineering and Information Services

7-5. Koury Residence Hall.
Source: UNC Housing and Residential Education

a street level convenience store. This multi-purpose structure replaced the former Rams Head surface parking lot. The landscaped commons on the roof of the parking deck serves not only as a front yard for the dining and recreation facilities, but also as a pedestrian bridge along the heavily-traveled student pathway from North to South campus.

Located in a valley along a heavily traveled student pedestrian route, the Rams Head project was designed to do more than simply integrate dining, recreation, and parking uses. The landscaped surface of the commons provides environmental benefits through rainfall capture/reuse, evapotranspiration, storage, and infiltration. The lawn and trees of the one-acre green roof plaza sit on a 56,000-gallon cistern that collects rain water for irrigation. An element of the UNC Stormwater Master Plan, the Rams Head design also includes an infiltration bed under the turf of an adjacent playing field and a day-lighted stream.

To further reduce the isolation of the Southeast Campus residence halls, the Registrar's Office, Housing Office, and other student services were relocated from the North to the Southeast Campus to bring them closer to the largest concentration of student housing. The new Student and Academic Services building group was constructed on the site of the former Chase Hall, a 1960s modernist cafeteria building demolished to

7-6. Rams Head Center.
Source: UNC Facilities Planning & Construction

make room for the new buildings. This location was carefully chosen to put it on the pedestrian path from the Southeast Campus residence halls to the Rams Head Center and on up to the North Campus. As a result of these strategic planning moves, the new Southeast Campus residence halls and apartments became part of a larger community where students could eat, work out, and pay their University bills within their own neighborhood. Not only did this make on-campus living more appealing, it also began to transform the Southeast Campus into a more functional and attractive location. By moving from the design of individual buildings to the design of an integrated community, the master planning process demonstrated the value of accounting for the big picture.

Investment in the South Student Residence Life and Services Community amounted to about $249 million (Appendix A). Some 410,000 square feet of new buildings were constructed at the Rams Head Center, and over 101,000 square feet were built at the site of the Student and Academic Services Building. The Ram Village housing added 985 undergraduate beds, and the four new residence halls along Manning Drive (Horton, Hardin, Koury and Craige) added approximately 1,600 new beds for undergraduates.

7-7. Student Academic Services Building. Source: Dan Sears, UNC

BUILDING A NEW STUDENT FAMILY HOUSING COMMUNITY

Family housing at UNC evolved from the Victory Village apartments, built by the Navy during World War II, to the Odum Village apartments built in the 1960s, to the current day Baity Hill Family Housing built during the dynamic decade. The new South Campus Family Housing Community is located beyond the existing campus boundary south of the Dean Smith Student Activities Center (basketball arena) and the Kenan Business School. It contains a row of apartments aligned along Mason Farm Road leading to a second apartment group situated on the Baity Hill property that had been donated to the University by the Baity family.

As the University planned to expand to the south on property it owned at Baity Hill and along Mason Farm Road, it encountered considerable opposition to its plans from its neighbors. Part of this opposition was directed at the proposal to open a major access road connecting to Mason Farm Road from the US 15-501 Bypass (Fordham Boulevard) and to locate the proposed right-of-way for a potential future regional rail transit line through the same area, both of which assumed that the University would acquire properties that it did not currently own.

The access road issue was so controversial that the approval of the Master Plan, originally set for the fall of 2000, was delayed until March 2001 so that alternatives to the access could be explored. The affected neighborhoods on the southern edge of the campus petitioned the Chapel Hill Town Council for a public hearing concerning their questions about the plan's impacts on the community. At a dramatic three-and-a-half-hour public hearing in September 2000, the University made its case for the Master Plan, and Ken Broun, a designated representative of the

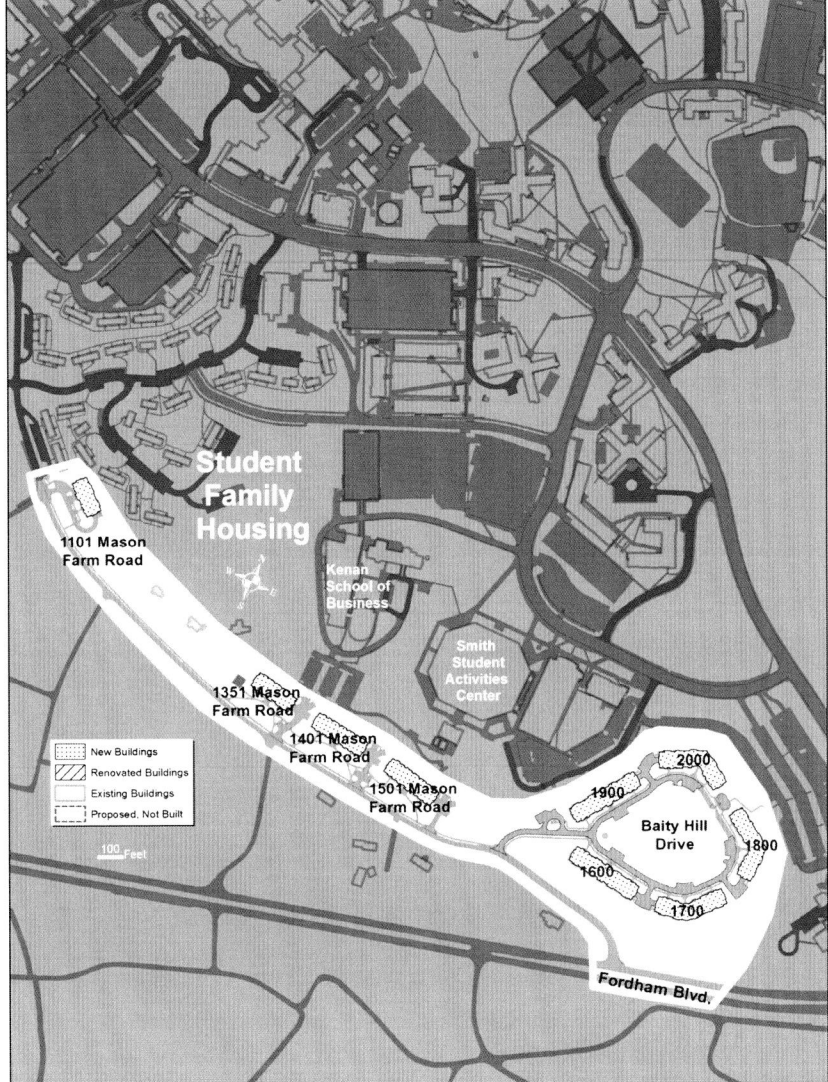

7-8. Student Family Housing Community. Source: UNC Facilities Planning & Construction

affected neighborhoods and former Dean of the UNC Law School, grilled the University representatives about issues of process and impacts.

At the hearing on the Plan, Adam Gross, the University's planning consultant, described the Master Plan's proposals for the South Campus, including meeting the community's demand for more student housing on campus. He expressed concern that the community viewed the planners as "bad guys" when they were trying to do the right thing for the University and the region. The access road and transit connection to US 15-501 would be necessary for hospital patient and employee access, since four-laning of South Columbia Street had been taken off the table at the Council's request. The most feasible location for new access was a relatively flat area south of the Smith Center connecting to Mason Farm Road.

Mayor Rosemary Waldorf presented the background information on the 15-501 Major Investment Study, which looked at the need for a new regional transit system that would extend from Ninth Street in Durham to the UNC Hospital on the campus. While the most optimistic scenario for construction to start would be ten to twelve years into the future, it was important to preserve rights-of-way, such as the one in question, in the interim.

Speaking on behalf of the affected neighborhoods, Ken Broun asked whether the University would acquire the necessary property through purchase or condemnation. University representatives answered that their preferred procedure was to purchase the property on the open market, although they declined to explicitly prohibit the use of Eminent Domain in the Plan. Broun then questioned the feasibility of changing the plan to lessen its impacts on Mason Farm Road, including moving the married student housing to the Horace Williams property near the airport, building new student family housing on the site of existing student family housing at Odum Village, and various other ideas. University representatives promised to study these alternatives, but did not commit to specific plan changes.

The final version of the 2001 Master Plan retained the proposed road and transit alignments as the major access to the UNC Hospital and medical center complex from the south. However, in the March 2006 *Update* to the Campus Master Plan, the new road plan was reduced to a single four-lane divided boulevard that used the existing Mason Farm Road for two of the lanes, retaining more buffer between the road and the new student family housing on its north side.

As developed, the South Campus Family Housing Community included two sections: a series of apartments ringing Baity Hill with a com-

7-9. Baity Hill Student Family Housing Complex. Source: UNC Housing and Residential Education

KEN BROUN, NEIGHBORHOOD ADVOCATE

At times, the minutes of the Chapel Hill Town Council meeting from September 2000 read more like the transcript of a courtroom drama.

On one side was Ken Broun: former mayor and trial attorney, law professor, and resident of the Mason Farm neighborhood, which sits on UNC's southern border. On the other, and on the receiving end of the bulk of Broun's questions, was the University's general counsel, Susan Ehringhaus.

The goal of Broun's relentless line of questioning, he recalls, was to get Ehringhaus and the University to publicly renounce the possible use of eminent domain to seize properties in the neighborhood for its development goals. "I wanted some statement that they wouldn't do that," he says. "I think I accomplished my purpose. The thought of the University being aggressive enough to use it was never raised again."

But the tense exchange was indicative of the rough start that the two sides got off to as the University rolled out its plans for South Campus, which included buying property along Mason Farm Road, bordering the neighborhood, to build new housing for married students. One flashpoint—"the incident that really provoked us," he calls it—was a letter from the University Counsel to one of his neighbors that raised the threat of eminent domain.

The neighborhood also feared that the University's advance to the border of Mason Farm might just be the first step. "There was a real concern that this was just the beginning of a University takeover of all of our homes," Broun says. "The concern was not simply the University buying up property on the north side of Mason Farm and intending to build there, but more that the University's manifest destiny was to expand to the Bypass."

Instead of attempting to allay these concerns, Broun says, the University first tried stonewalling, a tactic that left him and his neighbors feeling shut out. They also felt as though they were on the receiving end of a marketing pitch—this is what the University needs, and why—rather than engaged in a good faith exchange of ideas about how best to proceed. "The neighbors had the sense that it was not a give and take," Broun says. "It was a sales process. That was causing a lot of the concern, despite the personal respect we had for the (University) people up front; they were all people we knew and liked."

The process became more open and inclusive, he says, later on when Chancellor Moeser became directly involved. He adds that he has no complaints about how the married student housing project was ultimately carried out.

"However we got there, the outcome was a good one for everyone involved," he says. "Would my neighbor on Mason Farm Road rather have had the woods there? Sure. But if we were going to have anything at all, having married student housing there is great. They are very good neighbors."

Broun had a chance to try out his preferred approach to town/gown relations a few years later, when he was named chair of the Carolina North Leadership Advisory Committee. He says he applied the lessons learned in the Mason Farm debate to discussions between Townspeople and the University as they attempted to agree on a development vision. "I viewed myself as mediator between the people of the Town and the University, rather than as a spokesman for the University," he says. "I tried to make it a discussion rather than a sales project."

mons in the center and a row of apartments facing the newly widened Mason Farm Road. The three-story buildings, many with parking beneath, had a similar appearance with a brick base and gable roofs. There were environmental concerns over clearing the existing woods on the Baity Hill property, but the critical need for housing took precedence.

The new Student Family Housing Community included 246 apartments in five buildings, totaling some 400,000 square feet in the Baity Hill section, and 135 apartments in four buildings, totaling about 209,000 square feet in the Mason Farm Road section (Appendix A). The architect was Davis & Hining, and the total cost was over $46 million.

REIMAGINING THE ATHLETICS AND VISITORS' COMPLEX

Campus athletic facilities and visitor destinations should be designed to accommodate the special needs of peak demand during events, as well as to serve the day-to-day needs of student life. A sustainable athletic complex should seamlessly integrate playing fields, arenas, and stadiums into campus settings. Sustainable visitors' facilities should enjoy convenient access, as well as serving the needs of on-campus residents. New projects should be viewed as opportunities to connect visitors' facilities and campus life and to enhance ecological systems.

The Athletics and Visitors' Complex, while not a community *per se*, is a concentrated cluster of related destinations for athletic events and visitor trips. It saw major changes to several of its venues during the dynamic decade. With funding from its fan base, new sports projects were undertaken to update Boshamer Baseball Stadium, Kenan Football Stadium, Carmichael Auditorium, and Woollen Gymnasium. The Eddie Smith Field House replaced the old "Tin Can" building with a new indoor track and athletic practice facility.

The Daniels Student Stores building, another destination popular with visitors as well as students, got a major makeover, and the Rams Head Center parking deck, discussed as part of the South Campus Student Housing and Services Community, was an important addition for visitors attending sports events. Though not in the Development Plan, the Knapp Sanders Building, home to the School of Government and its frequent courses and events for off-campus visitors, received a new addition, interior renovation, and a new parking deck.

Located near the center of the campus, the Athletic and Visitors' Complex contains a mix of uses within walking distance of parking and services. The majority of its structures house various student recreation and University sports programs. Within its borders the sports fan can attend a football game, baseball game, women's basketball game, soccer match, swim meet, volleyball game, or field hockey match, and also stop by the Student Stores for UNC memorabilia. The student in search of recreation can find a gym, swimming pool, track, or outdoor field. In ad-

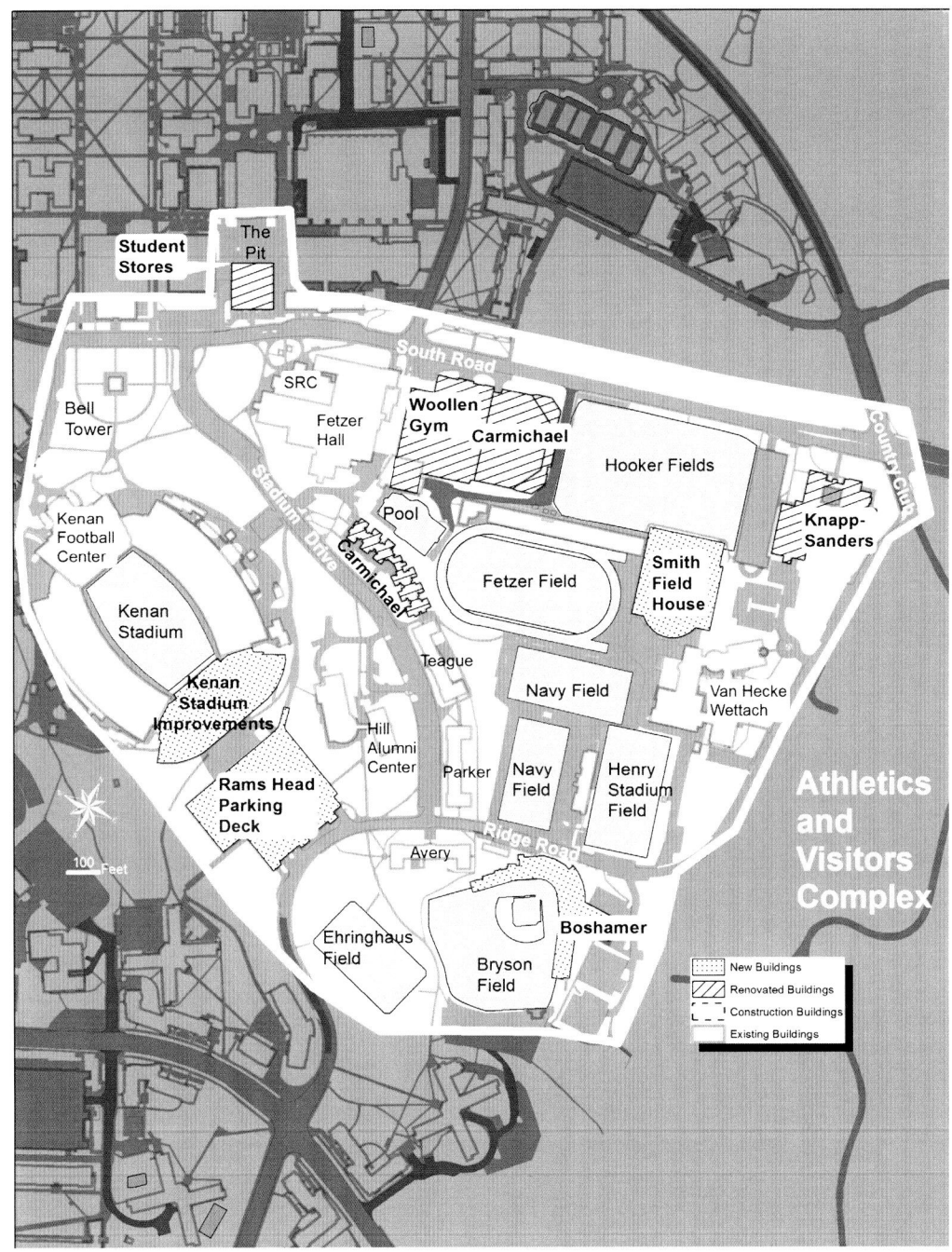

7-10. Athletics and Visitors' Complex Map. Source: UNC Facilities Planning & Construction

7-11. Boshamer Baseball Stadium, Rams Head Center, and Kenan Football Stadium. Source: Richard Tate, American Aerial Photos

dition, the visitor in search of continuing education courses can find a variety of offerings at the School of Government.

One of the most comprehensive athletic projects begun during the dynamic decade was the rethinking of the Kenan football stadium and the surrounding Kenan woods. The bold new vision not only expanded the seating and facilities of the stadium, but also opened the Kenan stadium concourse to make it a year-round pedestrian walkway between North and South Campus destinations and proactively managed the Kenan Woods to rescue its damaged trees and to channel game-day picnickers into planned seating areas. The master plan for Kenan Stadium by Robert A. M. Stern and Corley Redfoot Zack increased seating on the east end adjacent to the Rams Head Center, turned the former horseshoe shape into a fully enclosed bowl and added 3,620 new seats, bringing the total seating up to 63,000. The new architecture of the exterior features brick arches, similar in character to the nearby Bell Tower. The east end addition replaced the old 1927 Kenan Field House with a new Academic Support Center for Student Athletes and a new "Blue Zone" containing premium club and suite seating and lounge areas.

Hoerr Schaudt's landscape master plan for Kenan Woods applied the principles established in the Stormwater Master Plan, the Bell Tower Master plan, and the *Dignity of Restraint* report. The goal was to restore the historical and ecological integrity of the woods. The plan proposed enhanced circulation for both game- and non-game days, as well as security and lighting measures. Designated paths and picnic areas protected the woods from damage, and systematic tree replanting ensured the continued health of the woods.

Other sports facilities received major upgrades during the dynamic decade. Historic Boshamer Baseball Stadium, built in 1972, was demolished and rebuilt on the same site in 2009. The designers effectively fitted a larger stadium on a tight existing site while enhancing the streetscape along Ridge Road. With upgraded seating, concessions, offices, and training facilities, the new Boshamer provides a modern venue for the Tar Heel baseball program.

Carmichael Auditorium, home to the UNC women's basketball program and Olympic sports, was extensively remodeled in 2009. A new women's basketball museum and program offices were added and the entrance to the building was redesigned to link it to the adjoining Michael Hooker recreation field. Prior to this, a 70,000-gallon cistern and a 500,000-gallon infiltration bed were built as a regional stormwater facility below the adjoining Hooker Field recreation area to capture rain water runoff for irrigation use.

The Stallings-Evans Sports Medicine Center was added to Woollen gymnasium in 2010. This new facility gave UNC Sports Medicine a modern facility for its research and clinical practice. During the dynamic decade, Woollen also received some interior renovations, as did Carmichael Residence Hall.

While not part of the athletic facilities, the Daniels Building (UNC Student Store) serves not only students, but also campus visitors seeking Tar Heel memorabilia. Its 2007 renovation modernized the interior and opened a new entrance from the south, making it more convenient to access the store from the Bell Tower and Kenan Stadium area to the south and enhancing the north-south connection goal in the Master Plan.

Another important visitor destination is the Knapp Sanders Building, which houses the UNC School of Government. Started prior to the Development Plan and completed in 2003, the building received an addition, extensive interior renovation, and a 187-space parking deck. Located at a key campus entry point from the east, the Knapp Sanders building presents a dignified introduction to the historic campus. Inside its imposing portico lies a landscaped garden court.

All told, the Athletics and Visitors Complex projects added some 760,000 square feet of new and renovated buildings at a total cost of just over $192 million (Appendix A).

SOUTHEAST CAMPUS LESSONS FOR SUSTAINABILITY

Implementing the Development Plan for the new Southeast Campus projects demonstrated the volatility of proposed development adjacent to existing residential neighborhoods. Even though the University was pressured to provide more on-campus student housing and to improve automobile and transit access, its location on the edge of the Southeast Campus raised a storm of neighborhood protest. As a result, the design of the new projects went through numerous reviews with the adjacent residents and the Town before being approved.

Design of new projects presented valuable opportunities to link many goals and objectives beyond their obvious function. Planning the Southeast Campus so that student housing was located conveniently to student food service, recreation facilities, and administrative services increased the desirability of living on this part of the campus. Integrating stormwater management into the Rams Head Center and the new sports fields, and planning the Kenan Stadium and Kenan Woods together, served both human and natural environmental needs. Visualizing campus athletic and visitor facilities as parts of a linked visitor experience tied them into an accessible movement pattern. Developing new communities offered opportunities to upgrade and landscape the street corridors.

Important lessons from the Southeast Campus development were:

- Generating consensus is a critical part of the sustainability equation since unresolved conflicts linger and make future plans more difficult to implement.
- A sustainable student living environment should be designed to create mixed-use, walkable communities so that residence halls and apartments have convenient access to recreation, food service, and administrative services, as well as to academic facilities. Every new project should be viewed as an opportunity to foster opportunities for comprehensive community-based activities.
- Sustaining the natural environment should be an overriding priority for new development so that valuable natural resources are protected, conserved, and put to use. Every new project should be viewed as an opportunity to integrate stormwater management and energy conservation into green project architecture and landscape design.
- A sustainable athletic complex should be designed to integrate playing fields, arenas, and stadiums into campus settings that enable efficient access and egress and provide convenient supporting facilities for visitors. Every new project should be viewed as an opportunity to foster connections between sports facilities and campus life.

CHAPTER 8

Growing the Health Services Southwest Campus

The Southwest Campus is home to the dense Health Affairs and Health Research Communities. These two communities include four major North Carolina hospitals (Memorial, Women's and Children's, Cancer, and Neurosciences), the UNC Medical, Dental, and Public Health Schools, and a number of related research buildings, as well as parking decks and support facilities. Their large footprints, dense development, and architectural style reflect the different character of buildings needed to provide health services.

Clustered around the North Carolina Memorial Hospital, the Southwest Campus has grown steadily to accommodate the large increases in medical care and research over recent decades. It serves the needs of many types of users, including doctors and medical staff, patients, students, and research personnel. The form of the Heath Affairs and Health Research Communities reflects incremental growth that has occurred as new facilities are added, rather than being organized around common outdoor spaces and connecting greenways, as on the North Campus.

The sustainability challenge for the Southwest Campus was multi-faceted. Its layout had to be planned to allow future growth and adaptation without disrupting the ongoing activities involved in patient care, medical education, and health research. Its architecture had to be designed to house the latest upgrades of equipment and technology in research labs, operating rooms, and treatment facilities. Its dense network of buildings had to be opened up to add pedestrian connections and outdoor rooms to make it more livable. Its traffic flows, transit access, and parking areas had to be upgraded to handle increased future demands. Its landscaping

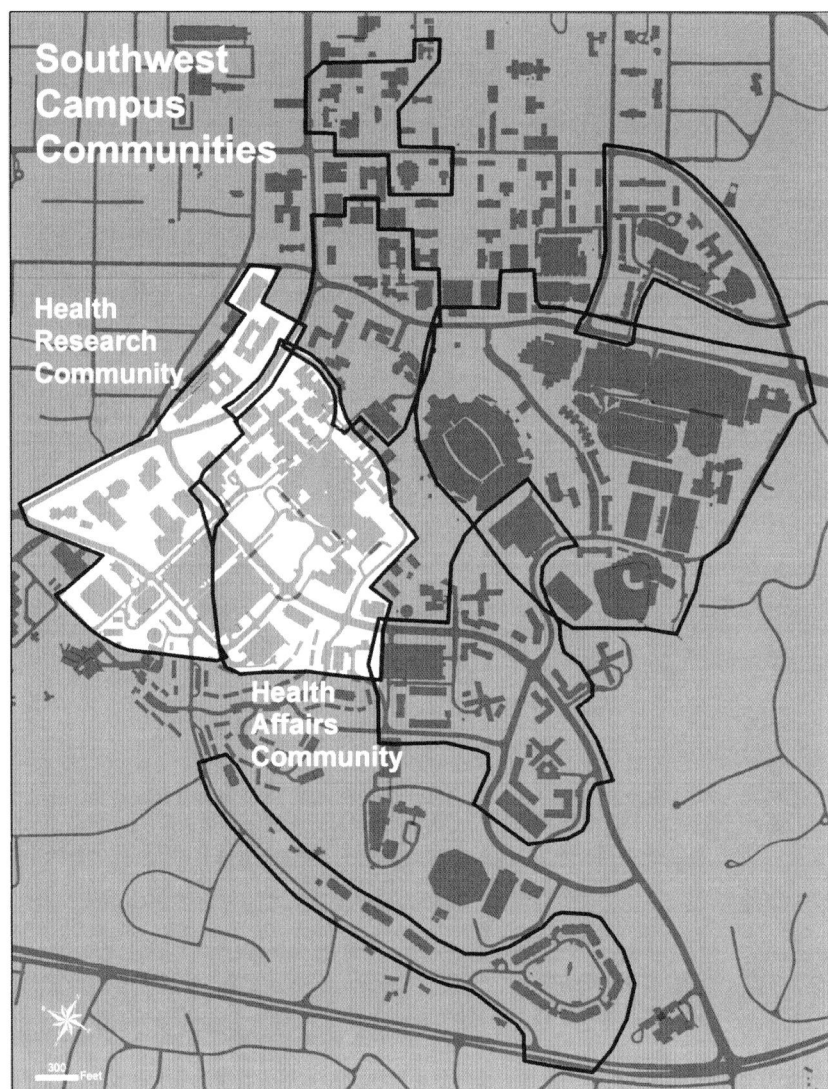

8-1. Southwest Campus Communities. Source: UNC Facilities Planning & Construction

and amenities had to be improved to humanize the scale of its expanse of steel and concrete. Its signage and directional guides had to be sharpened to enhance the way-finding of scores of patients and visitors and emergency personnel unfamiliar with the campus.

Planning for the Southwest Campus was complicated by the need to provide continuously modernized patient care, academic research, and teaching facilities in a limited area. It was a challenge to meet the overlapping needs of patients, visitors, doctors and nurses, and researchers; to plan, finance, and build new buildings; and to maintain older buildings. At the same time, infrastructure upgrades often disrupted access and scientific and technical advances changed the nature of the services offered. The Southwest Campus planner had to be sensitive to the needs of a health care enterprise in competition with other regional health care enterprises, and to balance its needs with the needs of the larger University. Achieving this balance was a challenging assignment for a health affairs planner.

The two Southwest Campus communities are closely related in terms of location, staffing, and building design. The primary difference is that the Health Affairs Community is distinguished by its orientation to patient care and hence the flow of people, while the Health Research Community is distinguished by its focus on health studies projects and hence the flow of data and science.

EXPANDING THE HEALTH AFFAIRS COMMUNITY

The Health Affairs Community must accommodate large daily flows of patients and visitors. Centered around two large parking decks for patients and staff, this community supports the UNC Hospital and medical programs. Its main access is along Manning Drive, with a secondary access from Mason Farm Road. Major additions to this community during the dynamic decade included the North Carolina Cancer Hospital and the related Physician's Office Building and Jackson Circle Parking Deck, the Carrington Hall School of Nursing, ITS Manning (the information technology services building), and the Manning Steam Plant and Substation. Though not included in the Development Plan, the North Carolina Women's and Children's Hospital also was completed during this period, and at the same time, a number of the existing Health Affairs buildings were renovated.

> The Health Affairs Community must accomodate large daily flows of patients and visitors.

8-2. North Carolina Cancer Hospital and Health Affairs and Health Research Communities. Source: Richard Tate, American Aerial Photos

GROWING THE HEALTH SERVICES SOUTHWEST CAMPUS

MARY BECK, SENIOR VICE PRESIDENT, PLANNING AND PROGRAM DEVELOPMENT, UNC HOSPITALS

For long stretches of the dynamic decade, no fewer than a half dozen major construction projects were underway within a block of Mary Beck's office at UNC Hospitals. As Senior Vice President for Planning and Program Development at the UNC Health Care System, it was up to Beck and her colleague Mel Hurston to ensure that many of those projects—including a new children's hospital, women's hospital, neurosciences hospital, cancer hospital, and a physicians' office building—were completed on time and on budget.

That meant navigating the Boards of Trustees of the University and of the UNC Hospital system, administrators, doctors, a design review board, and legions of architects and contractors, all while making sure that a very busy hospital, with an emergency room located right in the middle of the construction maelstrom, stayed open for business.

No wonder Beck calls that period of time "the perfect storm."

"By calling it that, I think everyone was acknowledging that if they didn't work together, they were going to have even bigger problems," Beck says. "Everybody had to be willing to collaborate and compromise."

The waters were tricky enough long before the first shovel went into the ground. Before the hospital could build anything, it had to reconcile its own master plan—one that focused on its clinical needs—with the University's overarching development strategy. "What we did was essentially accept the UNC Master Plan principles and then add some of our own," Beck says. "The difference in our master plan is that we are focused on patient care, and in one geographic area of campus. Our facilities need to link and connect and be part of an overall structure."

To that end, the new medical buildings have a number of features that set them apart from their academic counterparts. While brick construction dominates on the North Campus, for example, the hospital relied on pre-cast materials to let patients know that they were entering a medical facility, rather than an academic one. The designers also sought ways to make the buildings open up to the outside wherever possible—lots of windows and airy entrances, among other details.

"We wanted to change the way we welcome patients," Beck says. "A conscious and major effort was made to open up the entryways, to make children feel comfortable when they walk in the door, to give them an atmosphere that would be less intimidating and threatening."

Connectivity was another key element. In the finished product, visitors can follow a concourse all the way from the new cancer hospital through the women's and children's hospitals and into the original Memorial Hospital building. Again, the goal is to make people feel welcomed, oriented, and at ease in their surroundings. "This is (the patients') home while they stay here," Beck says. "We want them to feel comfortable. We want them to be able to see outside, commune with nature, see the sky."

Good communication was the key to weathering the construction process itself, which coincided with other nearby UNC projects such as a new steam tunnel, a power plant, and the renovation of Morrison dormitory. A regular meeting was instituted for key parties involved in construction. Builders submitted plans and schedules in advance of the meeting so that the timing of it all could be coordinated.

After a rocky start, Beck says, the system proved invaluable. "Site superintendents had a forum they could come to when they didn't like something. Contractors were often charged to work (a given issue) out together."

While the hospital has not yet met all its building needs—more patient beds and new operating rooms are on the horizon—that perfect storm is not likely to be repeated. Administrators have made a decision to move some services off campus to a facility under construction in Hillsborough. At the same time, they have just one building site left, in front of Memorial Hospital.

Beck also notes that the big storm came with a big payoff measured in terms of patient satisfaction. She says she regularly encounters University faculty and staff who were treated for cancer in the old Gravely Building, which was built in 1953 as a sanitarium for tuberculosis patients and replaced by the N.C. Cancer Hospital in 2009. They tell her how happy they are about the quality of the new facility. "Tearing Gravely down was kind of a great event," she says. "The people are the same. The care was always terrific. Now they have an environment to match."

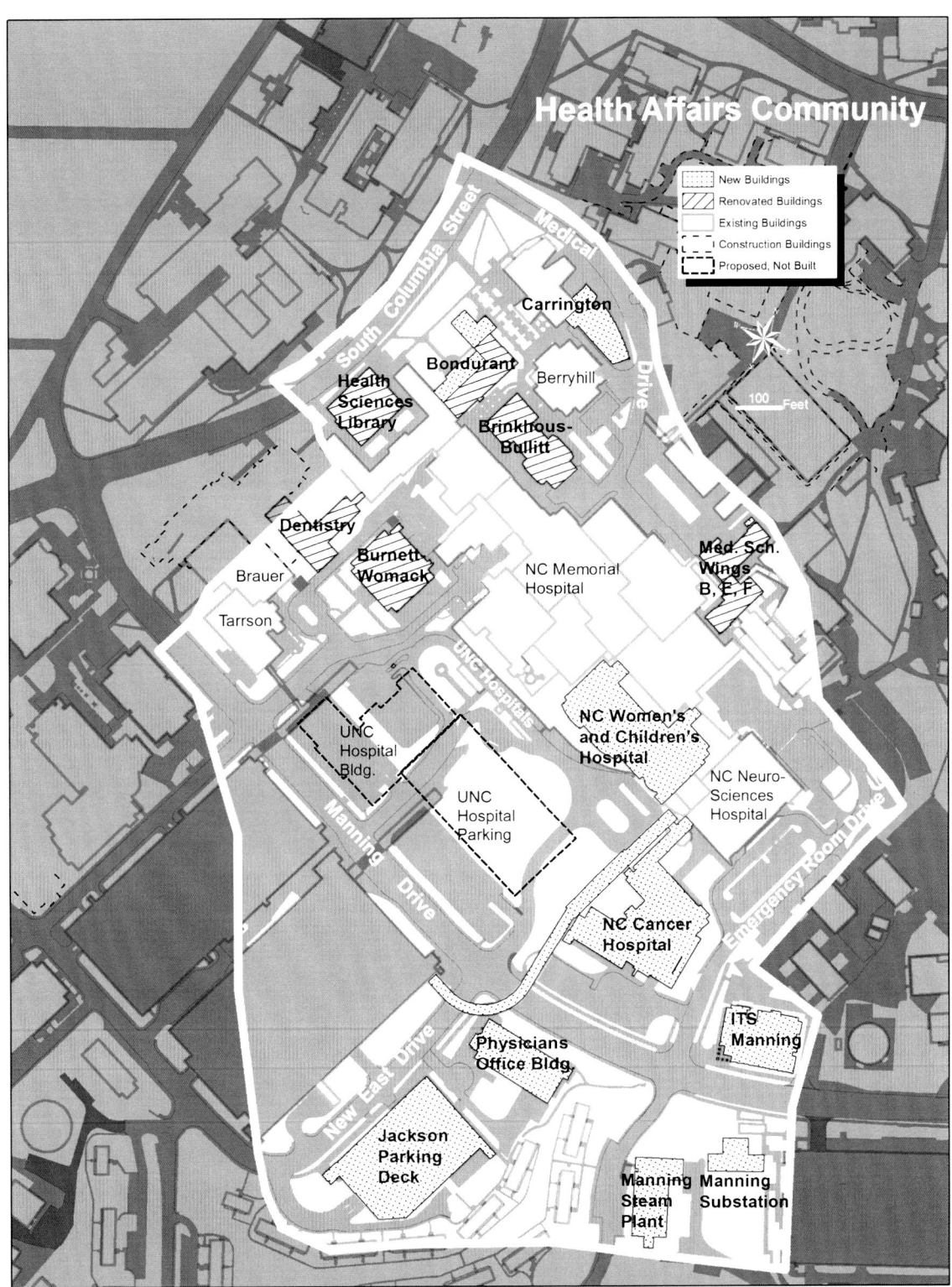

8-3. Health Affairs Community. Source: UNC Facilities Planning & Construction

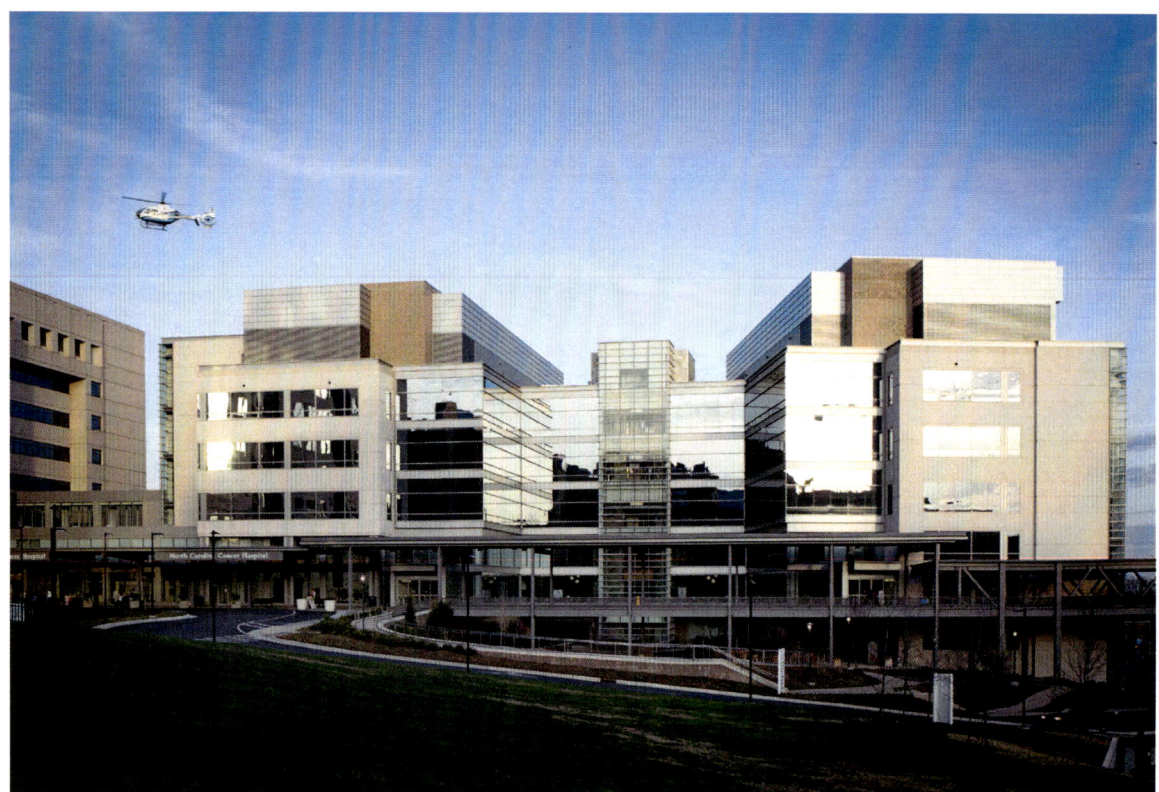

8-4. North Carolina Cancer Hospital. Source: UNC Facilities Planning & Construction

The North Carolina Cancer Hospital, completed in 2009, has 50 inpatient beds, 72 infusion stations, and 3 linear accelerators for radiation therapy. Connected by a pedestrian bridge to a patient parking deck across Manning Drive, the hospital was constructed as part of a larger project that also included the Physicians' Office Building and the Jackson Circle parking deck for staff. The State's only public cancer hospital project was built with a $180 million appropriation from the NC General Assembly.

When Dr. Jeffrey Houpt, former Dean of the Medical School, was called to testify before the State legislative leadership on behalf of building a new cancer hospital at UNC, he found that the legislators were already convinced of the need. About three-quarters of the leaders had had a loved one as a patient in the old Gravely Cancer Hospital and they understood the importance of modernizing the State's cancer treatment facilities. As one legislator said, "This is not Chapel Hill's hospital, this is *our* hospital." At that point, there was little argument about passing the appropriation to pay for the hospital.

Extensive Health Affairs construction took place during the dynamic decade. Construction of the Women's and Children's Hospital started before the Development Plan was completed in 2002. The eight-story Carrington Hall Addition to the School of Nursing was completed in 2005. As the first U.S. Green Building Council's Leadership in Energy and

Environmental Design (LEED) Certified building on the UNC campus, Carrington included a "green" roof to capture rainfall.

To support the heating, cooling, and information processing needs of the expanded campus, several new support facilities were built during the dynamic decade. The Manning Drive Steam Plant supplies steam heat for the system. ITS Manning, located at the hub connecting North Campus, South Campus, and Health Affairs, provides a central location for the UNC team of professional information technology workers.

Though not part of the Development Plan, extensive interior renovations were carried out to a number of the older Health Affairs buildings. These included the Health Science Library, Brinkhous Bullitt, Burnett Womack, and Old Dental.

Additions to the Health Affairs community under the Development Plan totaled some 1.7 million square feet at a cost of over $492 million (Appendix A).

INTEGRATING THE HEALTH RESEARCH COMMUNITY

Closely aligned with the Health Affairs Community is the large Health Research Community. Home to much of the UNC grant-funded research, this community includes: Genetic Medicine Research, Medical Biomolecular Research, Neurosciences Research, Biomedical Research & Imaging Center, Bioinformatics, Dental Sciences, Hooker Research Center, and the Kerr Addition to Beard Hall. Included in this community, due to their proximity, are the new Fedex Global Education building and the Thermal Storage Tank and Tomkins Operations Center.

The Health Research Community is located along South Columbia Street, Mason Farm Road, and Manning Drive. Because of their frontage on the main entrance roads to the campus from the south, many of these buildings are perceived as part of the gateway to UNC. A pedestrian bridge crossing from the new Dental Sciences building over Manning Drive furthers the gateway image. Taken together, these buildings, many up to eight stories in height, present a vista of contemporary architecture and design that is in keeping with their scientific mission.

To enhance the pedestrian connections in the Health Research Community, a major streetscape improvement project turned the South Columbia Street frontage into an attractive and safe walking environment. Decreasing the travel lanes on South Columbia and adding new landscaping, bollards, and sidewalks, not only created a more appealing visual environment but also improved pedestrian safety along this important entry route. Planners also designed a central greenway path from the new Dental Sciences building south to Mason Farm Road and the Ambulatory Care Center. Starting with the pedestrian bridge across Manning Drive to the plaza adjacent to the Thurston Bowles building, this route links a series of major research and academic buildings and planned out-

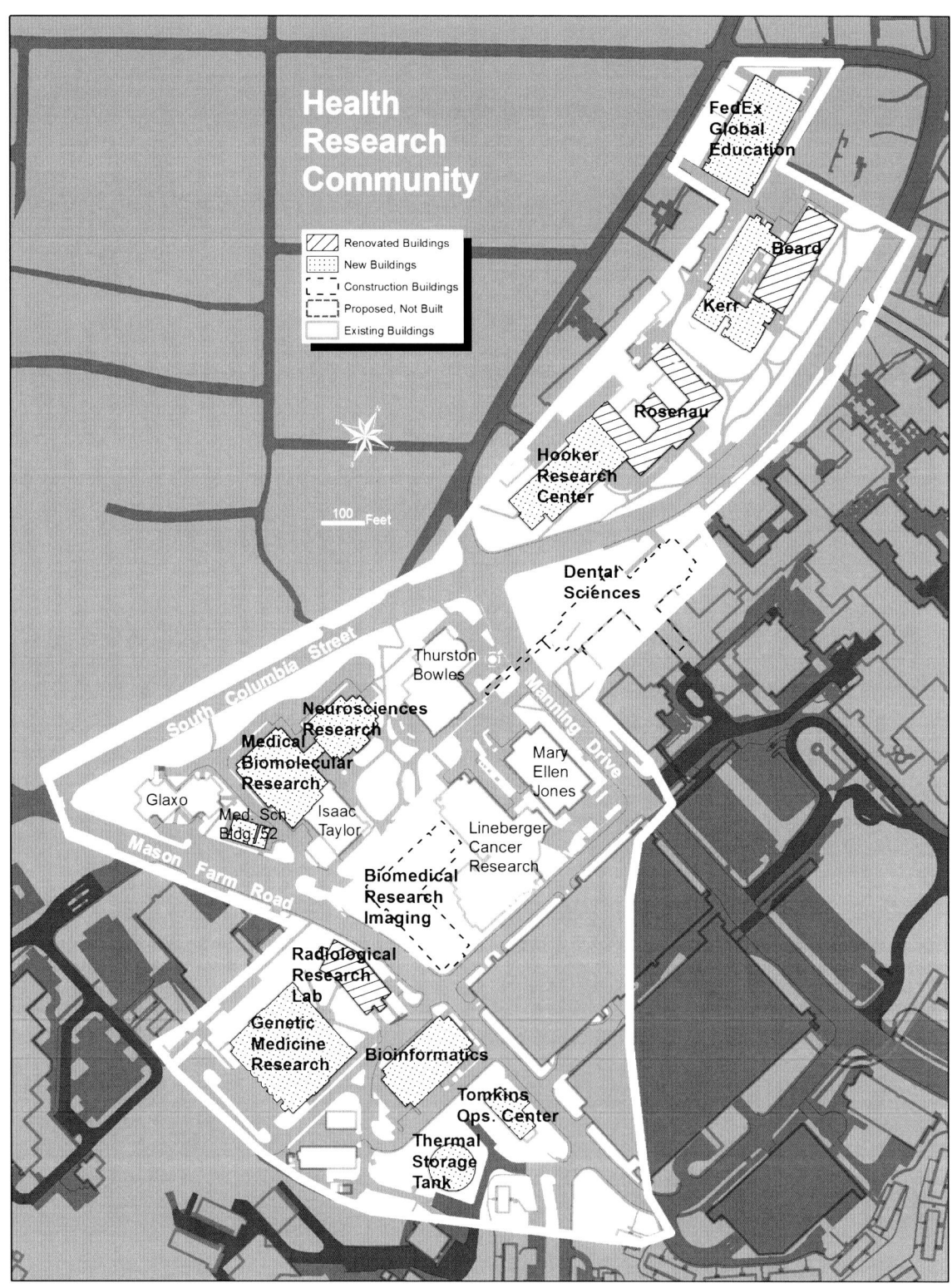

8-5. Health Research Community. Source: UNC Engineering and Information Services

8-6. Dental Sciences Building and Bridge over Manning Drive. Source: Flad Architects

door courtyards, including the Medical Biomolecular Research Building, completed in 2003, and the Neurosciences Research Building.

As a component of the new scientific approach to medicine, many of the buildings in the Health Research Community house interdisciplinary and multi-departmental research activities in fields such as pharmacology, genetics, pharmacy, biochemistry, and biophysics. Support facilities include the Biomedical Research and Imaging Center, a state-wide resource that supports image-based biomedical research across the UNC System; the Tomkins Operations Center, which houses the engineering staff that manages the heating and cooling of UNC building; and the five-million-gallon Thermal Storage Tank, which stores water cooled during off-peak electrical demand periods, reducing the need for electric purchases during peak hours.

Overall, the Health Research Community projects included some 1.96 million square feet of new and renovated building space and were constructed at a total cost of about $676 million (Appendix A).

SOUTHWEST CAMPUS SUSTAINABILITY LESSONS

Building UNC's Southwest Campus presented some of the greatest development challenges encountered during the dynamic decade. Because

8-7. South Columbia Streetscape Improvements. Source: UNC Facilities Planning & Construction

> To enhance the pedestrian connections …a major streetscape improvement project turned …South Columbia …into an attractive and safe walking environment.

it involved a mix of functions that served different clients, its planning required a higher level of coordination than other areas of the UNC campus. Sustaining this complex area demonstrated the special challenges of integrating land use, transportation, and infrastructure in a time of rapid construction.

Important sustainability lessons that emerged from development of the Southwest Campus include:

- A sustainable health services and research environment should be designed to create building arrangements that enable faculty, staff, and visitors to move safely and directly to their destinations and to enjoy attractive natural landscapes along their movement paths. Every new project should be viewed as an opportunity to foster a healing experience, along with interdisciplinary teaching, research, and patient care.
- Interdepartmental coordination groups should be established to sustain normal campus activities during periods of development. Infrastructure planning should be a central part of this responsibility.

CHAPTER 9

Visualizing a New Research Campus at Carolina North

Carolina North represents the next half-century of UNC's campus development potential. Located a mile and a half north of the main campus, the 250-acre Carolina North research campus holds the key to the University's future growth. Implementation of the 2007 *Carolina North Plan* and the 2009 *Development Agreement* between Chapel Hill and the University promises to open a new era in campus sustainability and in town/gown relationships.

The Carolina North site comprises about a quarter of the 979-acre Horace Williams property. The proposed development occupies the lower southeast part of the overall property extending west from Martin Luther King Jr. Boulevard to Seawell School Road, the boundary between Chapel Hill and Carrboro. Its southern frontage lies along Estes Drive Extension. Its major east-west orientation follows the alignment of the runway of the former Horace Williams Airport, a lightning rod for community controversy over the last portion of its sixty-year history due to safety concerns arising from its proximity to the Chapel Hill schools and neighborhoods that grew up around it.

Plans for Carolina North also faced controversy, generating considerable town/gown debate and taking more than ten years to reach final approval by the Town of Chapel Hill. The sustainability challenge for Carolina North planners was to create a future place to carry out the research and academic mission of the University while preserving the environmental resources and community values inherent in the land. The University, close to reaching the capacity of its main campus, needed

> Carolina North
> ... holds the
> key to the
> University's
> future growth.

space to accommodate its growing research activities, as well as some of its academic programs. The community, accustomed to enjoying the vast woods around the airport for recreation, was happy to see flight operations shut down but reluctant to see new development occur. Finding an acceptable balance between these opposing viewpoints took eleven years and required major commitments of time, energy, professional expertise, stakeholder participation, and good will on all sides.

To understand the forces that shaped the Carolina North Plan, it is necessary to review the history of the site (see Chronology in Appendix B), the various group efforts to find consensus, the final plan and the studies that supported it, and the development agreement that cemented its official approval and conditions.

HISTORY OF THE HORACE WILLIAMS SITE AND PLANS

Eighteen months before Pearl Harbor, UNC Chancellor Frank Porter Graham offered the use of the campus for national defense services. On learning in December 1940 that the University and the government wanted to use part of his land for an airport, Philosophy Professor Horace Williams donated his land adjacent to the 50-acre Martindale Airport for that purpose. Renamed the Horace Williams Airport, it became a Navy pre-flight school that trained over 20,000 personnel and whose instructors or trainees included future presidents Gerald Ford and George W. Bush, as well as Ted Williams, Otto Graham, and Paul Bear Bryant. It was the Navy who first paved Airport Road, later renamed Martin Luther King Jr. Boulevard.

Following its de-commissioning at the end of World War II, the airport became a civilian facility and eventually housed the local flying club and UNC's Med Air (later termed AHEC, an acronym for Area Health Education Centers program), a group of doctors who flew around the state providing medical training. Originally well outside the borders of development in Chapel Hill, the airport became the target of increasing protests as schools and residential neighborhoods located nearby. At a public hearing in 1989, neighbors demanded that the airport be closed for public use and limited to University flights only. In response, Chancellor Fordham agreed to phase out non-University use, but the airport continued to operate and occasional plane crashes during ensuing years kept the issue of closure alive.

Over time, the land adjacent to the airport became the location for various service uses. The Town of Chapel Hill built a municipal and transit operations center there and the Animal Shelter and recycling center were located there on land leased from UNC. A municipal sanitary landfill was located on 35 acres north of the airport runway until 1973, when it was closed and the Orange County Regional Landfill was established. The University also used it to store materials, including toxic wastes and construction materials. Concern that this valuable resource area was being nibbled away led to a call for a comprehensive analysis of the potential of the site for large scale University uses.

THE FIRST HORACE WILLIAMS PLAN: 1998. In 1998, the first of four plans for the Horace Williams property was prepared by the consulting firm of Johnson, Johnson, and Roy (JJR), who had also prepared the existing plan for the main campus. The Horace Williams site is covered in the *Outlying Parcels Land Use Plans: Summary Report* (Johnson, Johnson, and Roy, 1998), along with the Mason Farm property where the Friday Center and other uses are located. Even though the proposed land use plan for the Horace Williams site was based on retaining the airport and was not implemented, the JJR report highlights some important considerations that influenced future plans:

- Because the site is significant to, and falls under the zoning jurisdiction of, Chapel Hill, plans must be based on a town/gown consensus derived from extensive public debate and negotiation.
- A limited amount of the site (estimated then at 550 acres) is available for future development after the airport and significant natural features, such as Bolin Creek and Crow Branch are subtracted.
- Access to the site is limited by the roadway capacity of the Airport Road corridor.
- The University/Norfolk Southern rail corridor which passes through the site as it extends north to Hillsborough and south to Carrboro, presents an opportunity to establish a high-volume transit link from the property to the central campus.

After reviewing three alternatives, the JJR plan recommended a land use scheme based on use of the rail corridor as location for a transit line connecting to the central campus. As shown in the 1998 Plan in dark blue, the two major University Village areas focused on this rail corridor. Planning principles included promoting sustainable development by mitigating environmental impacts and conserving energy, promoting use of mass transit by clustering density within a five-minute walk of transit stops, and providing for bicycle and pedestrian connections. This conceptual plan established general uses but did not delineate specific development layouts. However, due to the assumption that the airport would remain open, this plan proposed development on the forested areas of the site, which would not be considered environmentally sustainable under current criteria.

THE SECOND HORACE WILLIAMS PLAN: 2001. In 1998 the University employed Ayers Saint Gross to revise its central campus plan and to consider the outlying lands as well. The Chancellor formed the Horace Williams Advisory Committee to work with ASG to develop a master plan for the Horace Williams site, using the JJR concept plan as a starting point. The work of this committee helped to establish more specific design concepts for the mixed-use research park envisioned on the site. A town/gown committee recommended using a Town/University development agreement along with a new zoning category to govern the future development.

The 2001 ASG land use plan assumed continuation of the airport. Similar to the 1998 plan, it proposed development extending west across the rail corridor into Carrboro, with the bulk of the new buildings in the center of the site. University Counsel Susan Ehringhaus and Chancellor's Special Assistant Jonathan Howes led the UNC team that worked on this plan.

Following two more Flying Club plane crashes, Chancellor Moeser announced in 2002 that Horace Williams Airport would be closed permanently to both University and private users. The North Carolina General Assembly delayed the closing until at least 2005 (and the actual closing would be further delayed until a new hangar could be built for UNC planes serving AHEC at Raleigh Durham International Airport). The closure decision opened the way for a third land use plan without the constraint of an operating airport on the site.

THE THIRD PLAN—CAROLINA NORTH: 2004. As understanding of the potential uses for the strategic Horace Williams site grew, a vision statement was prepared that elaborated on its expected nature. Renamed Carolina North, it was seen as first and foremost a university campus dedicated to serving the mission and ideals of the University. However, to meet the demands of contemporary competition in higher education, it also needed to be a place for public-private partnerships and public engagement, with flexible new spaces for research and education.

In the wake of the closure announcement, Chapel Hill formed the Horace Williams Citizens' Committee and charged it with developing principles regarding development of Carolina North, as the project had come to be known. Their 2003 report, updated in 2004, laid out the following principles, which were adopted as Town Policy.

- Manage development to minimize impacts on neighborhoods and the environment.
- Address community needs for housing, schools, and other facilities.
- Create a campus that is open, welcoming, and part of the community fabric while respecting the privacy and integrity of adjoining neighborhoods.
- Be either revenue positive or revenue neutral so that Town residents do not subsidize the costs of Town services.
- Assume leadership in sustainable water management and wastewater treatment and reuse.
- Ensure that development results in no net increase in stormwater discharge.
- Ensure no negative impact on air quality.

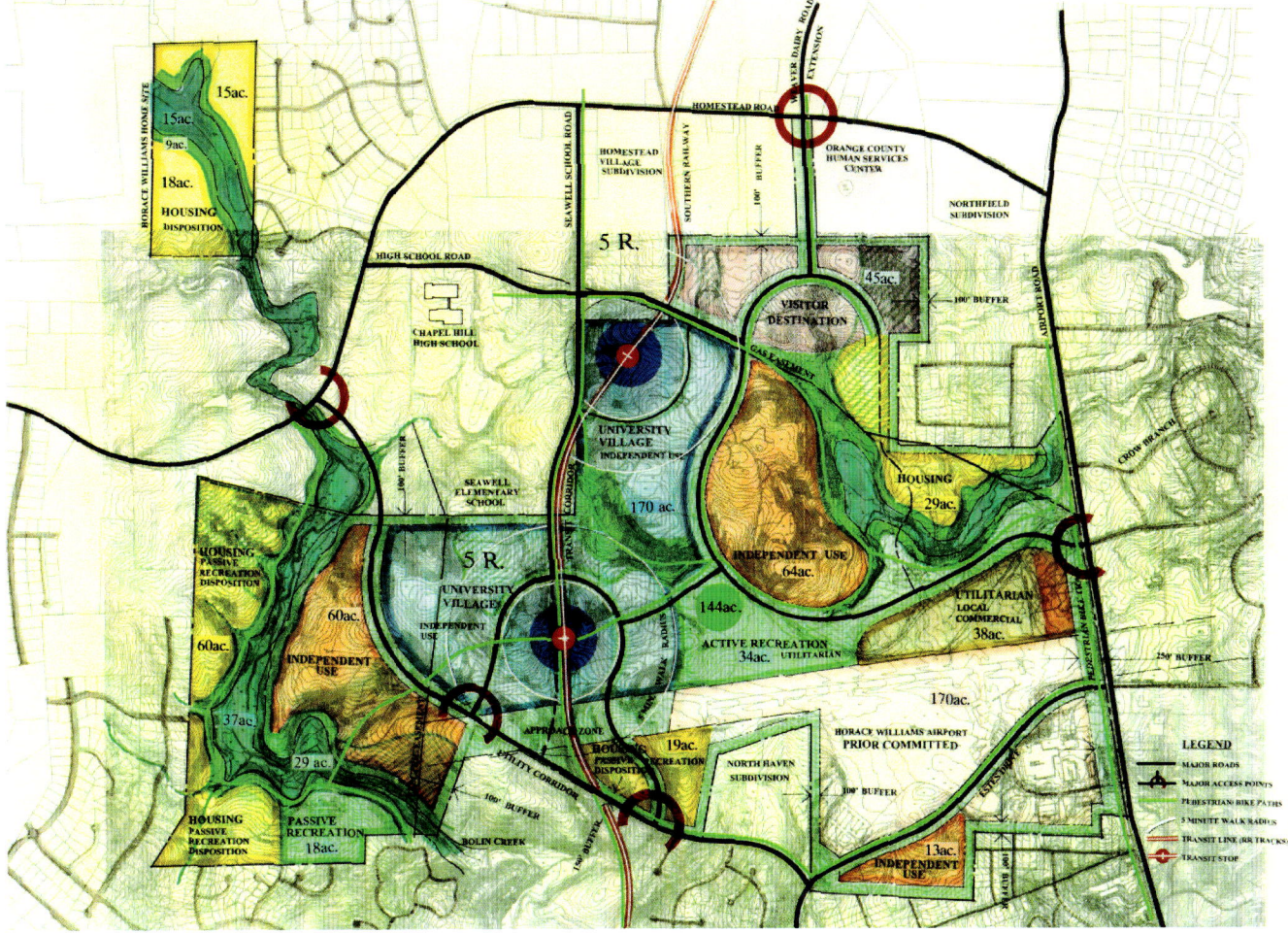

9-1. 1998 Horace Williams Land Use Plan. Source: Johnson, Johnson, and Roy, Inc. 1998.

- Preserve in perpetuity the maximum amount of open space possible, with a goal of 75 percent.
- Develop and maintain a network of trails and greenways.
- Maintain an inventory of natural resources as a guide for planning and development.
- Follow sustainable site design principles and goals.
- Create minimal impact on traffic and promote commuter safety.
- Comply with the Town's comprehensive plan.
- Create a new zoning district to apply to Carolina North.

With closure of the airport announced, ASG was able to place campus buildings on the area previously occupied by the airport runway. The 2004 plan concentrated the majority of its campus uses on the southeastern side of the property, but extended some development across the rail corridor into Carrboro. Similar to the previous plans, this plan left large areas of the site in their natural state. Vice Chancellor for Research and Economic Development Tony Waldrop led the University team that held town/gown discussions on this plan.

The Horace Williams Citizens' Committee continued to function through 2006, representing the Town's viewpoint. To broaden the discussion to include representatives of the University and other involved stakeholders, Chancellor Moeser appointed a broad-based Leadership Advisory Committee (LAC) in 2006, charged with creating guiding principles for the Carolina North development plan. The task of the LAC was to find agreement among the leaders on the thorny issues of fiscal equity, housing, transportation, the environment, and other relevant matters.

THE FOURTH CAROLINA NORTH PLAN: 2007–2010. The planning effort to prepare the final Carolina North plan involved an intense combination of leadership discussions, citizen participation, staff work, and consulting studies. While principles and tradeoffs were debated in various forums, expert consultants, funded by the University and jointly selected with the Town, analyzed the plan's fiscal impacts (TischlerBise) and transportation impacts (Vanasse Hangen Brustlin, Inc.). The University's master planning team included the following professional firms; Biohabitats, who analyzed environmental conditions on the site; RK&K Engineering and AEI Affiliated Engineers, who planned the energy and water systems; and Martin, Alexiou, Bryson, who planned the transportation systems. To help in pulling all this together, the Chancellor appointed Jack Evans as the full time Executive Director of Carolina North to lead this phase of the planning and implementation work. Evans, former dean of the UNC School of Business, worked closely with the Chapel Hill Town Manager, Roger Stancil, in the ongoing negotiations over the plan and development agreement.

The 2007 LAC report laid out a slate of principles representing the concerns of the involved parties. The report supported previously stated principles of neutral or positive fiscal impact, environmental sustainability, limiting development over the next 50 years, and encouragement of public transportation. While there was agreement on the broad sustainability principles, there was not complete consensus on all of the detailed statements on housing, provision of social services, cumulative impacts, extension of development limits beyond fifty years, and net negative air quality impacts. However, in the main the LAC effort was a significant advance in generating community-wide agreement on the parameters of planning and building Carolina North. The Leadership Advisory Committee report was submitted to the Chancellor in 2007.

Parallel to the LAC, starting in 2006 and running through 2007, the University held a series of Infrastructure and Sustainable Design Workshops with University staff, consultants, and invited community representatives to provide guidance for development strategies for Carolina North. The five working groups discussed principles, strategies, metrics and goals for transportation, natural habitat/landscape/water quality, water/wastewater/stormwater, building typology and energy generation/consumption/utilities. The resulting vision was "Carolina North will be characterized by continual discovery, assessment, learning, and improve-

JACK EVANS, EXECUTIVE DIRECTOR

When Jack Evans took over as executive director of Carolina North in 2006, the project wasn't going anywhere fast. Already, three cycles of planning—in the mid '90s, 2000, and 2004—had failed to yield a Town- and University-approved plan.

"What you had was a project that was being executed by 12 to 15 people with full-time jobs," Evans recalls. "And it wasn't moving."

Chancellor Moeser's appointment of a full-time executive director, instead of relying on the part-time efforts of other staff, helped jump-start the process; a deft touch with town/gown relations was also required. "We had to persuade the Town of Chapel Hill that we were willing to listen to the community voice as we developed the plan," Evans says. "We had to be very careful about now springing a full-blown plan on the Town and saying, 'Here is what we are going to do; don't stand in our way.'"

To that end, Evans and his colleagues made what is perhaps a counter-intuitive move: instead of using the public information sessions, which started in March 2007, to introduce one complete plan for land use, they introduced three incomplete ones. "We used those three as ways to illustrate different approaches," Evans says. "That way, we didn't early on find ourselves in an adversarial position, saying, 'This is our plan, we want you to agree with it.' We would always say, 'Please remember that this is a work in progress.'"

They refined the plan as the months passed, incorporating public feedback and adding specifics. By April 2007, they were down to two; by June, one. "This was our approach for creating a process through which the community voice could be heard, and the University could retain the initiative for the planning," he says.

While there were broad areas of consensus between the University and the community, discussions did bog down on occasion. When some Townspeople pushed to permanently ban development outside of a fraction of the property, for example, UNC dug in its heels. "That was a non-starter," Evans says. "There's no way we would tie the hands of future Trustees."

The University did, however, agree to limit development to 20 percent of the property over the next 50 years. It also gave ground in other areas. Recognizing the importance of the economic impact of Carolina North to the community, the University agreed to do a fiscal analysis. In response to community concerns about traffic, the University agreed to participate in a transportation planning study.

Evans says his relationship with Town Manager Roger Stancil was critical to the process. From the outset, the two men made a point of seeking out small problems they could solve together as a means of building trust. They would also warn each other about potential stumbling blocks. "In my opinion, we would not have been able to do this if we didn't have a Town Manager who was willing to work with us," Evans says.

When the Trustee-approved plan reached the Town Council in 2008, the University sought a development agreement with the Town to avoid having to rely on a series of special-use permits. "We had to have some stability in our relationship with the Town, so we could plan," he says. "If we had to take every project by itself to the Town council, project by project, we would have been forced to plan in a project-by-project way."

All the talks and trade-offs—some three-and-a-half years' worth—ultimately produced a deal that was fair to all parties, Evans says. "It took a long time, but I don't think we had anyone who felt they had been coerced, extorted or unable to express their voice," he says. "By taking small, inclusive steps, I think we avoided having someone run the whole thing into a ditch."

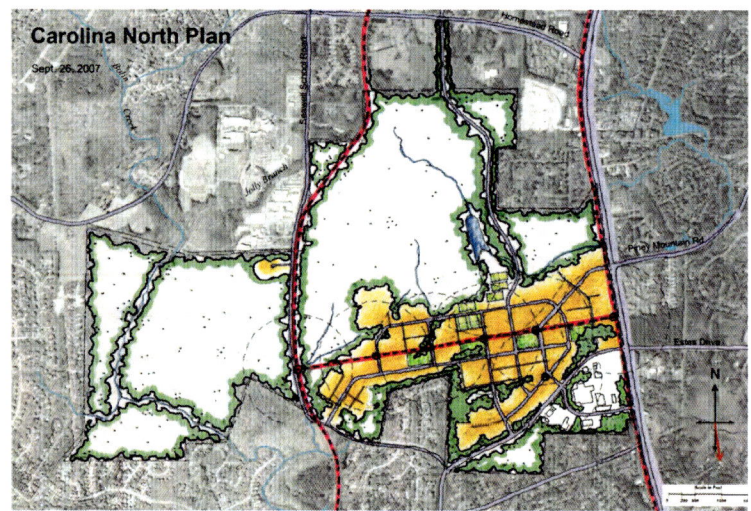

9-2. Carolina North Plan, 2007. Source: 2007 Carolina North Plan

ment. It will increase the vitality of people, the economy, and the planet, and it will teach through its activities, processes, and environment."

The discussions about principles, strategies, metrics, and goals were grouped under four major themes: 1) climate, culture and place, 2) climate neutrality, 3) conservation, efficiency and reliability, and 4) collaboration, education, training and outreach. These discussions reflected the integrated planning and systems thinking that were integral to the University's approach to sustainability planning.

Beginning in 2007, the University conducted seven monthly public meetings on the Carolina North plan for interested members of the community. The purposes were to provide information on the status of the plan, to provide an opportunity for questions, and to gather feedback that could be used in refining the plan. The early meetings included examples of the programmatic activities (research and teaching) that are likely to be located at Carolina North. Participants were encouraged to complete and submit comment cards at each meeting. All comment cards were transcribed and posted on the Carolina North web site. In the course of the meetings, various development design scenarios were tested, resulting in selection of a final scenario and fifteen- and fifty-year development footprints.

After reviewing various alternative layouts, the 2007 plan for Carolina North opted for an east-west layout. This land use pattern had the advantages of using the least undisturbed land, enjoying a solar south orientation (which at Carolina North is 8 degrees east of magnetic south), integrating a transit corridor as a central spine, and bringing more working landscapes with their contributions to stormwater management, low impact recreation, and natural habitats into the central core. In form, the central axis of the 2007 Carolina North Plan followed the alignment of the former airport runway and extended southwest from Martin Luther

King Jr. Boulevard to Seawell School Road. It had road access points at the Piney Mountain Road intersection, at two points along Estes Drive Extension, and from Seawell School Road and Homestead Road. Internal development areas were served by a grid pattern of roads and surrounded by open green space. A small school site was designated on the Carrboro side of Seawell School Road.

The 2007 Carolina North Plan was approved by the UNC Board of Trustees, some nine years and four planning attempts after formation of the initial Horace Williams Advisory Committee (see Trustees' Resolution of September 26, 2007 in Appendix B). The Plan states that:

> Carolina North will serve the mission of the University of North Carolina at Chapel Hill by creating a world-class research and learning campus in the heart of Chapel Hill. This new campus will be a vibrant, sustainable development that will attract and create exciting new opportunities for research and innovation in North Carolina. The implementation of this campus is a timely response to the surge in main campus development in the last decade. The need for this campus also reflects a trend toward public-private partnerships and economic development related to research efforts and innovations generated by the University. The Carolina North campus will provide a place for the University to grow and develop new models for research and education.

> The 2007 Carolina North Plan was approved … some nine years and four planning attempts after formation of the initial Horace Williams Advisory Committee.

SITE PLANNING STUDIES

The 2007 Carolina North Plan incorporated a number of findings from specialized studies. One of the most influential studies concerned the ecology of the site.

ECOLOGICAL ASSESSMENT. In July 2006, an ecological assessment of the Carolina North property was conducted by Biohabitats, hired by the University, to determine the suitability of the site to support development without compromising ecological stability and integrity. This assessment was based on the ecological, cultural, historic, and recreational characteristics of the site. Inventory and analysis included water resources, geologic formations, soils groups, approximate tree stand age, land use/land cover, morphology, landscape ecology, regional landscape ecology, state and local government natural areas designation, and cultural and historic resources. Data was collected on-site, through literature searches, and in interviews and meetings. These components were evaluated by an academic peer-review group and reviewed by staff. The multiple layers of analysis were then compiled.

The resulting assessment identified the portions of the site that were relatively more suitable for conservation or development. This ecological assessment was a critical foundation for the planning process, providing a physical basis against which development patterns, transportation, open space, connections, site management, and utilities infrastructure could be evaluated. The Composite Suitability Analysis displayed levels of suitability for development; the highest suitability area became the location of the proposed Carolina North development area.

TRANSPORTATION. Limited automobile access to the site is a challenge acknowledged in the plan, which sought to rely on various types of transit, including the fare-free local bus system, funded jointly by the University, Chapel Hill, and Carrboro. Regional transit is limited, although studies are underway to increase it. Pedestrian and bikeway alternatives are to be developed as implementation proceeds.

IMPLEMENTATION STAGING. The plan envisioned that the first 15 years of development would take place in the southeast corner of the site, where existing road access is the greatest. The program estimated that 2,475,000 gross square feet will be built during years 1–15.

CAROLINA NORTH 2009 DEVELOPMENT AGREEMENT

The capstone for the years of discussion, planning, and negotiation was the successful adoption of the Carolina North Development Agreement in July 2009. The agreement was prepared in accordance with the North Carolina General Statutes ("G.S.") 160A-400.20, which recognizes that large-scale development projects often occur in multiple phases extending over a period of years, requiring a long-term commitment of both public and private resources, and authorizes local governments to enter into agreements of up to 20 years with large scale developers on property of 25 acres or more.

Preparation of the development agreement was an unprecedented step for both UNC and Chapel Hill, whose past development proposal interactions had sometimes been wary if not in conflict. This was an institutional innovation of the same order as the 2001 adoption of the new Office/Instituional-4 (OI-4) Zoning District that allowed the Town to review and approve the proposed new campus plan as a whole, rather than in a series of building-by-building steps. Creation of the 2009 Development Agreement and its accompanying new University-1 (U-1) zoning district allowed the Town and the University to build consensus on a detailed plan and implementation program that comprehensively and proactively addressed the needs and concerns of both parties within the context of a binding legal contract.

A key role in the town/gown deliberations on the development agreement was played by David Owens, a professor in the UNC School of Government. Owens held the trust of both the Town and the University and acted as the honest broker in working out the details of the agreement. Trained as both a lawyer and a city planner, he understood the problems and potential solutions and assisted in the delicate negotiations between the UNC Chancellor and Trustees and the Town Mayor and Council.

Previous public discussions about the Carolina North plan had ad-

DAVID OWENS, HONEST BROKER

Pay attention to the big picture—and also to the details. Get the latest information out to every interested party—even those who are only interested once a month.

These phrases may sound a bit like Zen Koans, but to David Owens, they were two keys to success in his role as honest broker in the Carolina North negotiations between the University, the Town government, and the citizens of Chapel Hill. There's nothing mystical about his other bit of advice, however. "Plan on spending a fair amount of time," says Owens, a professor at UNC's School of Government, who dedicated some 60 working days to the negotiations over the 11-month negotiation. "This is not a simple process."

For Owens, who was hired by the Town of Chapel Hill to facilitate the deal, the process began with identifying all the systems that needed to come together—the big picture—and the order and timing required. As a starting point, he had a list of about 25 critical issues identified by the Leadership Advisory Council that had met the year before; he then prioritized those issues based on the degree of consensus that existed on them, among other factors.

Owens' strategy from the outset was to save the most difficult issues, like transportation and traffic, for later in the process. Comparatively easy ones like energy efficiency or carbon reduction goals were tackled early, giving the people involved a chance to build up trust in the process and in each other.

With an overarching calendar in mind, Owens could drill down to the details, which included items like deadlines to resolve the component legal and technical questions. He also built in reasonable amounts of time for public response.

Identifying the audiences involved was another crucial early step. A high-profile issue like this had a host of them, from the Town Council and UNC's Board of Trustees, to staff members on both sides, to highly concerned citizens, down to the general public. Some of those parties were dealing with the issues on a daily basis; others, like members of the community, might only focus on them—albeit very intensely—at a monthly public hearing.

"We asked who needs to be engaged and at what level, and made sure we built in appropriate levels of involvement all along," Owens says. "Who are the actors in this play, and how are we going to write them into this in a way that is appropriate and that they will appreciate?"

One of the big barriers to writing all the actors in was communicating with them effectively. To that end, Owens took advantage of technology whenever he could. Hearings were videotaped and televised, minutes and documents posted online, schedules and calendars updated weekly. Even so, the fluid nature of the negotiation made this task a difficult one.

"That was a real challenge, how to keep all of these audiences involved," he says. "Documents and proposals were changing as we went. One group would be commenting on one thing, but it had already changed."

As might be expected in a process that the Town and the University had tried and failed to resolve at least twice before, the negotiations did have some tenuous moments. Natural area protection, which came up about two-thirds of the way through, was one.

The University initially proposed that it would not develop outside of a third of its property in the first 50 years. Some Town Council members feared that plan would merely postpone development of land, not preserve it. They wanted an easement in perpetuity donated to a third party, an idea rejected by University Trustees on the grounds of fiduciary responsibility. "It was a pretty stark disagreement, and it was beginning to get a little heated," Owens says.

Rather than allowing high-ranking people on both sides to butt heads and bruise feelings, Owens' solution was to back off, regroup, then re-engage. "We said, 'Let us work on this at the staff level before the whole thing falls apart.'"

When staff reached a solution (which ultimately was to put a third of the least-developable land under easement), they ran it by the most concerned participants—Town Council member Jim Ward on one side, and University Trustee Roger Perry on the other—before reintroducing it to everyone involved. "That was a good helpful model as we got to even more difficult issues, where you needed even greater trust," Owens says.

As to the quality of the deal itself, Owens recalls telling Town Council members, six months into the process, that one measure of success would be if they got to the end of the process and said, "Of course this is the answer. It's not controversial. It's common sense."

And he notes that both the Town Council and the Board of Trustees approved the final version of the development agreement in less than 15 minutes. "Ultimately, in June, we got to that point," he says. "Everybody was on board."

dressed all of the major issues, setting the stage for a joint effort to invent an acceptable development agreement. The first step was a work session with the Town Council and representatives of the University Board of Trustees in January 2008, where they agreed to work cooperatively toward design of a new Town development review process for the Carolina North project. Senior staff from the Town and University formed the Joint Staff Work Group, which met regularly during 2008 and 2009 to work out the development review process. The Town Council asked the staff to develop a new zoning district and development agreement as the framework for reviewing Carolina North development proposals. The Town and the University then held ten joint work sessions during 2008 and 2009 to discuss the details.

The University submitted a request for a new zoning district, a 50-year Carolina North plan, and draft design guidelines in October 2008. The Town held public information sessions to get public input. The Town Council held work sessions on transportation and other issues. Drafts of a new University-1 (U-1) zoning district and a Carolina North development agreement were presented in February 2009, and Town advisory boards reviewed the zoning district and development agreement. In April 2009 UNC submitted its request for a zoning atlas amendment and development agreement and the Town staff submitted an amendment to the Land Use Management Ordinance creating the U-1 zoning district. This required concurrent review of a rezoning application and a proposed development agreement. After further public hearings and work sessions, along with consultant studies of parking, transportation, and other issues, the Town Council unanimously approved the agreement on June 22, 2009 and the UNC Trustees followed suit on June 25.

The 47-page agreement contains standards and procedures governing all aspects of the development of Carolina North, along with detailed design guidelines. While its preparation required large investments of time and energy by both parties, as well as major long-term commitments, the resulting Development Agreement was a win-win, which had major benefits for both the Town and University.

Its benefits to the Town included: implementation of the Carolina North plan with an appropriate mix of uses and densities on the site; protection of natural resources, minimization of adverse off-site impacts, and incorporation of sustainability principles; provision of an overall plan for transportation needs, including commitments to transit, bikeways, greenways, sidewalks, and road improvements; assurance that the project will be revenue neutral or revenue positive; integrated site plans, urban design elements, land uses, architecture, site engineering, and landscape architecture; commitments to public infrastructure and amenities by the University; and assurance of University provision of public improvements, facilities, and services.

Its benefits to the University included: obtaining sufficient certainty, timeliness, and predictability in the Town's development review and approval process to justify the required substantial up-front capital investment for a project that will require multiple years to build out; realization of the opportunity to implement the Carolina North development plan for a mixed-use campus development that is consistent with Town and University goals and needs; securing development rights for up to three million square feet of buildings and associated development in accordance with an approved plan of development; and integration of site plans, urban design elements, land uses, architecture, site engineering, landscape architecture, and mitigation measures.

The initial phase of the project, as allowed by the Development Agreement, included construction of some three million square feet of buildings on about 133 acres over a twenty year period. The 50-year plan anticipated development of 8 to 9 million square feet of floor space on 250 acres. A minimum of 25% of the total floor space covered by the agreement must be devoted to housing and preference for housing shall be given to UNC students and employees, with secondary priority to other public employees working within the Town. Some 300 acres of open space shall be protected with conservation easements. The maximum number of parking spaces allowed during the initial 800,000 square feet of building space shall be 1525; beyond the initial phase parking ratios shall be based on updated transportation impact analyses. A schedule of triggers and thresholds for action listed the times or levels of development that require certain reports or actions (Section 5.28.2).

2011 STATUS OF CAROLINA NORTH

The overall site land use arrangement is depicted in the 2011 Carolina North Development Agreement Annual Report. The 250-acre Development Area is located in the southeast corner of the site, adjacent to Martin Luther King, Jr. Boulevard. It is aligned with the former airport runway, which becomes a central open commons space. Until 50 years have elapsed, no further development is permitted in the surrounding 50-Year Limited Development Area. Development is prohibited in perpetuity in the Conservation Areas surrounding the streams on the site. It is prohibited for the next 100 years in the 100-year Limited Development Area.

Initial design of infrastructure and a research building began in 2011. Planners decided to extend the central green space axis, which follows the old runway alignment, through to Martin Luther King Boulevard in order to provide a clear and accessible pedestrian entrance to this central common space. The 20-year plan for the 133 acres of the initial phase envisions a mix of academic research, civic/retail, and housing in 3 million square feet of buildings.

Carolina North master planners envision a future campus setting of academic and research buildings connected by a strong landscape frame-

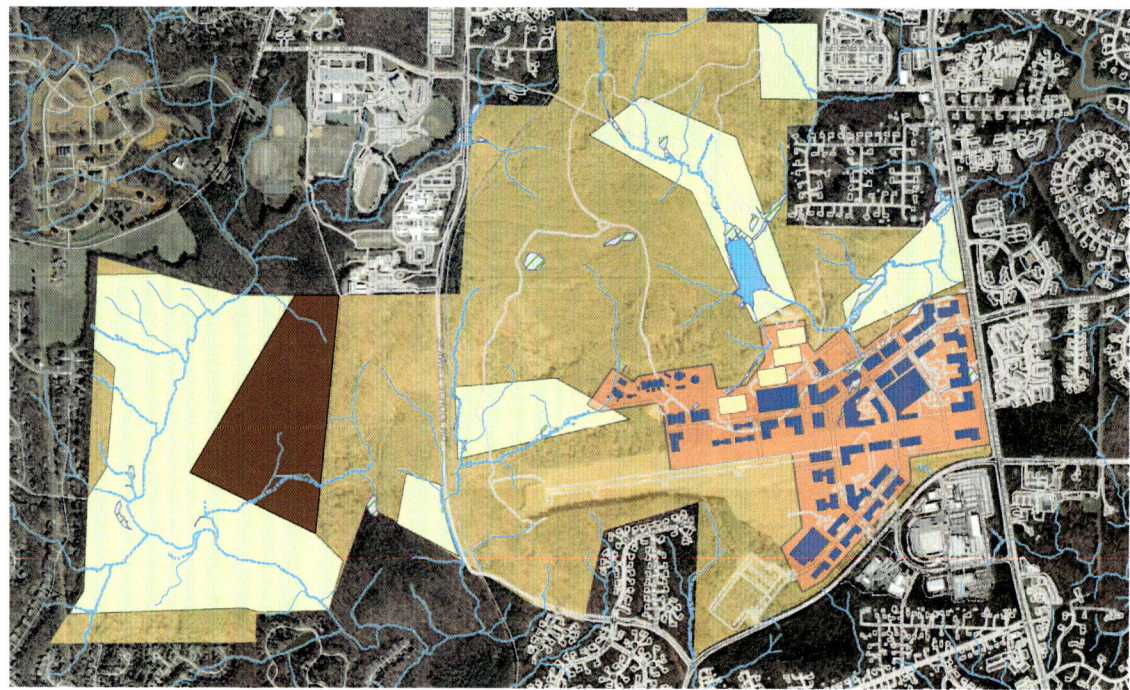

Development Agreement Plan

Legend

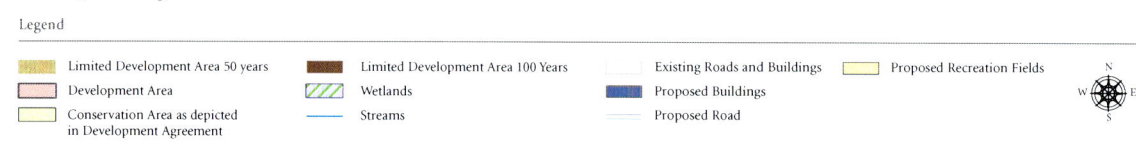

9-3. Land Use Arrangement in the Development Agreement Plan of Carolina North. Source: 2011 Campus North Development Agreement Annual Report

work. The most dramatic element is the central greenway leading from Martin Luther King, Jr., Boulevard on the east to the Carolina North forest on the west. Intersecting the greenway are working landscapes, naturalized stormwater management features that bring elements of the forest into the campus. Adjacent buildings are to be designed with green roofs to capture rain water and panels to capture solar energy. The whole campus is to be a model of sustainable development, from its architecture and landscape to its energy, water, and wastewater facilities.

SUSTAINABILITY LESSONS FROM CAROLINA NORTH

The experience of preparing the plan and development agreement for Carolina North was a case of patient negotiation and planning to combine the needs of the University and the Town. As in the process for preparing and approving the Master plan, the Carolina North planning process stretched over a number of years and engaged a wide group of actors. Looking back on this process, certain clear lessons are evident.

- A large campus planning initiative must expect to devote a high percentage of its time and effort in finding agreement among

diverse stakeholders on both the design and approval process for the plan. Transparency of decision-making is an absolute necessity during the planning process, in order to reassure the public and decision-makers that the process is open and committed to including all viewpoints.
- Leaders from both the University and the Town must be willing to collaborate and to negotiate in good faith if a successful public/private agreement is to be reached.
- Requiring advance planning and commitment does not impede innovation and creative thinking, but rather challenges planners and decision-makers to develop new pragmatic solutions.
- Large scale development plans must be based on solid evidence and analyses, such as in-depth ecological assessments, transportation impact studies, and fiscal impact analyses, in order to reassure decision-makers as to the logic and feasibility of the plans.
- Development agreements can provide substantial benefits to both universities and their home jurisdictions, but they require substantial up-front investments of resources.

9-4. Future Carolina North Greenway. Source: Ayers Saint Gross and Pylot Studios

CHAPTER 10

Lessons for Creating a Sustainable Campus

UNC and Chapel Hill learned important lessons about sustainable campus development from their experience in planning, reviewing, and building a huge campus addition during the dynamic decade. They learned to define sustainable campus development as a balance of historic preservation concerns, current development demands, and future potential needs. They learned to use the University's mission statement as a touchstone for assessing development proposals. They learned to collaborate on building consensus to solve problems arising from the unprecedented scale and impacts of the resulting growth. They learned to determine the responsible capacity of the campus in light of sustaining natural systems. Finally, they learned to use an ongoing review process to ensure that project designs respected broader needs for campus character and consistency. We present these lessons here not only to document the UNC experience, but also to make them available to other university campuses and their communities seeking to develop in a sustainable manner.

DEFINE SUSTAINABLE CAMPUS DEVELOPMENT

Typical definitions of sustainable development characterize it as a balance among economy, environment, and equity—the so-called triple bottom line, and hold that it must not put future generations at a disadvantage relative to present generations. For a university campus, the concept of sustainable development takes on a special perspective. Because the historic campus remains in place over generations, its maintenance must be a central focus of present and future planning. Therefore, the triple bottom line for a campus plan should be stated as *preserving the past, building the present, and anticipating the future*. It is the *intersection* of these concerns that determines the beauty and functionality of a contemporary university campus.

UNC's master planning process started with recognition of the great value of the traditional campus, and then linked this to the requirement for meeting the needs of the contemporary campus while anticipating the needs of the future campus. While not explicitly stated at the outset of the master planning process, this sustainable balance always was an underlying goal and it became more explicit during the dynamic decade.

In looking back over the experience of the dynamic decade, it is clear that sustainable campus development must be development that meets the needs of today's learning experience while respecting the need to preserve the educational evolution embedded in its historic resources and recognizing the need to anticipate future university academic objectives. Such development is sensitive to the needs of both current and future stakeholders, on and off the campus. In short, sustainable campus development is achieved by forward-looking planning that is based in the present but does not lose sight of the past.

Ask any group of university alumni about their campus memories and they invariably position their personal experiences within the historic buildings and outdoor spaces of their time at the university. The architectural and landscape fabric of the past comes to represent for them the precious history of their own individual growth narratives. While alumni recognize the need to continually repair and rebuild the campus environment, maintaining the historic campus helps to maintain their links to the soul of the university as they knew it. Tell them about adding six million square feet of new buildings within a ten-year period, and their biggest fear is that the old campus will be submerged under the new development.

One of the great triumphs of the dynamic decade was the preservation of the sacred spaces of the UNC campus. Polk and McCorkle Places lost none of their luster and patina, even while new construction was located on their flanks. The Arboretum and Kenan Woods, along with other historic open spaces, were maintained and enhanced in all their landscaped magnificence. At the same time, new student walking paths were extended from the North to the South campus, and new outdoors commons areas were carved out of the densely built-up South Campus precincts.

A second great triumph was the maintenance of the historic look and feel of the historic campus architecture. Rather than jettisoning the style and materials of the past, the new buildings achieved an aesthetic consistency without abandoning contemporary progress in construction and engineering. Design guidelines in the approved plan laid out proportions of mass, roof shapes, and fenestration to be followed by current projects. At the same time, some new modernist buildings were created where their function and location were appropriate.

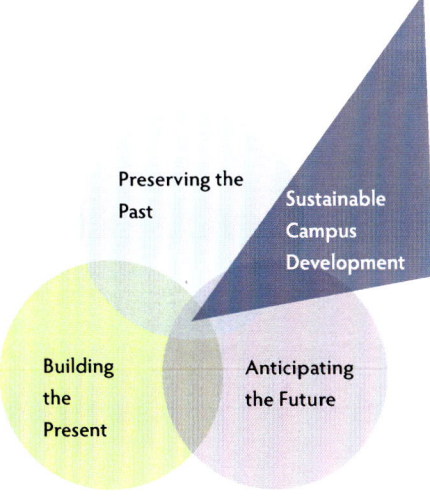

10-1. Sustainable Campus Development

Neither of these triumphs would have been possible without strong up-front planning and analysis. To build the case for preservation of historic buildings and landscapes requires a systematic analysis of their condition and value by a team of experienced historic preservation architects and landscape architects. Reports, such as UNC's *Historic Preservation Survey*, *The Dignity of Restraint*, and *The Report of the Task Force on Landscape Heritage and Diversity*, informed high-level decisions about what to preserve and how to carry out preservation programs. In a sense, they acted as the triage process for historic resources.

To build the campus needed for the present and to anticipate the needs of the future, planners turned to the principles laid out in the University's mission statement.

USE THE UNIVERSITY'S MISSION AS A TOUCHSTONE

One of the main principles established to guide the development of the Master Plan stated that the campus plan should allow for the University's physical growth to serve its threefold mission of teaching, research, and public service. Carrying out the University's mission became a touchstone for imagining and assessing new project proposals during the development process. The mission served not only to frame designs but also to defend them when disagreements arose.

A third triumph of the dynamic decade was the creation and linking of three types of campus communities: communities for student learning, living, and recreating; communities for faculty teaching and research; and communities for visitor and patient services. Made up of coordinated ensembles of structures, common areas, and circulation routes, these communities became the urban design modules for campus growth. They varied according to the existing nature of the three campus precincts: North, Southeast, and Southwest. The North Campus communities had to respect the beautiful 200-year-old context exemplified by Polk and McCorkle Places while surgically inserting modern facilities for the arts and sciences and for student living. The Southeast Campus communities had to reshape and give consistent form to a sprawling mix of sixties-type land uses while providing for a huge influx of student housing and support facilities and a raft of improved athletic and visitor projects. The Southwest Campus communities had to expand and modernize an operating cluster of health care and health research structures while maintaining its vital continuing patient care and funded research activities. At the same time, the underlying infrastructure framework had be extended and upgraded to support the new projects.

A fourth triumph was the modernization of the University's educational plant to position it for the challenges of the future. To meet the new demands of science and medicine, advanced laboratories and classrooms were built for emerging fields, such as bioinformatics, genome science, and medical bio-molecular research, as well as for state-of-the-art work in chemistry, physics, and computer science. At the same time, teaching facilities and offices within existing buildings were upgraded to incorporate digital teaching tools and other academic resources for the arts and humanities. Meanwhile, a new campus at Carolina North was envisioned and approved as an opportunity area for the disciplines and research of the more distant future, with an open framework to support a coordinated a new twenty-first century research, living, and learning environment yet to be designed.

Neither of these triumphs would have been possible without constant reference to, and guidance by, the University's mission of teaching, research, and public service. The mission's precepts encouraged creative thinking by participants in the planning and development process at the same time that they guarded against allocating precious State-owned University lands for projects that were only marginally related to the mission.

The mission set the grand goal for the dynamic decade, but its realization depended critically upon gaining agreement on the means to carry out the goal. This was the challenge of building consensus for the plan, for answering the criticism that the devil is in the details.

BUILD CONSENSUS FROM THE START

The success of a large and comprehensive campus master plan is directly related to the breadth and depth of stakeholder consensus supporting it. University growth and change affects both the academic community and the town, each of which calculates its own set of costs and benefits. If authentic participation is not built into each stage of plan-making, then the result may be festering conflicts that can derail the plan or weaken it through unwise concessions to vocal opponents. Although genuine town/gown collaboration is difficult and time-consuming, there is no other way to ensure that good plans will not be compromised, delayed, or shot down due by determined opposition. This is especially true when university campus development decisions are a matter of joint jurisdiction with the host community, as is the case with UNC and the Town of Chapel Hill.

A fifth triumph of the dynamic decade was the reformulation of the University zoning district to change it from a building-by-building approval process to a Master Plan approval process. Not only did adoption of the OI-4 zoning district do away with the cumbersome micromanagement of University development by the Town elected officials, it also demonstrated at the start of the decade that the Town and University could agree on a more efficient and effective process for deciding on campus development. It established the general principle that Town zoning approvals would be based on a jointly-negotiated overall plan and set the course for a series of further collaborative actions critical to the successes of the decade.

A sixth triumph was the joint agreement on the ten-year Development Plan itself, under the OI-4 zoning district regulations. This was a precedent-setting first for both the Town and the University. Neither had ever committed to a specific multi-year set of building types, sizes, and time schedules. To prepare the Development Plan, the University was forced to analyze and plan for a coordinated suite of large-scale building projects during the master planning process, rather than designing them incrementally as annual state funding appropriations were made. Thanks to the success of the North Carolina Higher Education Bond Referendum in 2000, along with major private contributions, some $1.5 billion in capital funding was available to implement the 2001 Master Plan. Prioritizing the expenditure of these funds and gaining Town approval of the Development Plan jump-started the plan implementation process.

Neither of these triumphs would have been possible without evidence of a deep commitment to sustainable campus development, as exemplified in the concept of "responsible capacity" of the campus. Town and University stakeholders had to be convinced by in-depth professional analyses that opening the floodgates to some six million square feet of new development would not drown the beautiful old campus and the historic surrounding neighborhoods in a gush of undesirable impacts.

LIMIT GROWTH TO RESPONSIBLE CAMPUS CAPACITY

Faced with a development budget of some $1.5 billion and a brand new master plan, some decision-makers might have been tempted to overbuild the campus without fully considering the limits of natural processes, space, history, and physical functions. After all, open spaces can be converted to sites for new buildings and older buildings can be torn down to make room for new growth. Densities can be pushed up by building more high-rise structures. Roads and parking lots can be expanded and additional infrastructure added. Build out is a subjective concept. Rather than going this route, however, the UNC planners stopped to ask, "When is it time to declare that campus development has reached the limit to its growth? When will additional development be unsustainable?"

The Master Plan was guided by a development strategy based on limiting growth to the responsible capacity of the campus. Responsible capacity is determined not only by the amount of land available for new construction, but also by the need to maintain the functions of natural systems that carry stormwater runoff, by the capacity of water, sewer, and other infrastructure systems to support new growth, and by the need to maintain the valuable historic landscapes and buildings on the campus. It is also determined by the need to limit impacts on off-campus neighborhoods, roads, and facilities. Balancing all of these needs and concerns demands high order planning skills, as evidenced by the role of Luanne Greene, the consultant who assisted the University in implementing its plans from from the start to the finish of the dynamic decade.

LUANNE GREENE, IMPLEMENTATION PLANNER

When crafting UNC's Master Plan, Luanne Greene and her team at Ayers Saint Gross looked to the past to develop a timeframe for completing all the projects. Checking off everything on the list, they concluded, would take about a half-century.

As it turned out, it took ten years.

"We told everyone what we thought was the truth during the Master Plan, but it came to fruition so much faster," says Greene, a principal and director of the campus planning studio at the design firm. "We told them it was going to transform campus, but not 'Hey, we're going to implement big hunks of the plan at one time.' Who could have predicted it?"

That wildly successful pace of implementation, driven by what Greene calls a "once-in-multiple-generations" influx of public and private funding, meant a speedy, dramatic makeover for the University, and heady days for designers and builders. But it also meant headaches for the University's faculty, staff and students.

"It is pretty common that you go through a plan, and you're going to build three buildings," Greene says. "Holy smokes—this was every area of the campus, all together, all the time. The whole campus was torn up, cranes everywhere. People couldn't walk where they wanted to walk."

The disruptions took their toll. When Ayers Saint Gross returned to UNC to update the Master Plan in 2006, Greene says, they found that some on campus were questioning its original principles. In response, the firm took the time to re-evaluate the goals it had set forth.

"We decided that these were big growing pains, but these goals were right for this institution," she says. "And not long after that, there was a bit of a breather and people started to see the fruits of the labor. Rams Head, the Campus Y, Memorial Hall: you started to see places on campus that had been really successfully enhanced."

The pace and scale of implementation also tested the patience and flexibility of the planners themselves. Ideas set forth in the plan were quickly put to the test, and changes were often necessary. One of the hot-button issues on the main campus, for example, was transportation. The original Master Plan was predicated on the idea that, on a campus with very little parking at its core, some people would switch to the park-and-ride system and others to public transpor-

tation. What they found is that park-and-ride—which was "much more effective and pleasant," Greene says —emerged as the clearly preferred option.

"Planning really is a process," Greene says. "It is very different from a design project, where you're developing one thing. Not all issues will come into focus at the same pace; not all people will get on board at the same pace. Certain things come into focus and then other things are snatched away from you and become confusing again. You need to be flexible and ride those highs and lows that come along with such a big effort."

Greene cites the Rams Head complex, designed by her firm, as a "stunning transformation" of what was once a hole in the campus. She also highlights the renewal of the historic core of campus—the Campus Y, Old East, Playmakers—as an enhancement that at times gets lost in the shuffle of the new buildings. Another standout is the Science Complex, which she says solves the problem of how to site very large academic buildings while retaining the human scale that defines college environments.

"It is so complex on one hand, and it looks so effortless," she says. "It feels good when you're walking around them, and you're walking around really big buildings."

Really big buildings will also be a dominating feature as the University builds out its Carolina North property. But Greene says that the growing imperative for buildings that are both high-comfort and high-performance will likely drive the look of the new campus in a different direction. Every building will have to take advantage of its setting, climate, and solar orientation to a degree that may make the comforting uniformity of a Polk Place impossible. "We should not assume going forward that all facades of a building will look the same," Greene says.

At the same time, plans for Carolina North will also have to integrate academic, corporate and institutional partners. "That is forging new ground," she says. "Some of those things happen on campus now, but they don't happen in an intensive way and in a consolidated place."

"There is no shortage of ambition at Carolina," she adds. "At every turn (in the dynamic decade), the University could have taken an easier path, and at every turn they chose to stick to their principles."

A seventh triumph of the dynamic decade was calculation of, and limiting development to, the responsible capacity of the campus. This involved more than simple engineering equations; it also involved positive actions to supplement the responsible capacity by building an innovative stormwater management system with large underground cisterns to allow re-use of captured rainwater, by instituting a free University/Town supported bus system to reduce the amount of single car usage and hence the amount of paved roads and parking needed, by creating a thermal storage system to extend the supply of chilled water, by replanting older trees whose life spans were ending, by carrying out an extensive waste recycling program, and by initiating and staffing a new office of sustainability.

An eighth triumph was crafting a plan for a second research campus around vigorous sustainability criteria. Instead of building on all 979 acres of the Horace Williams site, the University limited its development to only 250 acres of the least environmentally sensitive land. Extensive environmental analyses by objective professional ecologists documented the critical resources of the property and extensive public participation determined the location and type of building for the Carolina North campus. Expert consultant teams, some jointly funded by the Town and the University, analyzed environmental conditions on the site, energy and water systems, transit systems, and fiscal impacts. A robust negotiation process produced a formal Development Agreement spelling out the responsibilities of the University and the Town. This agreement was approved by the Town, along with the new University-1 zoning district, allowing the Carolina North campus to be developed as a future site for research, teaching, and living for students and staff.

These triumphs would not have been possible without a thorough planning and participation planning process that produced evidence that the existing campus was approaching its responsible capacity, along with a good faith effort by both the University and the Town to devise solutions that would respond to current sustainability needs while not constraining future development potential. To make that process work, the University increased the scrutiny of all proposed project designs to ensure that they met sustainability criteria.

REVIEW PROJECTS THROUGHOUT DESIGN

In recognition of the increased pressures resulting from the great increase in the number and size of new development projects during the dynamic decade, the University ramped up its project review process. Historically, all projects had been reviewed by the UNC Facilities Planning and Design staff architects and then by the faculty and staff members of the Chancellor's Buildings and Grounds Committee. This group made recommendations to the Chancellor, who then advised the Board of Trustees. The Trustees made the final decisions for the University. During that process, all projects typically underwent reviews at their preliminary and final stages, and often were revised substantially as a result of review comments. Once approved by the University, the projects were submitted to the Town of Chapel Hill for review and approval under its zoning regulations.

The ninth triumph of the dynamic decade was the establishment of a more comprehensive design review process guided by the design guidelines in the 2001 Master Plan. The Chancellor created a new Design Review Board of experienced architects and planners from outside the University staff and gave them broad powers to work directly with project architects to ensure design consistency and compatibility with the historic campus context. In essence, this was a *peer review* process, in which objective critiques by qualified professionals were employed to improve the quality of every design project. While University staff architects were constrained by their client status with the outside architects, and the Chancellor's Buildings and Grounds Committee members primarily offered lay perspectives, the Design Review Board had both the time and the capacity to give specific, broad-ranging professional design advice. They could ask the penetrating "what if" and "why not" questions. The effectiveness of their work is evident across the campus in distinguished projects, such as the Science Complex, the Rams Head Center, and the new student housing neighborhoods on the Southeast Campus. This ensured that all plans were thoroughly studied and reworked within the University decision system before going to the Town for formal hearings by community residents and elected officials.

This triumph would not have been possible without the Master Plan's design guidelines and the Development Plan's standards and criteria. The Master Plan states that the purpose of the design guidelines is to ensure that future buildings and grounds are as well-conceived as those of the past, and that its goal is to establish a framework for future designers so that the civic nature and beauty of the historic core is extended to the entire campus, combining tradition and innovation. The guidelines identified Carolina building styles, comparing plainer "background" buildings, such as Old East, with more elaborate "heroic" buildings, such as Wilson Library, to encourage architects not to think of each new design as a grand statement. They demonstrated how "transitional" buildings can incorporate both historical references and contemporary ideas. The Development Plan lays out site plan and impact standards that connect to Town zoning regulations for noise and light, environmental and transportation impacts, pedestrian circulation, stormwater management, public utilities, historic districts, and perimeter transition areas.

A WORK IN PROGRESS

Every campus is a work in progress. It is this unbroken historical thread that imparts the deepest meanings and values to a university campus. Sustaining that continuity while remaining open to the future is the basic charge of campus planning and development. In that sense, every campus is its own most important classroom, and the way that it handles the evolution of its buildings and grounds is its most valuable lesson for future generations.

Afterword

Holden Thorp, Chancellor

As the person who succeeded Chancellor James Moeser, I am extremely grateful for all that was accomplished in what the authors of this book have described as "the Dynamic Decade." The transformation of the UNC campus made possible by a carefully designed master plan, a strategically achieved development plan, a politically charged bond referendum and an ambitiously imagined fundraising initiative was at its height when I moved into the Chancellor's office.

Because of all the construction and the detours around it, getting to that office wasn't always easy. The Kenan Music Building was nearly finished, but Boshamer Stadium was in the midst of renovation and work was just beginning on the new genome sciences and dental sciences buildings. A deep pit was all that remained of Old Venable, the ancient and dilapidated building where I had spent so many hours as a chemistry student and professor.

Construction and renovation continued on schedule even after the economic collapse of 2008 and subsequent budget cuts because of the foresight of using the bond referendum as a funding mechanism. I was able to preside over the dedication of several new buildings, including the N.C. Botanical Garden Education Center, the Genetic Medicine Research Building, Taylor residence hall, and new Venable and Murray halls.

I was particularly proud of that last dedication because those two new buildings made the Science Complex envisioned in the campus master plan a brick and mortar reality. Joining with the recently completed Chapman Hall, Caudill Labs and Sitterson and Brooks Halls and flanked by the older Kenan and Morehead Labs, new Venable and Murray showed UNC's determination to create an environment worthy of the talented faculty and researchers we aimed to attract and keep here.

The work of the Dynamic Decade provides a fantastic foundation for the future here at UNC, yet it also presents certain challenges. We have increased our square footage substantially, which also means increased water and energy usage, especially in the high-tech laboratories. At the same time, we have pledged to stop using coal on campus by the year 2020 to reduce our carbon footprint. How will we be able to afford to power our new buildings in this time of budget cuts?

The answer is being smart about sustainability. In my first year in office, I named an Energy Task Force to look at the University's energy sources as well as our demand. The task force's recommendations as well as the continuing excellence of such campus organizations as the Office of Sustainability, Energy Services and Energy Management, led to a new energy use policy, adopted in July 2009. As a result of the energy conservation measures implemented, the University avoided more than $10 million in utility costs. We have introduced new technology, an energy dashboard, to help us keep tabs on energy usage in individual buildings, and we are using a new funding mechanism, the Green Revolving Fund, to encourage energy-saving projects. We are testing alternative energy sources, using reclaimed water and setting higher, greener standards for new construction and renovation projects.

Inspired by the Dynamic Decade and encouraged by the lessons learned during the campus master plan process, we have launched our next major project: the development of the Carolina North campus. University facilities planning staff and our partners at Ayers Saint Gross have designed a campus of the future on the Horace Williams site, a model of sustainability that will be home to the University's next generation of researchers, entrepreneurs, faculty, and graduate students. It's a campus meant to be created in stages over the next 50 years, so I look forward to more dynamic decades to come.

APPENDIX A

Development Project Chronology

NORTH CAMPUS

Science Complex projects. Source: UNC Facilities Planning and Construction

Building	Completion Date	Size sq. ft. Gross Area	Cost	Designer
Caudill Laboratories	2006	152,424	$59,445,360	Wilson Architects
New Venable Hall	2010	42,887	24,188,268	Wilson Architects
Murray Hall	2010	126,041	71,337,540	Wilson Architects
Chapman Hall	2006	142,351	55,516,890	Wilson Architects
Brooks Computer Science	2008	32,000	$40,423,146	Wilson Architects
Total		**495,703**	**$250,911,204**	

Bell Tower Complex projects. Source: UNC Facilities Planning and Construction

Building	Completion Date	Size sq. ft. Gross Area	Cost	Designer
Stone Center (prior to Development Plan)	2004	45,244	$9,509,827	The Freelon Group
Genomic Sciences	January 2012 (expected)	198,541	156,000,000	Skidmore, Owings, & Merrill
Parking Deck	2010	262,714	26,000,000	Skidmore, Owings, & Merrill
Central Park	Spring 2012 (expected)	65,340	1,100,000	Skidmore, Owings, & Merrill
Total		**571,839**	**$192,609,827**	

Arts Community projects. Source: UNC Facilities Planning and Construction

Building	Completion Date	Size sq. ft. Gross Area	Cost	Designer
Kenan Music Building	2008	43,486	$32,096,719	Perkins Will
Memorial Hall Renovation	2005	30,055	16,822,640	Calloway Johnson Moore West
Campus YMCA Renovation	2005	13,062	5,109,691	Pearce, Brinkley, Cease & Lee
Gerrard Hall Renovation	2007	4,220	2,350,000	Ann Beha Architects
Hyde Hall (prior to Development Plan)	2002	16,062	4,096,700	Cooper, Robertson
Total		**106,885**	**$60,475,750**	

North Student Residence Life and Services Community projects. Source: UNC Facilities Planning and Construction

Building	Completion Date	Size sq. ft. Gross Area	Cost	Designer
Parking Deck and Chiller Plant	2007	211,771	$46,700,147	Affiliated Engineers
Cobb Dormitory Addition	2006	103,265	829,045	Mitchell/Mathews
Winston/Connor/Alexander/Joyner Addition	2003	124,808	13,926,682	Pearce, Brinkley, Cease & Lee
Total		**439,844**	**$61,455,874**	

SOUTHEAST CAMPUS

South Student Residence Life and Services Community projects. Source: UNC Facilities Planning and Construction

Building	Completion Date	Size sq. ft. Gross Area	Cost	Designer
Rams Head Recreation	2005	47,414	$11,971,425	Ayers Saint Gross
Rams Head Convenience Store	2005	18,648	316,979	Ayers Saint Gross
Chase Dining Hall at Rams Head	2005	67,684	16,842,421	Ayers Saint Gross
Rams Head Center Parking Deck	2005	276,941	23,196,873	Ayers Saint Gross
Student & Academic Services-South	2007	27,213	5,192,761	Robert A.M. Stern
Student & Academic Services-North	2007	74,558	15,345,471	Robert A.M. Stern
Koury Residence Hall	2004	74,937	12,551,519	Hanbury, Evans, Newill, Vlattas
Horton Residence Hall	2004	74,403	12,551,519	Hanbury, Evans, Newill, Vlattas
Hardin Residence Hall	2004	59,537	9,794,917	Hanbury, Evans, Newill, Vlattas
Craige North Residence Hall	2004	75,582	11,657,312	Hanbury, Evans, Newill, Vlattas
Ram Village at 560 Paul Hardin Drive	2006	103,669	38,917,722	Clark Nexsen
Ram Village at 540 Paul Hardin Drive	2006	84,900	31,871,771	Clark Nexsen
Ram Village at 550 Paul Hardin Drive	2006	54,884	20,603,654	Clark Nexsen
Ram Village at 520 Williamson Hardin Drive	2006	142,903	19,519,133	Clark Nexsen
Taylor Residence Hall	2006	137,456	18,666,463	Clark Nexsen
Total		**1,320,729**	**$248,999,940**	

South Student Family Housing Community projects. Source: UNC Facilities Planning and Construction

Building	Completion Date	Size sq. ft. Gross Area	Cost	Designer
Baity Hill 1800	2005	81,191	$6,179,160	Davis & Hining
Baity Hill 2000	2005	81,191	6,065,904	Davis & Hining
Baity Hill 1600	2005	80,031	6,065,904	Davis & Hining
Baity Hill 1900	2005	80,031	6,179,160	Davis & Hining
Baity Hill 1700	2005	78,045	5,936,736	Davis & Hining
Baity Hill 1401 Mason Farm Rd.	2005	60,059	4,572,792	Davis & Hining
Baity Hill 1501 Mason Farm Rd.	2005	60,059	4,572,984	Davis & Hining
Baity Hill 1351 Mason Farm Rd.	2005	49,601	3,795,792	Davis & Hining
Baity Hill 1101 Mason Farm Rd.	2005	39,631	3,007,680	Davis & Hining
Total		**609,839**	**$46,376,112**	

Athletics and Visitors Complex projects. Source: UNC Facilities Planning and Construction

Building	Completion Date	Size sq. ft. Gross Area	Cost	Designer
Boshamer Baseball Stadium	2009	53,564, including concession stand & maintenance building	$17,589,848	Populous (formerly HOK Sport Venue), CRZ, Inc.
Kenan Football Stadium	2011 (est.)	200,000	105,000,000	Corley Redfoot Zack, Inc.
Carmichael Auditorium addition &	2009	15,606 addition; 86,303 renovation	31,500,000	Corley Redfoot Zack, Inc.
Woollen Gymnasium floor renovation	2004	35,000	584,485	Davis Kane
Stallings-Evans Sports Medicine Center	2010	20,390	6,807,891	Corley Redfoot Zack, Inc.
Eddie Smith Field House	2001	81,025	—	Daniel DiLullo
Daniels Building renovation	2007	56,297	11,196,251	Gurlitz Architectural Group
Knapp Sanders School of Government and parking deck not in Development Plan)	2003	74,731 deck; 22,000 addition; 115,375 renovation	3,348,000 deck; 16,403,465 building	Newman & Peterson
Total		**760,291**	**$192,429,940**	

SOUTHWEST CAMPUS

Health Affairs Community projects. Source: UNC Facilities Planning and Construction

Building	Completion Date	Size sq. ft. Gross Area	Cost	Designer
NC Cancer Hospital	2008	315,000	$150,000,000	Zimmer Gunsul Frasca Partnership
Physicians Office Building	2008	103,223	30,000,000	Zimmer Gunsul Frasca Partnership
Jackson Circle Parking Deck	2006	279,917	23,979,282	Pearce, Brinkley, Cease, & Lee
Carrington Addition School of Nursing	2005	86,327	18,682,737	Pearce, Brinkley, Cease, & Lee
ITS Manning	2007	97,181	28,262,398	Hartman Cox Architects
Manning Steam Plant and Substation	2008	34,354	27,885,317	AEI with Ayers Saint Gross
North Carolina Women's and Children's Hospital (not in Development Plan)	2002	440,750	164,700,000	HKS
Health Science Library (not in Development Plan)	2005	85,909	10,090,727	Cline Design
Brinkhous-Bullitt (not in Development Plan)	2008–2009	103,541 (New); 2,261 (Renovated)	12,724,267	Integrated Technologies Consulting
Burnett Womack (not in Development Plan)	2004–2007	4,330 (New); 172,554 (Renovated)	35,872,197	Lord, Aeck, & Sargent
Total		**1,725,347**	**$492,106,198**	

Health Research Community projects. Source: UNC Facilities Planning and Construction

Building	Completion Date	Size sq. ft. Gross Area	Cost	Designer
Genetic Medicine Research	2008	367,570	$93,151,562	Lord, Aeck, & Sargent
Biomedical Research & Imaging	Started 2009	343,000	245,000,000	Perkins + Will
Dental Sciences	Started 2008	216,130	118,293,960	Flad & Associates
Michael Hooker Research Center	2005	127,624	38,981,200	Anshen & Allen
Kerr Hall (Addition to Beard Hall)	2004	75,140	22,169,800	HDR
Beard Hall renovation	2007	86,600	9,290,881	Rotman Architecture
Rosenau Hall renovation	2008	229,358	11,517,213	Heery International
Thermal Storage Tank & Tomkins Operations Center	2006	31,415	15,883,879	AEI with Ayers Saint Gross
Medical Biomolecular Research (not in Development Plan)	2003	222,189	60,500,800	Lord, Aeck, Sargent
Neurosciences Research (not in Development Plan)	2003	108,380	27,713,696	HDR
Bioinformatics (not in Development Plan)	2000	152,782	33,677,000	BJAC
Total		**1,960,188**	**$676,179,991**	

APPENDIX B

Carolina North

BRIEF CAROLINA NORTH CHRONOLOGY

1940s–1950s

1940, UNC purchases Martindale Field and renames it for Professor Horace Williams, who had donated adjacent land to the University;

1942, Navy commissions pre-flight school at Horace Williams' Airport;

1945, Airport de-commissioned for civilian use; Portion of Airport land used as Chapel Hill landfill.

1960s–1970s

1961, Carolina Flying Club begins to use Airport;

1968, UNC MedAir (later AHEC) begins to use Airport;

1969, runway extended to 3,500 feet.

1980s–1990s

1989, neighbors protest use of Airport as public hazard due to concerns about nearby schools and neighborhoods at public hearing and ask for change from public to private use;

1989, Chancellor Fordham pledges to phase out all non-University use;

1993, jet crash at airport kills three;

1998, crash injures three;

1998, Johnson, Johnson, and Roy (JJR) report, *Outlying Parcels Land Use Plans,* proposed plans for Horace Williams Property and Mason Farm Property (Friday Center);

1998, Chancellor Moeser forms Horace Williams Advisory Committee;

1999, Town/Gown committee proposes MX 150 with development agreement.

2000–2011

- 2001, Ayers Saint Gross (ASG) land use plan for Horace Williams property assumes continued operation of airport and development on both Chapel Hill and Carrboro portions of property;
- 2001, two flying club plane crashes;
- 2002, Chancellor Moeser announces decision to close Airport, although NC General Assembly postpones closure until 2005 at earliest;
- 2003, Horace Williams Citizens Committee forms and issues report in 2004, which was adopted as Town policy;
- 2004, ASG prepares new 50-year development plan for Horace Williams property, based on decision to close airport;
- 2006, Chancellor Moeser forms Leadership Advisory Committee (LAC) to develop consensus principles for Carolina North planning and they submit report in 2007 recommending three "foundation studies," including an ecological assessment, a long-range transit study, and a fiscal impact analysis;
- 2006–2007, UNC holds Infrastructure and Sustainable Design Workshops with staff, consultants, and community representatives;
- 2007, UNC Trustees approve third ASG plan for Horace Williams property;
- 2007, University conducts meetings for interested community participants;
- 2009, initial research building plan rejected;
- 2009, UNC and Chapel Hill approve Development Agreement and new U-1 zoning district;
- 2011–2012, planning for infrastructure and initial research building commences.

VISION STATEMENT FOR CAROLINA NORTH, 2008

Carolina North will be first and foremost a campus, conceived in the academic mission and ideals of the University of North Carolina at Chapel Hill. As a flagship public research university charged with helping to lead a transformation in the state's economy, UNC must compete with national peers for the talent and resources that drive innovation. Today, that competition demands a new kind of setting—one that enables public-private partnerships, public engagement and flexible new spaces for research and education.

Carolina North will best serve the University and the State if it also strengthens the local community, enhances its quality of life, respects its character and values, and embraces its spirit of collaboration. Much more than a technology park or overflow space for main campus, Carolina North will be a tree-shaded campus for living and learning, where people can live, work and study in one place. This and other progressive measures will help make Carolina North a model of sustainability—a campus that is socially, environmentally, and economically sound.

Why Carolina North?

Rapid changes in education, research, and engagement mean that the university must pursue new opportunities in new ways:

- Carolina North will provide an ideal setting for collaborative research that advances new knowledge and attracts the talented researchers and students who enrich the intellectual life of the university and the community.
- Carolina has embraced the imperative of connecting the University's research programs to the economic well-being of the region and of the state. Carolina North will include facilities, shared resources, support services, a collaborative environment, and other assets essential for creating and nurturing new businesses and relationships with existing businesses focusing on commercializing UNC research discoveries.
- To accommodate expected increases in enrollment and research activity, UNC will develop clusters of closely related activities at Carolina North, making room on main campus for additional students, faculty members, and staff. For example, moving the Renaissance Computing Institute to Carolina North would attract research teams that benefit from high-performance computing, data visualization, and other strengths.
- UNC's recently adopted curriculum places strong emphasis on interdisciplinary studies, undergraduate research and entrepreneurship. Carolina North will help us offer a meaningful research experience to every student and will also provide a setting where students can pursue entrepreneurial endeavors that carry innovations into the marketplace.
- As federal funding for research levels off or declines, institutions are turning to the private sector to sustain their momentum. Unfortunately, UNC-Chapel Hill currently ranks 90th nationally among research universities in corporate-sponsored research as a percentage of total funding. By providing a setting for public-private partnerships that spur innovation, Carolina North will attract new funding, stimulate economic growth, and create jobs for North Carolina.

RESOLUTION SEPTEMBER 26, 2007

WHEREAS, on May 26, 2005, and May 25, 2006, the Board of Trustees expressed by resolution its strong support for the development of a campus at Carolina North designed to expand Carolina's multiple missions, boost innovation, and redefine the University's engagement with the region and the state; and

WHEREAS, the Carolina North Plan presented to the Board of Trustees today is the result of many months of study and deliberation and incorporates a wide cross section of community input as a result of Chancellor Moeser's leadership efforts to engage the community in a dialogue about Carolina North over the past 18 months. These community discussions have included the Carolina North Leadership Advisory Committee and the report with guiding principles it produced; the Infrastructure Workshops that explored sustainable models of development as a fundamental principle of development at Carolina North; and monthly community meetings that charted the course of an evolving land use plan; and

WHEREAS, to meet an urgent need for advancing University research technologies, on August 10, 2007, the University filed with the Town of Chapel Hill the initial concept drawings for a special use permit for the Innovation Center, the first building to be developed at Carolina North; and

WHEREAS, as a follow-up to the application for a special use permit for the Innovation Center, the Board of Trustees wishes to develop, in collaboration with the Town of Chapel Hill, the zoning mechanisms under which the remainder of the Carolina North Plan presented today will be realized.

NOW THEREFORE BE IT RESOLVED that the Board of Trustees commends the Chancellor for advancing the planning for Carolina North in such an open and inclusive manner; and hereby approves the Carolina North Plan; and

BE IT FURTHER RESOLVED that the Board of Trustees approves both the 50-year vision of the Carolina North Plan and the 15-year Phase 1 segment of the Carolina North Plan and directs the Chancellor to refine the Carolina North Plan consistent with the Board's discussion so that at the appropriate time the Chancellor may present the Carolina North Plan to the Town of Chapel Hill.

Mr. Winston moved approval of the resolution, which also approves the Carolina North Plan. The motion approved unanimously.

References

Abramson, P. 2010. "15th Annual College Construction Report." *College Planning and Management*, February.

Allcott, John V. 1986. *The Campus at Chapel Hill: Two Hundred Years of Architecture*. Chapel Hill, VC: Chapel Hill Historical Society.

Ayers/Saint/Gross. 2001. *Campus Master Plan: The University of North Carolina at Chapel Hill*. Baltimore, MD: The Authors.

Ayers/Saint/Gross. 2007. *Plan for Carolina North: The University of North Carolina at Chapel Hill*. Baltimore, MD: The Authors.

Biohabitats. 2007. *Ecological Assessment Report: Carolina North*. University of North Carolina at Chapel Hill. http://carolinanorth.unc.edu/Portals/CarolinaNorth/Documents/pdf/ecological_assessment.pdf.

Chapel Hill. 2009. *Development Agreement By and Between the University of North Carolina at Chapel Hill and the Town of Chapel Hill, North Carolina*. http://www.unc.edu/depts/trustees/MIN%20ATT%20609.pdf.

Henderson, Archibald. 1949. *The Campus of the First State University*. Chapel Hill, NC: University of North Carolina Press.

Hoerr Schaudt Landscape Architects. 2008. *The Dignity of Restraint: A Study to Preserve and Enhance the University of North Carolina at Chapel Hill's Majestic Tree Landscape*. UNC Historic Landscape Framework Plan. Chicago, IL: The Authors.

Johnson, Johnson, and Roy, Inc. 1991. *A Guide to Physical Development: Summary of the Campus Framework Plan*. Chapel Hill, NC: University of North Carolina.

Johnson, Johnson, and Roy, Inc. 1998. *Outlying Parcels Land Use Plans: Summary Report*. Chapel Hill, NC: University of North Carolina.

Kapp, Paul Hardin. 2003. *Historic Preservation Survey*. Chapel Hill, NC: University of North Carolina. Loose leaf notebook.

Perry, David C., and Wim Wiewel, editors. 2005. *The University as Urban Developer: Case Studies and Analysis*. Armonk, NY: M.E. Sharpe, Inc.

Powell, William S. 1992. *The First State University: A Pictorial History of the University of North Carolina*. Third edition. Chapel Hill, NC: University of North Carolina Press.

Morris Hickey Morgan, translator. 1914. Vitruvius. *The Ten Books on Architecture*. Cambridge, MA; Harvard University Press.

Shakespeare, William. *Julius Caesar*. Act 4, scene 3, 218–224.

Shapard, Rob. 2003. "Parking deck, plant figure in Council race," *Chapel Hill Herald*, October 11.

Stern, Robert A.M. 2010. *On Campus*. New York: The Author.

Sungu-Eryilmaz, Yesim. 2009. *Town-Gown Collaboration in Land Use and Development*. Cambridge, MA: Lincoln Institute of Land Policy.

Suttenfield, Nancy. 2005. *A Status Report to President-Elect Erskine Bowles*. University of North Carolina at Chapel Hill.

Task Force on Landscape Heritage and Plant Diversity. 2005. *Final Report of the Task Force on Landscape Heritage and Plant Diversity*. Chapel Hill, NC: University of North Carolina.

University of North Carolina. 2001. *Development Plan*. Chapel Hill, NC: University of North Carolina.

University of North Carolina. 2001. *Environmental Master Plan*. Developed as part of the 2001 *Campus Master Plan: The University of North Carolina at Chapel Hill*. Ayers/Saint/Gross. Baltimore, MD: The Authors.

U. S. Department of Interior. Nn.d. *Secretary of Interior Standards for Rehabilitation*. (http://www.hpo.ncdcr.gov/standard.htm.) Accessed 18 April, 2012.

Acknowledgements

Preparation of this book was a collaborative effort. Lesley Pories and Daniel Widis, both graduate students in City and Regional Planning at UNC, served as the Research Assistants. The manuscript was reviewed by Bruce Runberg, Anna Wu, Jill Coleman, and Paula Davis of the UNC Facilities Planning and Construction department, as well as by members of the UNC Design Review Board: Pete Anderson, Charles Kahn, Luanne Greene, and James Moeser. Sidebar interviews and write-ups were done by freelance writer Darv Johnson. Campus Community maps were prepared by Paula Davis, UNC Facilities Planning and Construction. UNC photographer Dan Sears generously shared images from his treasure trove of campus pictures. Richard Tate flew over the campus to record the book's aerial photos. Anne Kachergis created the book's unique design.

Authors' Biographies

DAVID R. GODSCHALK is Stephen Baxter Professor Emeritus in the Department of City and Regional Planning at the University of North Carolina in Chapel Hill. A Fellow of the American Institute of Certified Planners, he chaired the Chancellor's Buildings and Grounds Committee, chaired the Design and Operations Team for the 2001 Campus Master Plan, and served on the UNC Design Review Board during the planning and subsequent campus development processes. Previously, he served on the Chapel Hill Town Council and NC Smart Growth Commission. His co-authored publications include: *Sustaining Places: The Role of the Comprehensive Plan* (2012) and *Urban Land Use Planning* (2006).

JONATHAN B. HOWES served as Special Assistant to Chancellors Hooker, McCoy, Moeser and Thorp from 1997–2009. A Fellow of the National Academy of Public Administration, he chaired the Executive Steering Team of the 2001 Campus Master Plan and served as co-convener of the first steering committee for the Horace Williams tract. His previous positions include: Director of the UNC Center for Urban and Regional Studies, Research Professor in City and Regional Planning, and Adjunct Professor of Regional Planning and Public Policy. He served on the Chapel Hill Town Council and as Mayor of Chapel Hill, as Secretary of the NC Department of Environment, Health and Natural Resources, and as chair of the NC Parks and Recreation Authority.